Echoes of the Haitian Revolution
1804–2004

Echoes of the Haitian Revolution
1804–2004

Edited by

Martin Munro
and
Elizabeth Walcott-Hackshaw

University of the West Indies Press
Jamaica • Barbados • Trinidad and Tobago

University of the West Indies Press
7A Gibraltar Hall Road   Mona
Kingston 7   Jamaica
www.uwipress.com

© 2008 by Martin Munro and Elizabeth Walcott-Hackshaw
All rights reserved. Published 2008

12 11 10 09 08   5 4 3 2 1

CATALOGUING IN PUBLICATION DATA

Echoes of the Haitian revolution, 1804–2004 / edited by Martin Munro and Elizabeth Walcott-Hackshaw.

p. cm.

Includes bibliographical references.

ISBN: 978-976-640-212-9

1. Haiti – History – Revolution, 1791–1804 – Influence. 2. Haiti – History – Revolution, 1791–1804 – Fiction. 3. Haitian literature – History and criticism. 4. Haiti – In literature. 5. Haitians – Migration – History. 6. Haitian Americans – New Orleans – History – 18th century. 7. Haitian Americans – New Orleans – History – 19th century. 8. Haiti – History – Revolution, 1791–1804 – Women. I. Munro, Martin. II. Walcott-Hackshaw, Elizabeth.

F1923.E367 2008   972.94

Cover illustration: Édouard Duval Carrié, *Toussaint Louverture Ambaglo* (mixed media in resin, 16" x 18"). Detail of the installation *The Indigo Room, or Is Memory Water Soluble*, 2004. Collection of the Fort Lauderdale Museum of Art. Courtesy of the artist.

Book and cover design by Robert Kwak.
Set in Garamond.

Printed in the United States of America.

Contents

Introduction
Martin Munro and Elizabeth Walcott-Hackshaw — vii

1 Hidden in Plain View
Evasions, Invasions and Invisible Nations
Edward E. Baptist — 1

2 St Domingue Refugees in New Orleans
Identity and Cultural Influences
Nathalie Dessens — 28

3 Arguing around Toussaint
The Revolutionary in a Postcolonial Frame
Charles Forsdick — 41

4 The Haitian Revolution and a North American Griot
The Life of Toussaint L'Ouverture by Jacob Lawrence
Carolyn Williams — 61

5 Reading in the Dark?
Racial Hierarchy and Miscegenation in Heinrich von Kleist's *Die Verlobung in San Domingo*
Wendy Sutherland — 86

6	"Les Créoles Galantes?" White Women and the Haitian Revolution	
	Kathleen Gyssels	*95*
7	Revolutionary Acts of Translation Language and Freedom in Guy Endore's *Babouk*	
	William Scott	*111*
8	Letters Lost at Sea Edwidge Danticat and Orality	
	Brenna Munro	*122*
9	Being Haitian in New York Migration and Transnationalism in Edwidge Danticat's *Breath, Eyes, Memory*	
	Adlai Murdoch	*134*
10	Dancing at the Border Cultural Translations and the Writer's Return	
	Elizabeth Walcott-Hackshaw	*149*
11	Hatred Chérie History, Silence and Animosity in Three Haitian Novels	
	Martin Munro	*163*
	Index	*177*
	Contributors	*189*

Introduction

Martin Munro and Elizabeth Walcott-Hackshaw

The bicentenary of Haitian independence in 2004 triggered a renewed interest in Haiti, its history and its culture. In North America, well-known journals such as *Yale French Studies*, *Small Axe* and *Research in African Literatures* have published special issues on Haiti, while in a previous volume published by the University of the West Indies Press, *Reinterpreting the Haitian Revolution and Its Cultural Aftershocks*, we brought together essays that addressed the repercussions of the Haitian Revolution in Haiti, the Caribbean, the United States and Europe. In many ways, however, we as readers and researchers are only beginning to understand Haitian history and culture, and much work is still required in this neglected but fertile field. This present volume is intended to develop and complement the previous collection, and meet the growing demand for original scholarly work on Haiti. Our focus is again cultural, in the broad sense, and it touches on politics, history, diaspora studies, art, the question of race, and gender aspects of the revolution. Once again, our intention is to encourage further research into these and other areas of Haiti's complex culture and history. The history of Haiti has shaped our ideas of race, nation and culture in ways that we are often unaware of, while contemporary Haitian literature and thought address many issues that are of striking relevance to the broader world. Learning about Haiti is not, therefore, a static, one-way process, but it necessarily engages us in a dynamic dialogue that compels us to question and often alter our own ideas. Our hope is that the essays collected here will stimulate, engage and provoke in this way.

"Nothing is so invisible as that which is hidden in plain view"; so begins the first chapter by Edward Baptist. His case in point is the Louisiana Purchase, and

Introduction

the acquisition of that territory by Thomas Jefferson's delegates from Napoleon in 1803. Although the site of the Louisiana Purchase may be visible to the eye Baptist shows how its roots and meanings remain hidden. When Haiti won its independence, white authors and politicians attempted to erase the entire nation by excluding it from the community of international relations, bullying it into paying reparations to France and pretending that the nation either did not exist or was on the verge of collapse. But Baptist's chapter exposes further attempts, beyond the military and the political, effected through white historiography, to wipe the revolution off the map and to render it invisible in the epic accounts of the French Revolution and the Napoleonic Wars. Baptist's focus is on the historians of the United States who have also failed to acknowledge the debt owed to the Haitian struggle for independence. Few historical accounts, with the exception of that of Henry Adams, see the link between Napoleon's desire to take back the American territory, returning Louisiana to its pre-1763 role and the fight for freedom in Haiti. This conflict forced Napoleon to deplete his Louisiana mission in order to send more troops to St Domingue. The battle waged for freedom in Haiti, not the American political leaders of the time, helped to preserve the United States from foreign domination. It is long past time, Baptist argues, that Haiti's role is rendered visible.

Nathalie Dessens's essay continues the historical investigation into the forgotten effects of the revolution on the United States by considering the situation of the large community of St Domingue refugees in Louisiana. As Dessens says, between fifteen and twenty thousand refugees – white, coloured and black – arrived in Louisiana from St Domingue, the majority of whom went to New Orleans, whose population doubled immediately. Long in the shadows of American historiography, the history of this movement, and particularly of the situation of black and free coloured refugees, has finally begun to be interrogated. As Dessens shows, the white refugees contributed much to the development of journalism, education, the arts (theatre, opera, architecture) and to Freemasonry. The originality of Dessens's approach is however in her treatment of the three sub-elements of the refugee group not as disparate factions but as part of a single, organic group held together to some extent by their shared cultural and social factors. Beyond divisions of colour and class, the refugees shared common cultural features such as language, culinary arts and fashion that tied them together and gave them a relatively cohesive identity that in turn shaped the broader culture of Louisiana and New Orleans.

Charles Forsdick's chapter focuses on another St Domingue refugee, Toussaint Louverture. Forsdick reflects on the divergent uses and appropriations of the figure

Introduction

and the historical memory of Toussaint, the most enduring and evocative of all Haiti's revolutionaries. Basing his arguments on the contention that Toussaint Louverture has never been a fixed historical entity, and that Toussaint's Protean qualities seem only to intensify with time, Forsdick focuses on the postcolonial uses of the memory and symbol of Toussaint inside Haiti and also in broader theoretical and cultural debates. Forsdick's interest lies most particularly in the shifts in representational emphases that have taken place as the Toussaint figure has metamorphosed from an exemplum of anti-colonial struggle to a site upon which postcolonial anxieties (over the nation, class, colour and gender, for example) can be played out. Drawing on a wide range of historical, literary and critical sources, the chapter indicates the tendency in some recent historiography to underplay the primary importance of Toussaint to the revolution. It also discusses recent critiques of C.L.R. James's classic *The Black Jacobins* and how these critiques have used Toussaint to reflect on a number of issues related to postcolonial identity, such as gender, colonial mimicry and hybridity. As Forsdick concludes, Toussaint's spectral presence in colonial and postcolonial discourses indicates that the genealogy of postcolonialism must be traced back further than the 1950s and 1960s work of James, Lamming, Dadié and Glissant, as Toussaint embodied the dilemmas of the postcolonial long before the term postcolonialism was even coined.

Carolyn William's chapter looks at the artist Jacob Lawrence's visual narrative on the life of Toussaint Louverture. Lawrence, considered one of the most important American artists of the twentieth century, is heralded as a significant chronicler of the black historical experience in the New World. Williams illustrates the manner in which his 1939 work, the *L'Ouverture* series, went beyond telling the story of the heroic Toussaint to construct a visual history of Haiti from the arrival of Columbus to the birth of the the new nation. Lawrence, according to Williams, expressed the common desire of African Americans in the Harlem of the early twentieth century to tell the story of the ultimate triumph of the African diaspora. The forty-one paintings of the series constitute a narrative, each picture depicting an important episode in Haiti's history, culminating with the successful fight for independence. The panels articulate the tragic and the triumphant path towards victory. Through Williams's detailed analysis of Lawrence's methodology and technique we see the artist's desire to depict his essential view of Toussaint Louverture as the "George Washington of Haiti". The heroic Louverture occupies centre stage and is a compelling figure. In panel twenty, for example, the most famous of the series, the caption states, "General Toussaint L'Ouverture, Statesman and military genius, esteemed by the Spaniards,

Introduction

feared by the English, dreaded by the French, hated by the planters, and revered by the Blacks." Lawrence, this visual griot, as Williams notes, was able to weave pictures with words to create a story of Toussaint that remains didactic, expressive and imaginative.

Wendy Sutherland's chapter discusses Heinrich von Kleist's novella, *Die Verlobung in San Domingo* (*The Betrothal in San Domingo*) (1811) set during the slave revolt in St Domingue and argues that Kleist's conception of skin colour among the slaves reflects not only the colour hierarchy present in eighteenth-century German ideas of virtue and vice, but also the racial hierarchy, set up by German Enlightenment philosopher Immanuel Kant, to designate the human and moral being. As Sutherland shows, skin colour is for Kant an immutable trait established by climate and geography, and it not only designates race but also moral character and, therefore, humanity. In Kant's racial hierarchy, all races degenerate from the original white race, which he presents as perfection. The other races are rated inferior or superior according to their approximation to whiteness. As Sutherland's close analysis shows, the central conflict in the novella concerns racial mixing and the ambivalence that arises when skin colour and race are not fixed. In this case, racial hierarchy expressed in skin colour suggests a moral hierarchy revealed in the figures of the "pure" African slave, his "mulatta" wife, her "mestiza" daughter and the "pure" white victim of the slaves' brutality. As Sutherland shows, the line between appearance, *Schein*, and actual being, *Sein*, becomes blurred in the character of Toni, the "mestiza" youth used to seduce the white soldier to his death. Because of the ambiguity of her race, Toni possesses both the "virtue" of whiteness and the "vice" of blackness. The mutability of her skin, which changes colour depending on the lighting, also lends to her racial ambiguity and literally mirrors her volatile position among the black slaves and the white settlers. In revisiting this fairly obscure though fascinating novella, Sutherland's chapter reveals much about contemporary European interpretations of the revolution and how it was used to illustrate evolving ideas on race and colour.

William Scott's chapter similarly considers another non-Haitian text of the revolution, Guy Endore's *Babouk* (1934), and reflects on how the text uses the revolution to explore Endore's own historical and political context. Scott's argument is based on the idea that Endore presents the revolution in terms of a crisis of linguistic intelligibility, and that, for the novel's main characters, the revolution itself must, initially at least, be disguised in and through acts of linguistic dissimulation. Scott further shows that these acts of subversion and resistance can be fruitfully reread as acts of translation, which in turn point to the broader question of the politics of

INTRODUCTION

translation in general and the relation between translation and various imperialist discourses of "universal" rights. Within the United States, Endore's novel was not received as warmly as the author had hoped. Part of the reason for this, Scott asserts, was Endore's use of the Haitian Revolution to critique contemporary US imperialist interests. In spite of his efforts to mask this critique – that is, to translate it into a Haitian idiom – the message was nevertheless clearly expressed through the narrative's structure and culminating moments. As Scott shows, the Communist Party of the United States in 1934 reviewed the novel in a positive light, hailing it as a description – or rather as a historical prefiguration – of the revolution which was thought at that time to be imminent in the United States. In this respect, Scott says, the novel should be read as an adaptation of the events of Haiti in the 1790s that illustrates the need for a more inclusive revolutionary struggle in the United States during the mid-1930s. This meant, in other words, that Endore was attempting to show how a socialist response to the Great Depression would have to be, in addition, a struggle for the civil rights of African Americans and other marginalized citizens: those who, indeed, perceived themselves as marginalized to a great extent as a result of the discourse of universality that the Communist Party itself espoused at this time. As Scott concludes, to be "free" in the terms spelled out by the Haitian Revolution amounted to becoming included – through revolutionary acts of translation – in the "language" of freedom current among the left-wing US intelligentsia of the 1930s.

Like Sutherland's and Scott's, Kathleen Gyssels's chapter also deals with questions of colour and race, and with texts outside the established canon of literary and historical works on the revolution. Gyssels's perspective is informed by her realization that most writing on the revolution has focused on the heroism of the male slave leaders, and that there are few works that attempt to recapture the social ambiance, the colour and class contradictions, and the general chaos of the revolutionary years. Making a case for works that avoid both hagiography and demonology in favour of more nuanced versions of the revolution and contemporary St Domingue society, Gyssels discusses two recent novels: *Aube tranquille* (2000), a *spiraliste* novel by the Haitian author Jean-Claude Fignolé, and *All Souls' Rising*, a classic historical novel by the American Madison Smartt Bell. What these works have in common, Gyssels argues, is their common desire to "speak the unspeakable", to think of the revolution in terms other than of male heroism, and in particular to present the situation of white women – both Creole and European – within the maelstrom of the revolution. In shifting the emphasis away from the discourse of glorious black male revolt, these

Introduction

two authors, as Gyssels shows, imagine the particular alienation of white women caught in a situation that they understand little but which sweeps them up in all of its hatred, fury and madness.

Three chapters look at Haitian migratory and diasporic experience as explored in the works of contemporary writers of Haitian origin. Brenna Munro's "Letters Lost at Sea; Edwidge Danticat and Orality", focuses on the manner in which this transnational writer locates her work on the border between orality and writing. Danticat cultivates this liminal position, Munro argues, to re-create and articulate the migratory life that many Haitians experience. Accordingly, Danticat invokes a range of storytelling strategies, from television to paintings, as a way to chart this borderland. In her chapter, Munro focuses on what she sees as the chief among these tropes: the epistolary letter. Through a detailed analysis of letter-writing in *Krik? Krak!* (1995) and *The Dew Breaker* (2004), the letter is seen as a recurrent motif and a resonant sign for Haitian culture in an era of diaspora. The letter, argues Munro, is part of a fragile repertoire of connection that moves forth between the spoken and the written. She points to the many scenes in Danticat's works where the texture of the immigrant experience is evoked by depicting people recording and listening to cassette tapes, sending telegrams, receiving news of relatives over the radio, and using the telephone. Letters are a poignant synecdoche, as Munro illustrates in her chapter, for migratory life, bearing at once the stamp of origin, while also marked by their journey.

Adlai Murdoch continues the focus on displacement and migration to illustrate the ways in which this transnational movement has demanded a reformulation of Haitianness from beyond the island's borders. These migrant Haitian communities from Miami to Montreal affirm their culture of origin and that of their newfound, adoptive home, creating what Murdoch refers to as "a dual, double-voiced identitarian positionality". Murdoch is interested in this ongoing process of transformation and in its articulation by the migrant voices of these "new" Haitian communities. These voices include writers like Edwidge Danticat and Dany Laferrière, who employ subjective strategies of self-representation that engender new boundaries, spaces and frameworks for identity. Murdoch's chapter looks closely at Danticat's *Breath, Eyes, Memory* (1994), which evokes the tensions and dualities produced by an enforced separation from the Haitian homeland. The novel, according to Murdoch, is a paradigmatic example of contemporary Haitian novelistic discourse. It delineates the identitarian dilemma of these new communities that lack a sense of history and

Introduction

cultural continuity. Contemporary Haitian writers expose the complex case of Haitian writing beyond traditional borders and, as Murdoch argues, demand that we all revisit our traditional perspectives on and definitions of nationalism and cultural identity.

The third chapter in this discussion of migration and cultural transformation examines the treatment of the diasporic writer's return to the "native land". In Dany Laferrière's *Pays sans chapeau* (1996) and Edwidge Danticat's *Breath, Eyes, Memory* (1994), Walcott-Hackshaw interrogates the manner in which these two works reconstruct the island space and negotiate feelings of cultural indeterminacy and dislocation. The choices in the selection of location and the relationship between writer and landscape shape Walcott-Hackshaw's argument. With the passing of time, a natural distance has been created between writer and landscapes, both human and natural. The chapter uses the Césairean return as a *point de départ* for this discussion of self and territory. It is also framed by Stuart Hall's notion of culture as continual translation as each generation modifies and generates its own culture. Walcott-Hackshaw illustrates how this dynamic cultural process destabilizes concepts of fixed locations and is further complicated with the construct of return, as both Laferrière and Danticat discover that they must grapple with imaginary locations of return and the reality they face.

Martin Munro writes on the theme of interpersonal and self-hatred in Haitian literature. Beginning with the argument that colonial regimes invariably impose inferiority complexes on colonized peoples, Munro suggests that despite anti-colonial resistance and rhetoric, this sentiment of inferiority often persists in postcolonial states and is moreover complicated by internal class and colour divisions. In identifying the American Occupation of 1915–34 as the period in which modern Haitian nationalism was born, the chapter considers how in the post-occupation era national unity disintegrated into internal rivalry and discord, as Haiti's deep-rooted divisions once more came to the fore. The chapter attempts to understand the causes and manifestations of hatred and violence in Haiti and focuses on three novels – Marie Chauvet's *Amour* (1968), Yanick Lahens's *Dans la maison du père* (2000) and Lyonel Trouillot's *Bicentenaire* (2004). As Munro shows, far from reproducing nationalist visions of solidarity, these works focus on Haiti's internal animosities and violence and present the realities of a silenced people, alienated and exiled in their own nation. The chapter demonstrates that the works are connected by their representations of inter-class and colour mistrust and the contempt that manifests itself in cycles of violence and in the deep, unrelenting, though often disavowed, self-hatred of Haiti's people.

Chapter 1

Hidden in Plain View
Evasions, Invasions and Invisible Nations

Edward E. Baptist

Nothing is so invisible as that which is hidden in plain view. Case in point: the Louisiana Purchase, the territory that Thomas Jefferson's delegates bought from Napoleon Bonaparte in 1803, stretching from the Mississippi River west across the great plains and over the Rocky Mountains. This middle section of the United States is allegedly considered mere "flyover" territory by metropolitan intellectuals. The states of the old Louisiana Purchase may or may not be invisible to some travellers, but they are hardly invisible in either present or past histories of the American empire. These "red states" on electoral maps have certainly used their votes to support every aggressive extension of American power over the past few decades.

Yet the Louisiana Purchase has been, in countless other ways, the backbone of the American rise to world dominance over the last two centuries. Indeed one could hardly imagine a twenty-first-century United States *sans* the Louisiana Purchase. The 828,000 square miles of the Mississippi-Missouri Basin abounds with natural resources. Its iron and other metals built American industry and US military superpower. Its soil, though washing day by day to the sea, and increasingly parched by the over-tapping of aquifers, still feeds not only the United States, but also grows much of the 40 per cent of world grain exports supplied by the United States. Its land, which Jefferson predicted would become an "empire for liberty", was first an empire for slavery and the dispossession of Indians. Cotton created industrial revolution; stolen land lured immigrants flocking from troubled nineteenth-century Europe to labour-poor North America. The United States could not have gone on to conquer Texas, or California, without Louisiana. Indeed, the chances were good that, had New Orleans remained in the hands of Spain or France, the states west of the Appalachians would have split from those to the east. Even the American Civil War, which resulted in no small part from a regional dispute between groups of white people over the question of who would shape unsettled sections of the Louisiana Purchase, made the nation-state more powerful. The war centralized the federal government and placed the industrializing North and Midwest firmly in command of the reins of national authority. From gold to silt to iron to geographical space itself, the Louisiana Purchase has been for the American empire not flyover territory, but launching pad. No nation-state on Earth has grown more in power since 1803 than the United States, and the Louisiana Purchase has been the geopolitical cornerstone of that success.

The territory of the Louisiana Purchase is visible to both the eye and the mind, yet its roots and its meanings remain hidden. Michel-Rolph Trouillot argues that invisibility is not usually the status of the great and the powerful – at least not the subject of their greatness and the official narratives of their climbs to power. Instead, invisibility has been the status of the oppressed majorities of humanity. The subaltern peoples of colonized nations, women and others have remained outside the histories written by those who, at least in their times, thought of themselves as victors. Perhaps the more central the struggle of oppressed people for visibility is to the story of human freedom, the more assiduously the authors of official histories must work to render them invisible. Sometimes this work is conscious. One of Trouillot's cases shows that those in power anywhere might attempt to silence voices that dissent from their authorized, self-justifying stories of the nation. Trouillot's account of Haitian king Henri Christophe details the ways in which Christophe attempted to suppress public memory of his alleged 1802 betrayal of Toussaint Louverture.[1]

In other cases, the very unthinkability of phenomena derives from the fact that people have great difficulty admitting the existence of things for which they have no categories. They see things the way they want to see them and often refuse to see that which they are not able to classify, understand or explain through existing paradigms. For instance, as the German philosopher G.W.F. Hegel demonstrated, Europeans of the early nineteenth century could not conceive of African people as actors in history. Trouillot's key example of this kind of invisibility is the Haitian Revolution, which, he has argued, was ontologically unthinkable for the Europeans who witnessed it happening. Among their American cousins, imagined necessity compelled progenitors of the ideologies of revolutionary liberalism to define the Haitian Revolution and other forms of black resistance to white supremacy out of the realm of "thinkability".

The new forms of republican citizenship with which the American revolutionaries experimented were predicated on racial and gendered oppositions that fixed limits to access.[2] These in turn built on the long history of whiteness and blackness in the plantation colonies. The rise of plantation slavery had entrenched in the laws and vernacular beliefs of European colonists the argument that African men were insufficiently manly and African women insufficiently feminine. Slavery and racial caste laws then prevented African men and women from playing prescribed European male and female roles. Those who claimed black inequality could now point to men who did not head households, or near-naked women working in the cane fields as evidence from social reality that supported Europeans' claims about essential nature.[3]

As "man" came by the rhetorical and philosophical paths of the American and French Revolutions to mean "citizen", whites who already assumed that "black" could not mean "man" were unlikely to admit African people of any gender to the status of "citizen". While for many white people "slavery" served as the antithesis of "liberty", the roles of slaves as the negative references for free men demanded not that whites resolve this contradiction by freeing their slaves, but that they assume that no essentially free man could ever consent to such a state. The self-interested syllogism was to them obvious: black must mean not-really-man, and thus not essentially deserving of the rights of equality and citizenship.[4]

Citizens were not only white and male, but in both the rhetoric of the Revolutionary era and in that of its later historians, they were the actors who made political choices, stood up for their rights and, in the process, produced dramatic historical change. Contemporary white observers were thus almost compelled to first deny the existence of the events in St Domingue in late 1791. In Jamaica, France and the United States, they refused to believe the reports of general insurrection. When that became impossible, they sought to deny the revolutionary character of the massive slave rebellion. White observers ascribed its wide scale to white leadership. When the British and then Napoleon's French armies came to St Domingue, they assured themselves that white troops would defeat the mass of "undisciplined" blacks. Finally, when Haiti won its independence against all odds, white authors and politicians attempted to erase the entire nation. They excluded it from the community of international relations, bullied into paying reparations to France, and continually pretended that the anomaly either did not exist or was on the verge of imminent collapse – a failed nation composed of people who could not, after all, change the course of history.[5]

At last, white historiography did what the force of white arms could not, wiping the Haitian Revolution off the mind's map of the past. As Trouillot notes, and C.L.R. James insisted before him, historians – refusing to think the unthinkable – either ignored or banalized the revolution. Denying white defeat, they ignored casualties and losses that, for France and Britain, exceeded those of Waterloo. They left it out of their histories of the French Revolution and the Napoleonic Wars, epics that tell the creation and recreation of the imagined communities of France and Britain.[6] Haiti's revolution, as we shall see, too often remains absent from histories of the period. But the acquisition of the Louisiana Purchase by the United States has been no more invisible from the perspective of history than is its vast territory from the window of the plane flying over it today. From the very beginning, many Americans recognized that the future held grand possibilities only because of that purchase. Upon hearing that France had sold this vast territory to the United States, David Ramsay, one of the first nationalist historians of the American Revolution, said: "The establishment of independence, and of our constitution, are prior, both in time and importance; but with these two exceptions, the acquisition of Louisiana, is the greatest political blessing ever conferred on these states."[7]

Indeed, many had thought the geopolitical position of the United States in 1802, before the purchase, had reached its most untenable stage since the drafting of the Constitution fifteen years earlier brought federal order to the bickering state governments. Spain had closed the Mississippi to American trade, slamming to a halt the growth of the new communities along the western waters of the United States. Spain was intriguing to separate the western states and territories from the young republic. National interests and personal interests faced ruin without the reopening of trade routes for the west. Even Thomas Jefferson's personal problems with debt would look much more serious without the opportunity to sell "surplus" slaves to the western traders already driving enslaved African Americans across the mountains from Monticello towards Kentucky.[8]

Making matters worse were the swirling rumors that Louisiana would end up back in the hands of France. Napoleon Bonaparte, a particularly aggressive and successful military chieftain, now led that nation. It appeared that he planned for imperial France to return to the New World and reclaim what she had long ago stolen. Having subdued Guadeloupe and Martinique, Napoleon had now tackled the far more difficult task of returning St Domingue to the fold of empire and her people from the pastures of freedom to slavery. He had sent the greatest transatlantic expeditionary force ever assembled to destroy the republic led by ex-slaves and "gilded Africans". The news soon emerged that in 1800 Napoleon had in fact imposed on Spain the secret Treaty of San Ildefonso, which returned Louisiana, after four decades of Spanish control, to France. Napoleon planned to yoke Louisiana back into its pre-1763 role of provision ground for a reconstituted plantation colony. France's reoccupation of Louisiana would place an army of soldiers, forged in the fire of revolutionary Europe and tested in Egypt, on the banks of the Mississippi.[9] Indeed, the Louisiana-bound force that Bonaparte had assembled in Flanders by fall 1802, ready to board a fleet of transports that waited in the mouths of the Scheldt, was, by some accounts, larger than the entire US Army. Once this force reached the mouth of the Mississippi it would be able to block America's western trade at will. They could destabilize the tenuous links between the eastern states and the trans-Appalachian frontier settlements, and swallow the new republic piecemeal.[10]

Napoleon had destroyed one revolutionary republic from within – France. In St Domingue, his troops were attempting to reconquer another one and to re-enslave its citizens. US policymakers feared that Louisiana would then become the staging area for an invasion aimed at bringing down a third revolutionary republic. Jefferson's response, especially once he heard rumours of the secret clauses in the 1801 Treaty of San Ildefonso, was negotiation. He had already dispatched Robert Livingston to Paris in an attempt to purchase the city of New Orleans (even before public admission of France's reacquisition). Now Jefferson sent trusted deputy James Monroe with another offer of purchase. Monroe was to offer more money for the city and with it access to the sea. As an alternative, if rejected, Jefferson and his emissaries could display only the threat that if Napoleon held possession of New Orleans, America would regard France as its "natural and habitual enemy".[11] Yet this threat was bluster; American warfighting potential was small before Jefferson's inauguration, and it was essentially nil once Jefferson eviscerated the heavily Federalist armed forces and mothballed the Federalist fleet. Jefferson recognized that "The day that France takes possession of New Orleans fixes the sentence which is to restrain [the United States] forever within her low-water mark. . . . From that moment we must marry ourselves forever to the British fleet and nation." Rejected by an aggressive Napoleon, Jefferson and his republic would have to crawl back into the fold of France's enemy, the British.[12]

In February 1803, Jefferson's political enemy Alexander Hamilton lambasted the president's policy in an editorial in the *New-York Evening Post*. Jefferson, he suggested, had emasculated American arms, putting the United States in the power of

Bonaparte's reaching, grasping fist. Hamilton was essentially correct. Jefferson could not stop Napoleon from taking possession of Louisiana; or, for that matter, of any other point west of the Appalachian mountains. Negotiations, especially from such a position of military weakness, were unlikely to sway such a man as Bonaparte from his aim. Despite Livingston's cajoling, by the end of 1802 Bonaparte appeared poised to launch his Louisiana expedition. Monroe's mission to France in the early days of 1803 thus took on a note of desperation.[13]

Monroe arrived in sight of the French coast on 7 April 1803. On that same day, the jailer of Toussaint Louverture, hundreds of miles away from Monroe in the Jura Mountains near the Swiss border, found the captive warrior dead in his chair. Pneumonia had slowly strangled a man who had survived a half-century of slavery and a decade of war. Yet his people by that time had already won, in effect, their war of independence. In almost a year and a half since French troops had arrived in St Domingue, they had died by uncounted thousands both in battle and in the hospital wards where the yellow-fever victims piled up. After Leclerc tricked and betrayed Toussaint into captivity in 1802, local leaders, and then Louverture's disciples Dessalines and Henri Christophe, rose in open warfare. Once rumours of Bonaparte's planned reimposition of slavery leaked out, almost all of the black and mulatto population turned actively against the French. Reverse after reverse forced Napoleon to bleed dry his Louisiana mission in order to send more troops into the meat grinder of St Domingue. Among the forty thousand or more French troops lost by 1803 was his brother-in-law Leclerc, dead of yellow fever.[14]

The cost paid by the Haitian people was incalculable, and they would pay it in a myriad of ways for years to come. Even today they are still paying the price for claiming the right to act in history. In the simple terms of death, we know that battle killed many thousands, but the French also murdered tens of thousands. Even before the full-scale resistance began in late 1802, Leclerc drowned four thousand men, women and children in the harbour of Cap Français. Thousands died of disease and starvation in the course of a scorched-earth war that raged over the countryside. The thirteen-year struggle from 1791 to 1804 would ultimately cost the lives of at least one hundred thousand of St Domingue's pre-revolution population of half a million.[15] The price paid bought freedom and independence, however. Months would pass before the last French troops left St Domingue, but Bonaparte could see his own checkmate staring up at him from the pieces on the board. After receiving the latest catalogue of bad news in early 1803, he grumbled at dinner in the Tuileries: "Damn sugar, damn coffee, damn colonies."

He no longer had sufficient troops to occupy either St Domingue or Louisiana and, while the 1802 Peace of Amiens had given him a respite from war in Europe, Britain was making warlike noises once again. By the beginning of March 1803, at the latest, Napoleon admitted to himself that there would be no American empire for him. He turned back towards European dominion.[16]

Neither Jefferson nor Monroe yet knew of Napoleon's decision. On 11 April, before Monroe (in that day of stagecoaches) had even reached Paris, Napoleon's minister Talleyrand asked US envoy Robert Livingston if he was willing to buy *all* of the Louisiana territory – the entire drainage of the Mississippi and its western tributaries. A day or two later, sitting in his bathtub, Napoleon sent a servant to summon his hapless brothers Lucien and Joseph. One of them had negotiated the Treaty of San Ildefonso, and the other expected to be his brother's American viceroy. He gave them the bad news. They were displeased. But Napoleon did not care.[17] The US commissioners actually signed the treaty of the Louisiana Purchase on 2 May. For $15 million, Napoleon sold all of the vast Louisiana territory to the United States because he did not think that he could control it or make it profitable without the still more tantalizing Pearl of the Antilles, St Domingue. In the fall of 1803, the last French troops retreated from St Domingue. On the first day of 1804, Dessalines declared the independence of Haiti.[18]

Here one returns again to the question hidden beneath the soil of the Louisiana Purchase: why has the United States become a superpower? David Ramsay had no doubt. The blood of the Haitian people, fighting a desperate war for their independence, their lives and, most of all, for their freedom from slavery, paid the real price of the Louisiana Purchase. They made the United States a continent-sized power and preserved it from foreign domination, as Alexander Hamilton knew. "To the deadly climate of St Domingo," he wrote in June 1803, "and to the courage and obstinate resistance made by its black inhabitants are we indebted. . . . The real truth is, Bonaparte found himself absolutely compelled by situation, to relinquish his daring plan of colonizing the banks of the Mississippi." The Purchase did not, he charged, come about because of the actions of American political leaders. Indeed, Hamilton ridiculed Jefferson for his lack of historical agency and the inability of his policy to achieve an outcome: "the United States, by the unforeseen operation of events, gained what the feebleness and pusillanimity of its miserable system of measures could never have acquired". The United States ended up receiving an unmerited gift: salvation "from the consequences of our errors and 'perverseness'" – in Hamilton's judgment, of course, one of those failures was Jefferson's attempt to strip the pro-Federalist Army and Navy of their power.[19]

This sequence of events is no shock, I am sure, to anyone educated in Haiti, or to anyone who has read C.L.R. James. Somehow, however, historians of the United States have ignored and forgotten the judgments of two early observers, Ramsay and Hamilton, to whom they defer on so many other subjects of nationalist history. Even when American historians grudgingly present at least the bare facts of the sequence of events I have described, they deny their meaning. They refuse to make the obvious deductions. They quickly turn to other subjects. Blinded by generations of invisibility, they simply do not see what it is that they are missing. Or perhaps they refuse. For instance, Tim Matthewson's 1995 article on Thomas Jefferson and Haiti purports to bring the wars on St Domingue into the history of the United States, but instead turns the Haitian Revolution's outcome into a product of American decision making. Rather than arguing that Haiti's defeat of Napoleon shaped American policy and American outcomes, he asserts "the Haitians probably would not have won their independence without American aid". This claim, which returns the capacity for decisive action to the hands of white and American actors, is a persistent one in the historical literature, or at least that portion written by American historians. From Brenda Gayle Plummer, for instance, we find that Jefferson "secretly provid[ed] the rebels with military supplies". However, no historian has presented any evidence to back up assertions that the US government presented essential and covert aid to the rebels, especially after LeClerc's invasion. True, Jefferson did not stop the trade of private merchant vessels to St Domingue, so complained Pichon, the French envoy to the United States. But the American president probably could not stop such trade, both because of the political difficulty of angering powerful mercantile interests further than he had already done, and because in 1802–3 the government did not have the ability to do so stop trade any more than it would during the failed 1807–9 embargo.[20]

The claim that American supplies purchased from private traders were the essential factor that enabled the rebels to win seems untenable as well. In the course of his article, Matthewson demonstrates that US trade to St Domingue actually suffered a dramatic decrease in volume during the course of the French invasion. What still arrived may well have been mostly intended for the French, who held most of the ports well until 1803. By this time, the rebels had been conducting an often-successful campaign of guerilla war in the interior of the country, away from the ports, for (depending on the region and the particular group of rebels) between six months and a year. The rebels were thus perhaps not so dependent on outside supplies in order to wage war as the American-aid school seems to assume. Their independence should be no real surprise. As one French officer remembered, "the Africans . . . set out for a campaign with nothing to eat but maize", which they could get from the farmers whom, the officer continued, the rebels allowed to come to market "without pillaging". After more than a decade of continuous warfare, the population was also not lacking in firearms. British interdiction of French supplies may have been significant in the final months of late 1803, after the May declaration of war between the two European powers, but Matthewson cannot demonstrate significant American aid to the rebels.[21]

The attempt to make Haitian victory dependent on nebulous quantities of American trade fails the test of Occam's razor. This logical postulate holds that the most likely explanation is the simplest one that fits all available facts. We know the effect of Haitian victories and French losses on Napoleon's decision-making process; we know little or nothing about the size, nature or effects of American trade on the strength of the rebels fighting in St Domingue for their freedom. Some of the other claims by such historians simply do not fit the available facts at all. Matthewson, for instance, asserts that Jefferson's refusal to loan Bonaparte money was decisive in the Haitian Revolution. But this rejection came in the late summer of 1803, after the issue of French defeat was decided. By this time, Bonaparte had already abandoned his American vision, as the Louisiana Purchase signalled, begun a war with Britain, and allowed Rochambeau's ever-shrinking force to drop below ten thousand men. Historians who attempt to shift agency away from the ordinary Haitians and their leaders in the final phase of the Revolution never attempt to think through the question of what sort of aid, and at what time, would be decisive in this kind of war. The presence of American trade becomes "aid", and the supposed presence of aid alone suddenly becomes the decisive factor. So it is – but only in the shift of focus back to the decisions and actions of white Americans.[22]

With the claim that Jefferson was the agent, the active force in the events of 1802–4 in St Domingue, American academic historians attempt to invert the causation of the Louisiana Purchase. If the American government caused the rebel victory in the Haitian Revolution, then it does not matter if French defeat in St Domingue led to Napoleon's fire sale of Louisiana. Jefferson and white America were still the actors, still in charge of their own fate. More recently, Matthewson depicted Jefferson as the all-powerful doctor who "presid[ed] at the birth of Haiti".[23] Some might see the American president who refused to recognize the new nation in 1804 and instead imposed a crushing embargo on independent Haiti as something rather more like a would-be infanticide. Other historians, looking back with vision even more tinted by the stars and stripes than Matthewson, have assumed that Napoleon realized that the United States would inevitably grow to be the most powerful nation on earth and that resistance would be futile. Alexander DeConde's monograph on the sale of the Louisiana Purchase says that "in the final analysis Napoleon recognized the reality of the situation . . . . He could not, any more than the decaying Spanish monarchy, stop the westward tide of American expansion." By using the metaphor of an uncontrollable natural phenomenon, DeConde obscures the contingency of this crucial event. A French army on the Mississippi would certainly have wreaked tremendous havoc, not just on American plans for expansion, but also on the still-shaky connection of the states west of the Alleghenies to the United States. This was of course the very possibility that Jefferson was desperate to avoid, but he was unable to prevent without the intervention of the Haitian people.[24] While Matthewson simply asserts something unlikely about Haiti, DeConde moves to the realm of a nationalist inevitability that makes the efficient cause of Napoleon's decision to sell irrelevant.

The type of denial exhibited by DeConde represents a broader tendency among American historians, who consistently forget that there was any possibility that the Louisiana Purchase would not take place, or outside forces helped force the cession. Not all of them agree with DeConde and the others. However, the truest measure of these few voices' inability to undermine the implacable nationalist certainty of American independence of influence comes in the way in which the most widely read works of American historians continue to render invisible Haiti's role in the Louisiana Purchase. That most basic and in some ways significant of works, the bread-and-butter of many college publishing houses in New York, is the textbook of national history intended for the US "survey course". This course is meant to introduce university "freshmen" to college-level study of history. Hundreds of thousands of undergraduate students take such courses every year in the United States, and they buy hundreds of thousands of textbooks (the publishers carefully guard the information, so one cannot be more precise than this) at as much as one hundred dollars per volume. In some institutions this course and a course on "Western civilization" are the two "gateways" into a major, the series of courses that entitle one to claim a bachelor's degree in history. Yet the survey course also serves as a kind of one- or two-semester-long civics lesson.

Professors, departments, universities and the historical profession look to the survey course to ensure that college students will know about subjects considered important to being "American" – the Revolution, the Constitution and its ideology, the Civil War, and perhaps more than a few years ago, the roles of slavery and race in shaping American citizenship. The survey itself is both artefact and artificer of the idea of the nation, and so are the textbooks typically used in these courses.[25]

The survey text is also supposed to serve more than nationalist purposes. It is supposed to sum up and present in easily digested, synthetic terms the current state of historical study on everything that happened in the chronological period covered by that particular volume. The survey text seeks to present to a relatively large but fairly specific public composed of eighteen- to twenty-two-year-olds (and also the self-appointed invigilators of the supposed left-wing heresies of the American academy) a distilled and summarized version of professional scholarship. Critics often charge textbook authors with "mentioning everything and explaining nothing". Yet this seemingly formless grab-bag of historical and historiographical knowledge has a broader, deeper shape, one that molds the textbook into the form of a story about the nation that also tells the nation who it is. In fact, to be more precisely critical, it tells the nation, or at least dominant elements thereof, what the nation has already agreed that it is willing to know. The economic incentive to do so is tremendous, since, on the one hand, every textbook represents approximately two million dollars in direct costs expended by the publisher before a single copy is shipped. On the other hand, there are those hundreds of thousands of pairs of hands, each one of which may fork over large sums of money for a textbook. The desire to please a broad audience comes from both the fear of losing the massive investment made by the publisher and the desire to reap the substantial rewards that can accrue to those who hit the right note.[26]

Even as the survey text teaches us about historical knowledge along the fault line between academy and lay public, it also tells us about the state of assumptions in the field itself. It comes, in a sense, at the end of a Great Chain of Historical Scholarship, from dissertation to monograph to reviews accepting or rejecting said monograph's findings, to footnoted citations in other works influenced by said monograph, to accepted/orthodox interpretation. Even for professional historians, the textbook's categories can both reflect and, in subtle ways, shape the prevailing questions and assumptions of the field. One of those assumptions is that the discipline of American history is still wedded to the national history narrative.

While academic historians in the United States may intend to create survey texts that lead student-citizens to question some aspects of US history, their textbooks may still reproduce the assumption that the United States acts alone, that it created its own current status through hard work and deserved success, and that it owes no one – least of all darker peoples inside or outside the United States – any compelling debt.[27] Almost all US history textbooks incarnate in both the questions they ask and the answers they offer a certain set of assumptions about the nation and about national expansion. Those that refuse to celebrate a process that takes place at the expense of the Native Americans, as well as underpaid immigrant labourers from Ireland, China and Mexico, still tend to see the geographical and consequent economic growth of the United States as destiny, manifest or otherwise.[28] This destiny, in most tellings, appears to proceed from an internal logic, rather than only within or even only because of the logic of events external to the United States.[29] Rarely if ever do the history books emphasize the contingency of this process – the very real possibility that it would not happen. Still less do they argue that the United States only survived and grew because of the efforts of rebellious, freedom-loving people who were not white colonists in powdered wigs and knee breeches, but African-born black revolutionaries who had survived life in the bellies of two beasts.

Such conclusions, though seemingly evident from the actual narrative of events leading up to the sale of the Louisiana Territory, are not to be reached and would have to proceed from questions that one must not ask; or so one must conclude from a survey of the discussion of the Louisiana Purchase found in some of the most popular textbooks being used today. In recent editions, a few texts do admit something approaching the sequence of events that I have detailed already. If you already know, you can find in a stray word or sentence confirmation that Haitian resistance forced Bonaparte to abandon his plans for a revival of France's American empire. In some of the textbooks, Bonaparte then sells Louisiana – all of it, much more than Jefferson had hoped to acquire – to the United States for a pittance. For instance, John Murrin et al's *Liberty, Equality, Power* notes that "accidents of French and Haitian history had given the United States a grand opportunity". While both France's invasion of St Domingue and the resistance of the Haitian people were intentional rather than accidental, at least this text notes that there was a causal connection.[30] Similarly, John Mack Faragher's *Out of Many* notes that "in the wake of the French defeat, and in need of money for European campaigns, Napoleon offered the entire Louisiana Territory".[31] And Joseph Conlin's *The American Past: A Survey of American History* reports that "[Napoleon's] remarkable turnabout had nothing to do with American wants and needs. Louisiana had become worthless to Napoleon. . . . Some 30,000 French troops were killed in battle or incapacitated by tropical fevers. 'Damn sugar,' Napoleon said on hearing of the debacle. 'Damn coffee. Damn colonies! Damn niggers!' " Conlin himself adds the last two-word sentence, perhaps, to Bonaparte's words, which is an interesting thing to do. And here Haiti leaves the story again and for good, and Conlin turns, one hopes with relief that is not too evident, to decisions made by Americans: to constitutional debates about the acquisition of territory and the addition of states.[32]

These connections would not have been made even ten or fifteen years ago, a change which reflects the fact that some Americanists now read C.L.R. James in graduate school, for instance. Other textbooks, however, continue to fail to tell what actually happened. One major textbook, *The American Promise*, says merely that in 1803 "the French negotiator simply asked Livingston to name his price".[33] The text offers no explanation for the sudden turnabout. Many textbooks of US history also commit careless factual errors that reveal their essential lack of interest in those phenomena, people and places that they do not believe contributed to the destiny of the United States. For instance, Faragher's *Out of Many* reports that "in 1804, under the leadership of Toussaint L'Ouverture, the former colony, renamed Haiti, became America's first independent black nation".[34] Toussaint had been gone from the island for two years and dead for almost one by 1804. Admittedly, historians of the Revolution have expanded our understanding of the role of Vodûn, but this is perhaps taking the role of *les morts* too far.

In the same vein, Conlin's *The American Past*, ignoring the fact that rebellion and abolition had already ended slavery in St Domingue, states that "black rebels in Haiti, France's most valuable West Indian colony, both slaves and free men, had battered a crack French army".[35] The rebels, now free, were in fact fighting to prevent the reimposition of slavery on St Domingue. Once black, always a slave to Napoleon and many other whites through history, but surely historians should not repeat that assumption. And just like the historians criticized a decade ago by Michel-Rolph Trouillot, those who write textbooks like *Out of Many* often continue to emphasize yellow fever above everything else as the cause of French defeat. Indeed, disease played an important role, but yellow fever had been present on St Domingue and other Caribbean islands for more than a century, and it had not defeated planter rule in all that time. White troops in the Caribbean had always suffered high death rates, but maintained control over colonial territories all the same. Between 1802 and 1803, something seems to have been different. Perhaps that something was not yellow fever, malaria, or even a few merchant ships from Boston, but the resistance and sacrifice of hundreds of thousands of Haitians.[36]

Oddly, the textbooks do a better job in some cases than does the specialist literature on the Louisiana Purchase. The recent spate of works on the Louisiana Purchase, many issued just in time for the 2003 bicentennial of the doubling of American Empire, do not make up for the errors and omissions of the textbooks.[37] Peter Kastor's *The Louisiana Purchase: Emergence of an American Nation* is part of the series *Landmarks in American History* – published for Congressional Quarterly Press, no less, which might both explain and add extra interest to its astonishing omissions. The term "Haiti" does not appear in the index or the text. "Louverture", "Toussaint", "Dessalines", "Rochambeau", "LeClerc" – all these are absent. So, too, is "St Domingue", except in the discussion of the refugees from St Domingue who arrive in New Orleans from 1791 to 1804 and again in 1809. The text, however, focuses on the white and to a lesser extent, free coloured refugees. To all this silence about causation, credit and consequence, there is only one exception – a single footnote in James Sofka's article "Thomas Jefferson and the Problem of World Politics", which admits that the war in St Domingue limited Napoleon's options. But in the text of the article, of course, the author argues that Napoleon made his decision to sell Louisiana because of Jefferson's "intimidation" of France.[38]

Charles Cerami's *Jefferson's Great Gamble: The Remarkable Story of Jefferson, Napoleon, and the Men Behind the Louisiana Purchase* admits that Toussaint opened the way of the Purchase for Jefferson, but his discussion of St Domingue is brief. Cerami's discussion of the Haitian Revolution focuses on what appears to be a garbled apologia for the French attempt to reimpose the Code Noir. Their special legal system appears as just another morally neutral variant in a diversity of ideas. This is another kind of invisibility imposed on rebellion, which Cerami achieves by rhetorically normalizing and equalizing the moral rights of freedom fighter and genocidal tyrant, as if France had just as much right to inflict slavery as enslaved Africans had to resist it.[39] Before a few pages have passed, the diplomatic narrative of Livingston, Monroe and their French counterparts – these are the "men" – rises up to conceal the unthinkable possibility that Haiti should be the subject, the main actor, of the "remarkable story" that Cerami is telling. While this literally puts half a million men/people "behind the Louisiana Purchase", where one cannot see them, clearly Cerami does not intend to refer to this process in his title. The "men" who act, who are visible in his history, are neither black nor Haitian.[40]

As always, most significant are not the mere errors and omissions but the questions not asked and the stories not told, whether by the textbooks or the more specialized works on the Louisiana Purchase. Jon Kukla's *A Wilderness So Immense*: *The Louisiana Purchase and the Destiny of America* and Roger Kennedy's *Mr Jefferson's Lost Cause* acknowledge the connections between Bonaparte's Caribbean defeat and his Paris decision about the Louisiana Territory. And yet each of these ends up rendering the relationship between Haiti and the United States invisible after 1803, irrelevant to the "destiny" of the United States that they seek to explain. Kukla and Kennedy obscure the role of Haiti by turning from her as soon as she has fulfilled what appears to be her sole purpose: making necessary the sale of Louisiana. The destiny of the United States proceeds and Haiti's act disappears from their conclusions. Imagine a discussion of American constitutional principles with no reference to the acts of the "Founding Fathers" or New England culture without a mention of the Puritans. In the growth of the United States, however, this particular set of internal consequences and external causes have no meaningful connection.[41]

The purposes of US scholarship and, indeed, of white scholars in general have never included granting credit to a small, black and fiercely independent nation for their role in the survival of a vast white one. Yet in his *American Historical Review* assessment of Kukla's text, Jeffersonian scholar Peter Onuf dismisses even Kukla's inconsiderable reference to the Haitian causation of the Louisiana Purchase, saying, "His emphasis on the centrality of the Haitian Revolution does not break new ground."[42] One might find it puzzling that Onuf criticizes an historian for discussing something that actually happened. More ominous is the fact that Onuf is wrong: even the limited claim that Kukla makes has never had its day of full discussion in the academic or public historiography of the United States and its expansion. Onuf's erroneous assertion that we have discussed and are now through with discussing this phenomenon provides a perfect conclusion to American scholars' long effort to cloak with invisibility the origins of the Louisiana Purchase. They have avoided substantive discussion of the issue for decades. From time to time the unavoidable factuality of Haiti's role has squeezed a sentence up through the surface of accounts that present the Purchase as part of a seamless narrative of American destiny. Yet now, apparently, those accidental, partial and incomplete accounts provide both a justification and an occasion for contemporary scholars to dismiss even the weakest latter-day discussions of Haiti's agency as repetitive.[43]

I am afraid that on the question of Haiti's role in the Louisiana Purchase, all the texts of American historians – save one – fail utterly. Whether textbook or monograph, article or review, US history inevitably gives the shortest, briefest account possible of Haiti's role in causing the Louisiana Purchase to take place. They never interpret the process by linking cause to consequence. Texts move immediately to the next subject, that of American occupation and control of Louisiana. The decision to evade, ignore and render invisible suggests a number of causes and motives. Clearly, white commentators have long been uncomfortable with the idea of independent black people.[44] One wonders whether white observers in the nineteenth-century United States were more sceptical that black independence could persist, or afraid that that an independent Haiti might actually succeed. The latter motivation may have driven the American attempts to deny Haiti membership in the community of western hemisphere nations from the Panama conference of 1826 onward. Southern pro-slavery writers viciously criticized Haiti, not only for the failures of its unstable politics, but for simply existing as a nation of self-emancipated black inhabitants that might suggest to North American slaves the possibility of successful rebellions.[45] But even among non-Southerners, white doubt that an independent black people could persist and succeed in Haiti has remained remarkably consistent for two centuries. J. Michael Dash's description of the "constant scepticism that characterized American attitudes to Haiti in the nineteenth century" could as easily characterize government officials who speak about Haiti today. Scepticism also permeates the crocodile tears, stern talkings-to and befuddled accounts of exotic primitives that permeate the accounts of journalists who have visited Haiti during the repeated crises of the last twenty years.[46]

Haiti's relationship to US history remains as invisible in American discussions of the Caribbean nation's long-standing state of crisis as it does in histories of the Louisiana Purchase. Certainly, race helps render Haiti's role in US national expansion invisible. This is not, however, a simple question of inattention, of the passive inability to notice the role of black people doing something at the corners of history. Nor does the plain racial malice that has driven white America's hostile attitude necessarily explain everything about this silence. Of course, nationalists, including America's purveyors of white nationalism, are often reluctant to credit the assistance of those whom they openly or unconsciously consider their mortal enemies. Yet racial liberals have written much history as well, and one might hope that the evidence, the blatant factuality of the sequence of events that led to the Louisiana Purchase, might be too strong for either simple ignorance or malice to deny. White anti-racists from the

United States have indeed decried from time to time the active hatefulness of American attitudes towards Haiti and Haitians. But they cannot see the historical evidence of passive American dependence on Haitian action in 1803 because they do not want to see it. Instead, the demands of the (white) American national myth, which require that the United States succeeds on its own without the help of anyone – especially of the darker sort – necessitate an active and contorted process of rendering invisible Haiti's contribution to US expansion. American historians must work hard to avoid seeing the chain of cause and effect. American historians must refuse to say the simple words "Haiti won the Louisiana Territory for the US", even though they are as plainly true as any judgment of American history, because the logical next statement of the syllogism could well be "perhaps therefore the US owes Haiti a substantial debt".

Such a possibility is invisible to them. They can pillory the attitudes of Southern slave owners who feared the export of slave revolt to their shores without loosing themselves from the assumption that white people are history's actors. No one says that the United States doubled its size and became a truly expansive, continental empire only because Haiti – on its own – achieved its independence. No one, it seems, whether in dense professional text or grab-bag survey textbook for the millions, may break the surface of this historiographic nationalism, because the very admission of American dependence is absolutely contrary to the prevailing narrative of the exceptionalism of America and the independent agency of its white actors in history. With one exception, no one says that the ex-slave rebels, who defeated LeClerc and Rochambeau, saved the United States from the humiliating choice between submission to Bonaparte and a shotgun marriage to the British fleet. Again with the same single exception, no prominent American historian takes the next step of saying that the United States in consequence owed Haiti a debt, in whatever terms one might want to construe that debt.

The single exception, oddly enough, is Henry Adams. A frosty Boston intellectual, who was also a member of the generation of Northern Republicans who abandoned Southern African Americans to the tender mercies of the white South, he seems an unlikely candidate for such a role. He wrote at the end of the nineteenth century, in an era in which white Americans had redoubled their efforts to read African Americans out of American history, erase enslaved and free blacks' active roles in bringing about the emancipations of the US Civil War, and rehabilitate Southern slaveholders as members of a white nation that shaped its own destiny without any outside aid.[47] Yet Adams wrote these apparently forbidden words:

> Toussaint never knew that St Domingo had successfully resisted the whole power of France . . . but even when shivering in the frosts of the Jura his last moments would have glowed with gratified revenge, had he known that at the same instant Bonaparte was turning into a path which the negroes of St Domingo had driven him to take, and which was to lead him to parallel at St Helena the fate of Toussaint himself at the Château de Joux. . . . That the "miserable negro" as Bonaparte called him, should have been forgotten so soon was not surprising; but the prejudices of race alone blinded the American people to the debt they owed to the desperate courage of five hundred thousand Haytien negroes who would not be enslaved.[48]

Adams's assessment, long-ignored by other American historians, is not only unique, but is also of interest here because it explicitly uses the word "debt".[49] Some might wonder how much the Haitian defeat of Napoleon's forces was worth to the United States. We cannot measure the benefit gained by the United States by not having to fight Napoleon, not having to marry herself to the British fleet, or not losing Kentucky and Tennessee to secession and Aaron Burr. The simple way to assess these outcomes is to say that they might have made the difference of survival. We could also measure in some way – financial or otherwise – the vast wealth and power opened to the United States and its citizens by the Louisiana Purchase. We might wonder if Haiti did not deserve at least a "finder's fee" for this windfall.[50] But perhaps Haitians would not want to associate themselves with the colonization by force of over eight hundred thousand square miles. After all, in 1804 this land really belonged to a hundred different Native American peoples. The United States would proceed to spend the century ejecting, starving and killing them. Perhaps more to the point is the question of what the American denial of indebtedness has led to, in terms of costs for Haiti and Haitians.

Although they are students of a society in which market relations of exchange and debt have become all in all, American historians have systematically refused to analyse either the value of Haiti's gift to the United States or the possibility that the United States thus incurred any obligations to Haiti. Yet the metaphors of gift-giving and resulting obligation or indebtedness are inherent in the way in which the United States thinks about its relations with other countries. While many Americans have successfully excised France's contribution to American independence from their historical memories, they have been eager to decry France's ingratitude for liberation in 1944 on each subsequent occasion when French leaders have contradicted the wishes of American presidents. DeGaulle's expulsion of American troops in 1966, or the

Chirac regime's refusal to accept Bush and Powell's assertions that Saddam Hussein's Iraq was brimming with missiles, fissile material and nasty bacteria, evoked in response the cold anger of the loan shark denied repayment.[51]

Commonplace assumptions about the role of the United States in the world drive both US policy towards Haiti and the absence within US historiography of Haiti's gift to the United States. In American discussions of foreign policy, US commentators and state actors have consistently depicted Haiti as even more of a debtor, in both the financial and the moral sense, than France. This alleged indebtedness has consequences, for the United States has used it to justify aggression. From the beginning, the United States treated independent Haiti as if it had not paid its admission fee into the community of nations. The US government did not object to France's successful effort to exact reparations from the Haitian government in the 1820s, recompense for the "crimes" committed by Haitians who destroyed the property of French citizens – St Domingue slave owners – in the process of seizing their freedom from plantation slavery. The United States itself threatened Haiti with invasion in 1850 if she did not meet its monetary demands for debt repayment, and – despite the Monroe Doctrine – supported similar forms of extortion by other European nations. In 1915, the United States justified its invasion of Haiti with the claim that only thus could the safety of American creditors be guaranteed.[52]

Haitians have resisted American ventures, as in the Caco and other rebellions against the 1915–34 US occupation or the *dechoukaj* of the remnants of the US-backed Duvalier regime, but they have experienced tremendous suffering as the consequences of intervention, invasion and exploitation. In more recent years, the giveaways signed by Jean-Bertrand Aristide at Governor's Island in 1994, the price charged by the protector of world democracy for sweeping aside the anti-democratic military monster it had created and returning an elected president to office, turned vast sections of the Haitian economy over to outside exploitation. Allegedly similar to the "structural adjustment" that the World Bank and other institutions have forced on African nations, in the end they protected neither the Haitian people's right to choose their own government, nor Aristide himself. Yet here is how the script reads: despite the investments by the United States in Haitian nation-building over the previous years, the lucky recipients have failed. The insistent demands of American commentators and academics that we should analyse Haiti's situation as if American acts are completely irrelevant to the state of permanent crisis is simply another form of rendering Haiti's realities invisible.[53]

The completely unthinkable nature of America's historic debt to Haiti has allowed US decision makers to round up domestic support for imperialist and neo-imperialist ventures in the Caribbean. Surely American domestic support at some times, and convenient apathy at others, would have been less likely if a central part of national-historical consciousness was an acknowledgment that, in 1803, the United States had depended on Haiti for protection. For even if one consented to view as immaculate the American involvement in late-twentieth-century Haiti, putting aside an accounting of the crimes inflicted by American occupiers and neo-imperialists, the United States, in its relations with Haiti, is the one that has never paid its debts. Yet it is the very fact and magnitude of that debt that makes the US historian unable to come to the most obvious conclusions about the sequence and significance of causation in the case of the Louisiana Purchase. To admit those things would then be to admit that white America depended, perhaps for its survival, on the group of black people whom Americans seem to despise most and seem to think the least competent and independent – the most childish – in all the world. Perhaps the need to make more certainly invisible the history of US dependence acts and has acted as an incentive, however subconscious, for American people and policymakers who have rendered Haiti dependent in the past and present. And as the years go on, the mental costs of confronting this invisibility seem to mount. Despite the vaunted new willingness of American historians to incorporate African Americans and the history of slavery into their narratives, despite the expansion of cultural histories of the ideologies of whiteness, and despite the constant use of phrases like "Atlantic history", the stubborn refusal to repeat the words of Henry Adams remains. In the face of all the evidence, their persistent aversion to admitting the significance of Haitian victory for US survival and expansion, thereby recentring the narrative of the Louisiana Purchase, may be the best evidence of all that the debt exists and that many Americans find it too painful to acknowledge.

Much less will Americans be willing to render recompense. As always, when one comes to speak of Haiti, there is no easy solution. Were we to rewrite all the textbooks, we could not undo all of the foul things that have passed, all that the United States has done to Haiti. Given the long-established effort to hide the past, rendering visible Haiti's gift to American national wealth and comfort would take some doing. Yet the truth is always relevant. And by acknowledging a past in which Haitians decided the fate of the United States, perhaps more Americans might recognize that their two-centuries-old *a priori* assumption – that Haiti should not exist and that it cannot change its own fate, even with assistance from the United States – is not only incorrect, but has destroyed US–Haitian relations. Acknowledging this truth might also put more Americans on the road to acknowledging the injuries inflicted by the United States on Haiti, and perhaps to acknowledging some debt in the matters of invasion, occupation, support of dictators and coups, systematic attempts to subjugate the Haitian economy, and the unequal treatment of Haitian nationals. It is long past time for Americans to acknowledge what they owe to Haiti.

Notes

1. Michel-Rolph Trouillot, *Silencing the Past: Power and the Production of History* (Boston: Beacon Press, 1995), 40–69.

2. Ibid., 70–107; Sibylle Fischer, *Modernity Disavowed: Haiti and the Cultures of Slavery in the Age of Revolution* (Durham: Duke University Press, 2004).

3. Kathleen M. Brown, *Good Wives, Nasty Wenches, and Anxious Patriarchs: Gender, Race, and Power in Colonial Virginia* (Chapel Hill: University of North Carolina Press, 1996); Jennifer Morgan, *Laboring Women: Reproduction and Gender in New World Slavery* (Philadelphia: University of Pennsylvania Press, 2004); Kirsten Fischer, *Suspect Relations: Sex, Race, and Resistance in Colonial North Carolina* (Ithaca: Cornell University, 2002); Edward E. Baptist, "The Absent Subject: African-American Masculinity and Forced Migration to the Antebellum Plantation Frontier", in *Southern Masculinities*, ed. Craig T. Friend and Lorri Glover (Athens: University of Georgia Press, 2004).

4. Indeed, as much of the literature in the previous footnote argues, it was the denial of manhood status to male Africans, and citizenship rights to all Africans generally, that made white men into both men and citizens. Trouillot illustrates the implicit dichotomies at work here with the example of the French slave ship captain who, upon hearing that the *Société des Amis des Noirs* had offered support to the claim of *les gens de coleur* to citizenship, labelled himself " 'l'Ami des Hommes.' The Friends of the Blacks were not necessarily the friends of Men." Trouillot, *Silencing the Past*, 81–82. Cf. Susan Buck-Morss, "Hegel and Haiti", *Critical Inquiry* 26 (Summer 2000): 821–65.

5. J. Michael Dash, *Haiti and the United States: National Stereotypes and the Literary Imagination*, 2nd ed. (New York: St Martin's Press, 1997), 23.

6. Trouillot, *Silencing the Past*, 95–107; C.L.R. James, *The Black Jacobins: Toussaint L'Ouverture and the San Domingo Revolution* (1938; repr., London: Allison and Busby, 1980). Many histories of the Atlantic revolutionary period either ignore the Haitian Revolution (for example, R.R. Palmer) or depict it as a mere offshoot of the French Revolution. Cf. Fischer, *Modernity Disavowed*, 7; Walter Johnson, "Time and Revolution in African America: Temporality and the History of Atlantic Slavery", *Rethinking American History in a Global Age*, ed. Thomas Bender (Berkeley and Los Angeles: University of California Press, 2002), 148–67.

7. Epigraph from Jon Kukla, *A Wilderness So Immense: The Louisiana Purchase and the Destiny of America* (New York: Knopf, 2003).

8. Herbert Sloan, *Principle and Interest: Thomas Jefferson and the Problem of Debt* (New York: Oxford University Press, 1995); Roger Kennedy, *Mr Jefferson's Lost Cause: Land, Farmers, Slavery, and the Louisiana Purchase* (New York: Oxford University Press, 2003), 108–9; and Kukla, *Wilderness So Immense*, 245–49, discuss the suspension of the privilege of deposit of New Orleans.

9. I believe that this formulation comes originally from James, *Black Jacobins*.

10. Theodore Crackel, *Mr. Jefferson's Army: Political and Social Reform of the Military Establishment, 1801–1809* (New York: New York University Press, 1987), 100, reports that the US Army had only two companies of artillery and four of infantry stationed along its Mississippi River border with Spain.

11. Quoted in Kukla, *Wilderness So Immense*, 245; Thomas Jefferson to Robert Livingston, 18 April 1802.

12. Ibid., 232 (quotation).

13. Cf. Alexander Hamilton's February editorial: "For the *Evening Post*", 8 February 1803, in *The Papers of Alexander Hamilton*, ed. Harold C. Syrett, Jacob E. Cooke and Barbara Chernow (New York: Columbia University Press, 1961–87), 26: 82–85; Alexander DeConde, *This Affair of Louisiana* (New York: Scribner's, 1976); Peter Kastor, *The Nation's Crucible: The Louisiana Purchase and the Creation of America* (New Haven: Yale University, 2004); François Barbé-Marbois, *The History of Louisiana, Particularly of the Cession of that Colony to the United States of America*, trans. William B. Lawrence (Philadelphia: Carey and Lea, 1830), 251–52. Pushed by Federalists, Jeffersonians in the US Senate belatedly passed a resolution in late February, allowing Jefferson to call up 80,000 militia in the western and southern states. Cf. Walter LaFeber, "An Expansionist's Dilemma", *Constitution* 5, no. 3 (1993): 4–13. The House of Representatives approved the resolution on March 2. *Senate Journal*, 7th Cong., 2nd sess., 117 (Washington, DC: A. and G. Way, 1802; repr. Wilmington, Del.: Michael Glazier, n.d.); *Journal of the House of Representatives*, 7th Cong., 2nd sess., 359 (Washington, DC: S.H. Smith, 1802; repr. Wilmington, Del.: Michael Glazier, n.d.). They did not actually appropriate any money to do so, and survivors of the American Revolution surely knew that militia troops against hardened regulars would face long odds. In a letter sent to Monroe right before his departure on the French mission, Secretary of State James Madison admitted that this resolution was for show and represented no real investment: "[these were] measures of expenceless or cheap preparation". Madison to James Monroe, 1 March 1803, *Papers of James Madison: Secretary of State Series*, vol. 4, *1802–1803*, ed. Nancy Hackett et al. (Charlottesville: University of Virginia, 1998), 361–62. This has not stopped American historians from arguing that Jefferson tricked Bonaparte into backing down: a sort of "enchantment", according to Arthur P. Whitaker, *The Mississippi Question, 1795–1803: A Study in Trade, Politics, and Diplomacy* (New York: Appleton, 1934), 216–36; cf. E. Wilson Lyon, *Louisiana in French Diplomacy, 1759–1804* (Norman: University of

Oklahoma, 1934), 203. Unfortunately, Napoleon did not hear the news about this army, whether it was a real prospect or empty threat, until he had not only already decided to sell Louisiana but in fact had informed the American emissaries of his decision: Albert H. Bowman, "Pichon, the United States, and Louisiana", *Diplomatic History* 1 (Summer 1977): 257–270, esp. 267 and 267n32. For those willing to face facts, this should put the *quietus* to the claim that American military posturing in February 1803 had any effect on Bonaparte's decision.

    14. Carolyn Fick, *The Making of Haiti: The Saint-Domingue Revolution from Below* (Knoxville: University of Tennessee Press, 1990); David P. Geggus, *Haitian Revolutionary Studies* (Bloomington and Indianapolis: Indiana University Press, 2002); Laurent Dubois, *Avengers of the New World: The Story of the Haitian Revolution* (Cambridge, Mass.: Belknap, 2004).

    15. Cf. Dubois, *Avengers of the New World*, 302. David Geggus does not give an estimate of black deaths in the Haitian Revolution, though he concludes that the population was "decimated". Geggus, *Haitian Revolutionary Studies*.

    16. P.L. Roederer, *Oeuvres Du Comte P.L. Roederer* (Paris: Firmin Didot Frères, 1854), 3: 461; Comté Barbé-Marbois, *History of Louisiana* (Philadelphia: Carey and Lea, 1830), 174–75, 263–64.

    17. DeConde, *This Affair of Louisiana*, 161–66.

    18. Cf. Dubois, *Avengers of the New Worlds,* 297–301 for a concise account of the Haitian declaration of independence.

    19. Alexander Hamilton, in the *New-York Evening Post*, 5 July 1803, in Syrett et al., *Papers of Alexander Hamilton*, 26: 130–31.

    20. Tim Matthewson, "Jefferson and Haiti", *Journal of Southern History* 61 (May 1995), 209–41, quote 231; Brenda Gayle Plummer, *Haiti and the United States: The Psychological Moment* (Athens: University Press of Georgia, 1992), 19; see also the "nationalists" identified in Robert L. Paquette, "Revolutionary Saint Domingue in the Making of Territorial Louisiana", in *A Turbulent Time: The French Revolution and the Greater Caribbean*, ed. David Barry Gaspar and David P. Geggus (Bloomington and Indianapolis: Indiana University Press, 1997), 204–25.

    21. "The Africans . . . . without pillaging" quoted in Gordon S. Brown, *Toussaint's Clause: The Founding Fathers and the Haitian Revolution* (Jackson, University Press of Mississippi, 2005), 207; Rayford W. Logan, *The Diplomatic Relations of the United States With Haiti, 1776–1891* (Chapel Hill: University of North Carolina Press, 1941), 146–47; Jan Pachonski, *Poland's Caribbean Tragedy: A Study of Polish Legions in the Haitian War of Independence, 1802–1803*, trans. Reuel K. Wilson (Boulder: East European monographs; New York: Distributed by Columbia University Press, 1986), 58–59. DeConde, *This Affair of Louisiana*, argues that Jefferson initially supported Bonaparte's invasion as an attempt to rein in a potential source of black independence. Later, DeConde asserts he "stepp[ed] up aid to the rebels" as Louisiana negotiations stalled [101]. Both DeConde and Matthewson depend for

their claim on a couple of official letters from the French minister to Washington (Pichon) complaining that American merchants are supplying the rebels. One might also weigh these letters – written neither in St Domingue or one of the major commercial ports of the US – with some acknowledgment of their rhetorical nature, but in any case one might observe the slippage from merchants' independent decisions into the contention that Jefferson was supplying the rebels with the material needed to create the decisive margin of victory.

22. Matthewson, "Jefferson and Haiti"; see Logan, *Diplomatic Relations*, 147–48 for the timing of the loan rejection. Logan, in contrast to those who have cited (and, I would say, misinterpreted) his careful work on the diplomatic archives in their attempts to depict American aid as decisive, rejected any attempt to assert such a conclusion when the facts appeared inconclusive: "I find it impossible to evaluate the four factors responsible for this extraordinary event, namely, yellow fever, Jefferson's policy, the British blockade, and the courage and determination of the Haitian troops" (Logan, *Diplomatic Relations*, 150–51). Perhaps the fact that Logan was not white was a mere coincidence, and had nothing to do with his willingness to concede some agency to the Haitian rebels.

23. Tim Matthewson, *A Proslavery Foreign Policy: Haitian-American Relations during the Early American Republic* (Westport, Conn.: Praeger, 2003), 114; cf. the similar interpretation offered by Thomas O. Ott, *The Haitian Revolution: 1789–1804* (Knoxville: University of Tennessee Press, 1973).

24. DeConde, *This Affair of Louisiana*, 159. See the critique of the inevitability of Manifest Destiny in Peter Kastor, *The Nation's Crucible: The Louisiana Purchase and the Creation of America* (New Haven: Yale University, 2004), 39–40. Hamilton considered his February demand in an editorial – that Jefferson increase the size of the army to 10,000 men – was likely to be considered wildly excessive. In 1802, the US Army was approximately 4,436 men in strength. See Hamilton's February editorial "For the *Evening Post*"; and on US Army strength in Syrett et al., *Papers of Alexander Hamilton*, 26:14–15n9. See note 13 above for the claim that a proposed calling-out of the militia in the western and southern states was essential to forcing Bonaparte's hand.

25. See Daniel J. Cohen, "By the Book: Assessing the Place of Textbooks in a US Survey Course", *Journal of American History* 91, no. 4 (2005): 1405–15; Steve Forman, "Textbook Publishing: An Ecological View", *Journal of American History* 91, no. 4 (2005): 1398–405.

26. "Mentioning everything" from Chester E. Finn, Jr., president of the Thomas E. Fordham Institute, quoted in Gary Kornblith and Carol Lasser, " 'The Truth, The Whole Truth, and Nothing But the Truth': Writing, Producing, and Using College-Level American History Textbooks", *Journal of American History* 91, no. 4 (2005): 1382. The basic perspective on nationalism outlined by Benedict Anderson, *Imagined Communities: Reflections on the Origin and Spread of Nationalism* (London: Verso, 1983) is obviously important for the architectonics of my own thought here. On the American case, see the work on the exclusion of black agency in historical accounts of the Civil War summarized by David Blight, *Race and Reunion: The Civil War in American Memory* (Cambridge, Mass.: Belknap, 2000).

27. A text would have to be aggressively anti-nationalist indeed not to risk replicating the idea that there is a broad community called "Americans" who all have in common the identification with American nationality as a desirable quality. The one exception that comes to mind is Howard Zinn, *A People's History of the United States: 1492–Present* (New York: HarperCollins, 2003). The contrast between this and Eric Foner, *The Story of American Freedom* (New York: W.W. Norton, 1998) is instructive.

28. They rarely see the domestic slave trade and forced southwestward migration of enslaved people generally as an essential component of the story of US expansion. Instead this falls under the category of Southern history, usually confined to a chapter on the "Old" and presumably slow-to-change or -expand south. The role of slavery is often seen as a "contradiction" and a problem for future "race relations" rather than as a massive process of exploitation that built white wealth in both South and North. Perhaps that is both cause and consequence of the fact that only 6 per cent of white Americans support reparations to African Americans for slavery. See Gregory W. Streitch, "Is There a Right to Forget: Historical Injustices, Race, Memory, and Identity", *New Political Science* 24, no. 4 (2002): 525–42, esp. 540n59.

29. See the still-accurate observations of D.W. Meinig, "Continental America, 1800–1915: The View of an Historical Geographer", *History Teacher* 22 (February 1989): 189–203. "My theme is grounded on the elementary fact that the US has neighbors." But as he notes, in the textbooks he surveyed, he was "surprised [by] the paucity of treatment [of neighbouring countries and their interactions with the United States], the rigidity of focus, the narrow internal exclusiveness of concern". Ibid., 189–90.

30. Murrin et al., *Liberty, Equality, Power*, 281.

31. Faragher et al., *Out of Many: A History of the American People*, 4th ed. (New York: Pearson Group/Prentice Hall, 2002), 250. The textbook *A People and a Nation* does perhaps the best job of any of this lot in connecting the Louisiana Purchase to Haitian success in resisting Napoleon, as consequence to cause: "Napoleon had lost interest in the New World. Once he failed to recapture independent Haiti, the idea of a New World empire dissolved and Louisiana became superfluous. At the same time he needed money for renewed warfare against Britain." Mary Beth Norton et al., *A People and a Nation* (Boston: Houghton Mifflin, 2002), 220. One should note that high school history textbooks are apparently no better, and perhaps worse, on this question. Cf. Greg Dunkel, "Haiti's Impact on the United States: What 'Voodoo Economics' and High School Textbooks Reveal", in *Haiti: A Slave Revolution: 200 years After 1804*, ed. Pat Chin et al. (New York: International Action Center, 2004), 45–57, esp. 52–53.

32. Joseph Conlin, *The American Past: A Survey of American History*, 7th ed. (New York: Thomson, Wadsworth, 2004), 167. Cf. George B. Tindall and David Shi, *America: A Narrative History*, 5th ed. (New York: W.W. Norton, 1999), 1: 378, which manages to not come down on any side of the question.

33. James Roark, Michael Johnson and Patricia Cline Cohen, eds., *The American*

Promise (Boston: Bedford/St Martin's, 2001), 1: 294. My notes indicate that my reader's report for the publisher on the first edition of Roark et al. raised this question in insistent tones, but evidently there was not much of a response.

34. Faragher et al., *Out of Many*, 240. See Murrin et al., *Liberty, Equality, Power*, concise 2nd ed. (Fort Worth: Harcourt, 2001), 1: 244, which refers to the "sugar island of Saint Dominique [*sic*]" and a slave revolt that occurred there between 1802 and 1803. I am not familiar with the island or the slave revolt.

35. Conlin, *The American Past*, 167. Of course, "specialists" do no better at times than synthesists, for example, Ronald D. Smith, "Napoleon and Louisiana: Failure of the Proposed Expedition to Occupy and Defend Louisiana, 1801–1803", *Louisiana History* 12 (Winter 1971): 21–40, esp. 38.

36. Faragher et al., *Out of Many*, 240; Trouillot notes that white authors habitually emphasize the role of yellow fever in French defeat, while black authors acknowledge that black rebels may have had something to do with French losses as well.

37. Earlier works on the Purchase and on the geographical expansion of the United States and its empire often avoided discussing the Haitian Revolution at all. Drew McCoy, *The Elusive Republic: Political Economy in Jeffersonian America* (New York: Norton, 1982), which manages to describe national expansion as the key to Jefferson's political economy without mentioning the Haitian Revolution, is one such example. The alternative response to the argument that defeat in St Domingue spurred Bonaparte's decision to sell is ridicule of the idea that Haiti could influence the course of history. See William M. Sloan, "The World Aspects of the Louisiana Purchase", *American Historical Review* 9 (April 1904): 513.

38. James Sofka, "Thomas Jefferson and the Problem of World Politics", in *The Louisiana Purchase: Emergence of an American Nation*, ed. Peter J. Kastor, Landmark Events in US History (Washington DC: Congressional Quarterly Press, 2002), 59.

39. Charles Cerami, *Jefferson's Great Gamble: The Remarkable Story of Jefferson, Napoleon, and the Men Behind the Louisiana Purchase* (Naperville, Ill.: Sourcebooks, 2003), 53.

40. Ibid., 47–51, 70.

41. Kennedy, *Mr Jefferson's Lost Cause*; and Kukla, *Wilderness So Immense*. I except from this generalized critique the works of two recent historians of slave rebellion, Robert Paquette and Douglas Egerton.

42. Peter S. Onuf, review of Kukla, *Wilderness So Immense*, in *American Historical Review* 109, no. 2 (2004): 519.

43. Similarly, Tim Matthewson dismisses the question of Haiti's role in the Purchase as a "hardy perennial" of historiography – perhaps not a flower but a weed, to some American historians: Matthewson, "Jefferson and Haiti", 209. Alfred Hunt, *Haiti's Influence on Antebellum America: Slumbering Volcano in the Caribbean* (Baton Rouge: Louisiana State University Press, 1988), 190–91.

44. Trouillot, *Silencing the Past*.

45. Hunt, *Haiti's Influence on Antebellum America*, 129–39. Traditionally authors have

seen Southern commentators on Haiti as operating from a panicked fear of slave revolt, but the angry attempt to silence something that simply does not fit their world view must also be considered an element of the antebellum South's approach to Haiti.

46. J. Michael Dash, *Haiti and the United States: National Stereotypes and the Literary Imagination*, 2nd ed. (New York: St Martin's Press, 1997) 3; Paul Farmer, *The Uses of Haiti* (Monroe, Me.: Common Courage Press, 1994).

47. See Blight, *Race and Reunion*.

48. Henry Adams, *History of the United States in the Administrations of Jefferson and Madison* (New York: Scribner's, 1889–91), 1: 2, 20–21.

49. Thomas Bailey, *Diplomatic History of the American People*, 8th ed. (New York: Appleton/Meredith, 1969), 114, does say "John Adams and Toussaint L'Ouverture, in whose honor statues should be erected in appropriate spots, are the forgotten purchasers" of Louisiana. One might assume that if someone else purchases something that you then hold, you owe them a debt of either payment, thanks or a gift in return. However, Bailey then insists that Bonaparte's decision came from a desire to keep the United States out of an alliance with Britain, and, of course, "averting future wars with this boundary-bursting young nation" (ibid., 108). In other words, Napoleon feared the United States – although apparently he did not fear them until the Haitians had defeated him. Bailey's racist discussions of Toussaint Louverture also leave much to be desired.

50. I addressed this issue in an paper presented at the Haitian Bicentenary Conference at the University of the West Indies, Trinidad and Tobago, 15 June 2004. My short answer is one might argue that the Haitian defeat of Napoleon's army could be said to have saved the United States the equivalent of $641 million in 1803. The Purchase cost the United States approximately four cents per acre, while the US federal government typically sold land at a minimum price of $1.25. None of this money has ever been repaid, so, with 201 years of 5 per cent annual interest, the US benefit from Haitian victory could now in this way be calculated at $15.25 trillion.

51. The recent nonsensical book by John J. Miller, *Our Oldest Enemy: A History of America's Disastrous Relationship With France* (New York: Doubleday, 2004), seems to emanate directly from the resentment of "conservative" Americans at France's effrontery in the Bush-generated Iraq crisis. The resentment runs so deep that the author produces a text whose essential premise is a *prima facie* falsehood, an attempt to have shrill polemics wipe away the reality of France's crucial support for the United States at the latter nation's founding. If you are not going to accept our lead, the book seems to say, and we cannot define you as dependent, we must define you as a mortal enemy.

52. Alex Dupuy, *Haiti in the World Economy: Class, Race, and Underdevelopment since 1700* (Boulder: Westview, 1989), 126–42; Hans Schmidt, *The United States Occupation of Haiti, 1915–1934* (New Brunswick: Rutgers, 1971).

53. Dash, *Haiti and the United States*, 166–68; see Sibylle Fischer's critique of Samuel Huntington's comments on Haiti in *Modernity Disavowed*, 7.

CHAPTER 2

St Domingue Refugees in New Orleans
Identity and Cultural Influences

Nathalie Dessens

The repercussions of the revolution that ended with the foundation of Haiti, the second republic in the Americas, were both strong and manifold. Among them was the constitution of a diaspora of refugees who settled in the neighbouring West Indian islands (in the Spanish part of the island – Santo Domingo – in Cuba, Jamaica, Trinidad, Puerto Rico and many other islands, although in smaller proportions) and also on the northern continent. Many inhabitants of St Domingue found refuge in the Atlantic harbours of the United States and many more still ended up on the Gulf Coast and in Louisiana, especially in New Orleans.

Whites, slaves and free people of colour from St Domingue poured into New Orleans between the early 1790s and the 1810s. Some came directly in the 1790s and at the time of the independence of Haiti, but for most of those fifteen thousand or so migrants, New Orleans was a secondary destination. They arrived there from the eastern United States and from the Caribbean, especially Jamaica, from where a thousand Haitian migrants came in 1803–4 and Cuba in 1809–10. The Cuban wave was the largest and brought to Louisiana ten thousand refugees, doubling at once the population of the Crescent City. Composed of three numerically equal groups of whites, slaves and free people of colour, the wave of immigrants had enormous repercussions on the social fabric and culture of Louisiana.[1]

The impact of the refugee community on the economy, social organization and political life of their host territory was significant. Many areas of Louisiana society were influenced by the Haitian migrants, and domains such as sugar cultivation, education, journalism and the arts especially benefited from their expertise.

The three-tiered organization of society was reinforced and the political life was enriched by their unusual dynamism and tradition of activism.

The Haitian migrants' most enduring influence was undoubtedly in the cultural field. All three categories of population brought specific cultural traits to Louisiana. The whites developed education, journalism, architecture, the theatre and many other fields, but also implanted a strong tradition of Freemasonry. The slaves influenced all aspects of the vernacular culture from cooking to oral literature, from Voodoo to the Creole language. As for the free people of colour, they gave a dynamic impulse to the cultural expansion of nineteenth-century New Orleans and a clear tradition of contestation.[2] There is no doubt that these ten thousand new arrivals had an enormous influence on a city whose population in 1805 was only eight thousand.[3] A long historiographic silence has surrounded this refugee movement. Whenever allusions have been made, in the past two centuries, to their presence in Louisiana, the possible influences of the three groups on the Louisiana culture were mentioned separately. No research of these influences has ever been attempted without dissociating the three groups. Although it makes the study more difficult, it seems, however, closer to reality and far more intellectually challenging to consider the cultural continuum created by the three interdependent Haitian migrant groups and their common influence on the Louisiana culture. After a brief survey of the main identified cultural influences of each of the various refugee groups, this chapter will focus on the development of a common identity among the refugees that may in turn lead to considering them as a community. The emphasis will thereafter be placed on the features that justify my challenge to the traditional division between the three groups as far as cultural influences are concerned.

Although the historiography has long been silent on the refugees, it is easy to draw a global picture of their main fields of cultural influence in Louisiana.[4] Some influences are better known than others. The slaves from St Domingue brought with them and passed onto the Louisiana slave community many cultural traits that had been first creolized in St Domingue. A first syncretism had indeed been operated in the island between various African cultural bases, as well as Amerindian and French cultures.[5] The specific culture that emerged from this fusion and adapted to the local surroundings had many features in common with the Louisiana slave culture, but the difference in the milieus where this creolization had occurred also induced many differences. When the St Domingue slaves came to Louisiana, they brought their very specific culture with them, and a two-sided acculturation occurred. They imported some cultural traits and revitalized others that existed in a latent state. When they reached Louisiana, they brought with them an organized Voodoo cult and their own Creole language, which influenced the Louisiana Creole.[6] They also added to all aspects of Louisiana folk culture. Their Caribbean rhythms infused the local music and gave birth to a very specific style of music described by all the travellers who attended the dances on Congo Square throughout the nineteenth century.[7] The St Domingue slaves added certain specific traits to the oral literature of the Louisiana slave community. They altered cooking and clothing practices, vernacular medicine and all the fields of daily life, including architectural traditions.[8]

The free refugees of colour are said to have, by their occupational patterns, added much to the culture of Louisiana. They were mostly artisans and their main fields of influence were confectionery, house building and furniture making.[9] They thus greatly influenced the main building practices of Louisiana, as well as the fashion domain. The Haitian free people of colour were extremely active artistically, leaving in Louisiana a very deep cultural legacy.[10] Famous poets, writers and musicians were refugees or were descended from refugees. Edmond Dédé, Constant Debergue, Eugene Arcade and Samuel Snaër were highly considered musicians in Louisiana. Louis Victor Séjour, Michel Séligny, Camille Thierry, Armand Lanusse and Rodolphe Desdunes were among the most famous and most prolific writers of nineteenth-century Louisiana.[11] There is no doubt that the free refugees of colour left a tremendous cultural legacy to Louisiana and that they endorsed the leadership of the politically active free group of colour in nineteenth-century New Orleans.[12]

The white refugees' most influential role bore on the development of culture in general. In the early nineteenth century, Louisiana was still lagging somewhat in most cultural fields and was considered to be very close to a frontier society, although the Spanish regime had left the marks of some improvements and refinements on the French Louisiana society. This lack of cultural development was particularly palpable when Louisiana was compared to St Domingue, especially in the areas of education, cultural entertainment, the press, and all the fields pertaining to the improvement and transmission of knowledge.[13] The refugees immediately tried to draw the society and culture of their new homeland closer to that of their birthplace. They founded, directed, edited and wrote for all the newspapers of early American Louisiana. From the first Louisiana newspaper, *Le Moniteur de la Louisiane*, founded in 1794, to *Le Courrier de la Louisiane*, which ran from 1807 to 1860, to the *Louisiana Gazette*, the first bilingual newspaper of Louisiana, to *L'Ami des Lois, Le Propagateur*

Catholique, *La Lorgnette* or *L'Abeille*, the Louisiana press was entirely in the hands of the refugees.[14]

The white refugees also founded schools at all educational levels, primary and secondary schools for both black (free and slave) and white children, but also the first establishment of higher education in Louisiana, the *Collège d'Orléans*.[15] They founded, managed and acted in the theatres of Louisiana. They founded the French opera, the first opera in the United States that could emulate the European opera houses.[16] They opened bookstores and music stores. By means of all these new ventures, they brought much cultural and educational vitality to New Orleans and ensured the survival of Gallic culture – even if it was already creolized, adapted to the situation and place in which it emerged – and French language in American Louisiana. They also developed other forms of entertainment, mainly balls, gambling and duelling.[17] They founded places for socializing, from café bars (the famous *Café des Réfugiés*) to coffee shops. Moreover, they brought an active tradition of Freemasonry to Louisiana, founding the main lodges, becoming Grand Masters, and ensuring a very porous relationship between Freemasonry and society at large.[18] It is thus easy to find the areas of influence of all three groups. It is also easy to examine them – at least superficially – separately. When working on them, however, so many overlapping areas appear that it seems much preferable to deal with them without entirely separating the three refugee groups, all the more so because there seems to have existed among them a real sense of community.

The three groups shared a strong feeling of ethnic community. They all travelled together, on the same boats, after living through the difficult stages of the migration.[19] They were connected in many ways, sometimes by blood ties (in particular the whites and the free refugees of colour), or at least by years of living side by side, since the slaves the refugees brought with them were domestic slaves, oftentimes very close ones. Many a tale of refugee flight – whether real or romanticized – is about the Mammy smuggling her master's children onto a boat and hiding them until the vessel left St Domingue for safer refuges.

They had lived together in St Domingue, had shared the same cultural experiences, were interconnected and had fled together to their various asylums. This might already suggest the idea of community. They were also all confronted with the challenges of settling in an altogether new environment, and lived in the same areas of New Orleans, essentially the French Quarter and the faubourgs Tremé and Marigny.[20] Although slaveholding refugees sometimes rented their slaves out to ensure their own survival, many kept their slaves with them, which meant that coexistence was maintained between them. Relationships also continued between white refugee men and free women of colour. In general, historians mention the "close personal relationships" developing between the two groups.[21] Paul Lachance, for instance, speaks of "quasi-familial relationships between some masters and their slaves".[22] There are even examples of philanthropic assistance between the different groups. Rodolphe Desdunes, himself of refugee descent, mentions Julien Déjour, a free philanthropist of mixed African ancestry born at Les Cayes, in St Domingue, who made a fortune in Louisiana and gave part of it away to the needy. Desdunes writes: "The white, the black, the yellow – all were the same in his eyes and all received from him equal compassion and monetary assistance."[23]

Of course, all this is hardly sufficient to justify the idea of a continuum between the three groups. But there was also, quite visibly, among all the refugees, whatever their race and status, a certain common pride of being from St Domingue. All legal and sacramental documents bear testimony to this fact. There is hardly a marriage contract or a will passed before a notary, a certificate of baptism or marriage recorded by the Catholic Church that does not bear the mention of the St Domingue origins of those who signed them, be they whites or free people of colour. While most other notarial acts and sacramental records rarely mention the place of birth of the parents, for instance, this information is contained in all the documents concerning St Domingue refugees' descendants. In the sacramental records, the links with St Domingue are sometimes indicated by a marginal note added by the two priests who kept the records, Thoma and Koune, both St Domingue refugees. Tombs also display the refugees' habit of indicating their origins, sometimes very late into the nineteenth century and sometimes for persons who were not even born in St Domingue, but who lived there for a while.[24] The St Domingue refugees obviously constituted "a distinct ethnic group for two decades after the major influx of 1809", although this feeling of shared ethnicity decreased after 1830, partly because the indemnification of the refugees by the French government had shattered any faint hope of return, and partly because the first generation refugees were progressively disappearing.[25] The three decades were sufficient, however, to activate the cultural continuum between the three groups and the transmission of their specificities to Louisiana. According to Gabriel Debien and René Le Gardeur, at a time when Louisiana was a favourite place of settlement for Americans and when Americanization was jeopardizing the Creoles' Gallic culture of Louisiana, "united by their Creole language and culture and by their common misfortune, these newcomers from the islands permitted New Orleans to preserve for a few more years its colonial character, its exotic charm and a life-style similar to that of an island just offshore from the continent".[26]

Although the differences and oppositions had been strong in St Domingue between the different racial groups, essentially because of the very different statuses they had been granted, a common cultural ground had existed, be it in matters of language, architecture and culinary or musical tradition, for instance. An initial creolization process had occurred between them all in St Domingue, characterized by a blending of various ethnic traditions with adaptation to the very specific Caribbean milieu. Their common flight and resettlement in a strange land had reinforced the cultural continuum they had brought with them to their new homeland. They all spoke the Creole language together, ate the same food (cooked by slaves or not), grew, sold and consumed the same products, listened to the same music, and lived in the same houses. Together they followed or created clothing fashions. Whatever part they played in the chain, the result was that they were used to the same cultural features and thus participated together in its transmission in Louisiana.

This idea of a common cultural continuum transmitted by a community derives both from the existence of a certain spirit of community among them and from the fact that, even when one group was more influential in certain areas, the others also participated in the transmission. Education, for instance, has always appeared as a privileged area for white cultural transmission. Many free persons of colour, however, also opened schools and taught.[27] The press was certainly another area of white prestige. There were, however, newspapermen who were free refugees of mixed ancestry working for the white refugee press.[28] The free people of colour were also very active in the development of Freemasonry. There were several non-segregated lodges and many masons, sometimes very influential ones, were of mixed ancestry as, for instance, Pierre Roup, who played an essential role in the foundation of the *Loge de la Persévérance* in 1820 and became (and remained for years) a high-ranking officer of the lodge.[29] In the same way, among the refugee actors were several quadroon actresses. As for the transmission of Caribbean or St Domingue musical traditions, this was ensured mainly by the refugee slaves who danced on Congo Square on Sundays and thus spread their rhythms, dances and musical instruments to Louisiana folk culture.[30] Some free composers of colour, however, like Edmond Dédé, and white composers, like Louis Gottshalk, also participated in the transmission. Gottshalk clearly says, in his autobiographical book *Notes from a Pianist*, that his aim when writing compositions such as his most famous tune "Bamboula" of 1848 was to record the West Indian music heard in his childhood on Congo Square.[31]

Architecture was another example of mixed influences beyond any notion of race and status. When considering the example of the Creole cottage (or of the shotgun house, which some specialists say is derived from a process of creolization occurring in the West Indies between Amerindian, African and European influences), the responsibility for introducing architectural features cannot be attributed to the white community alone.[32] They participated, of course, by having this type of house built, but the main artisans were free men of colour, and the builders were slaves. Although some refugees rented out or even sold their slaves to survive, most of them kept with them the slaves they had brought from St Domingue, and those slaves participated in all the ventures their masters started in their new homeland. Similarly, all three groups played a role in introducing new tastes and new fashions in clothing, jewels and decoration. If the whites ordered these products and partly chose the style they wanted, the main artisans were free refugees of colour, and slaves very often participated in the confection. The same could be said about cooking, which would be performed by white women, free women of colour and slaves. The refugees' culinary traditions had emerged from the combination of Caribbean products with products imported from the other continents by the various populations, and from the mixing of Amerindian, African and European preparation and cooking traditions.[33] Influences on the Creole cooking of Louisiana can thus hardly be attributed to a single group. Similarly, the Creole language of Louisiana was doubtlessly influenced by the St Domingue Creole speakers. The introduction of some words and syntactic structures pre-existing in St Domingue Creole is concomitant with the arrival of the refugees.[34] It is clear that in the linguistic field, the transmission was ensured mainly by the black refugees, slave and free. The whites, however, also used this idiom to communicate with their slaves and with the free refugees of colour. Therefore, we can justifiably state that the whole group participated in the transmission of the language.

To take but one last example, the introduction of Voodoo is generally attributed to the St Domingue migrants that came to Louisiana in the early nineteenth century. The slaves, of course, as the original practitioners of this religion in St Domingue, were the main vectors of its transmission to Louisiana. The religion, however, apparently crossed all racial barriers. Many New Orleans Voodoo figures, like Dr John, as well as the main Voodoo queens of New Orleans (Sanité Dédé, for instance), were free refugees of colour or were connected with the free refugee group (the first Marie Laveau was twice married to free refugees of colour and the second Marie Laveau, her daughter, who is sometimes mistaken for her mother, was thus a descendant of refugees). At lower levels of the organization, many free refugees of colour were involved in rituals and practices. The St Domingue whites also participated, and Marie Laveau's career is said to have begun while she was an itinerant hairdresser for white women. The descriptions of Voodoo ceremonies also most often include white spectators and participants.[35]

Finally, the refugee community as a whole reinforced the Creole tradition of New Orleans and enabled it to resist much longer the Americanization that followed the Louisiana Purchase. To quote Paul Lachance, "the persistence of a Gallic community in New Orleans for over three decades after the Louisiana Purchase was in large part owing to its reinforcement by racially and socially heterogeneous French-speaking immigrants".[36] Because their schools and newspapers were francophone, they ensured the persistence of the French language until the late nineteenth century, all the more so, since they were intent upon preserving their Gallic culture. The Books of Wills of New Orleans prove that in the 1830s, while most wills were written in English, even by Creoles and "foreign" French, the refugees and their descendants still wrote theirs in French.[37] In the second half of the nineteenth century, the main intellectuals descended from the free refugees of colour still produced literary works exclusively written in French. The collection of poems whose authors were mainly descended from refugees, *Les Cénelles*, published in 1845 by Armand Lanusse, himself of refugee ancestry, was written in French.[38] Rodolphe Desdunes also wrote exclusively in French, even as late as 1911, when *Nos hommes et notre histoire* was published. Louisiana folk culture in general resisted the sudden American invasion, to the point that, two hundred years later, Louisiana is still somehow not mainstream in America. In such fields as cooking, music or Mardi Gras traditions, Louisiana's exceptionalism has persisted into the twenty-first century, and a traveller to New Orleans today has no doubt that something in the historical culture of the city has conferred it a unique character.

The influence of the St Domingue refugee community on Louisiana's culture has long been neglected by the historians of Louisiana. When they were explored in the twentieth century, these fields generally occasioned studies that bore on one of the three groups of St Domingue migrants. Each of the main influences was attributed exclusively to one group. If it is true that one community generally had more influence in specific domains (the slaves for music or Voodoo, the free people of colour for literature, the whites for the press, education or Freemasonry), it is impossible, most of the time, to entirely dissociate the three groups. This is probably partly due to the Louisiana social fabric, which tended to favour this kind of cultural fluidity, but also and mainly to the refugee group which tended to build one cultural community. Having black people in schools, theatre plays or Masonic lodges did not shock the white refugees. The whites' attendance at the Congo Square dances or the Voodoo ceremonies was accepted by the black communities. The most probable explanation for this lies in the fact that the culture that the refugees brought with them was the result of a creolization process started in St Domingue as well as of the conditions of their migration, which tended to seal the common bond between all the different refugees. The two-way acculturation that followed the refugees' arrival in Louisiana was in fact a second creolization process – a recreolization perhaps – in which each and every individual member of the migrant group participated to his own degree.

There is still much to do to fully assess the influences of the St Domingue refugees in Louisiana. What is important, however, is to avoid any artificial division when assessing this cultural influence, even if the traditional historiographic treatment is easily understandable. Most nineteenth-century American historians tended to focus only on the white communities, and they dealt with the Americanization of Louisiana rather than with the forces that held in check the cultural homogenization of the nation. The following generations, attempting to fill in the gaps of a historiography that had so long focused solely on the white majority, quite naturally tended to deal exclusively with the black communities. It seems today much preferable to consider that they exerted a common influence, beyond race, status and class, and that they developed a certain "symbolic" ethnicity that they transmitted to Louisiana society through a complex and intricate process of creolization.[39]

Notes

1. The mayor of New Orleans gave the following official figures for the 1809–10 wave: 2,731 whites, 3,102 free people of colour and 3,226 slaves. Report of the Mayor of New Orleans to Governor Claiborne of 18 January 1810, published in *Le Moniteur de la Louisiane*, 27 January 1810.

2. For more details, see Caryn Cossé Bell, *Revolution, Romanticism, and the*

Afro-Creole Protest Tradition in Louisiana, 1718–1868 (Baton Rouge: Louisiana State University Press, 1997).

3. Detailed figures are available on the United States Census website, http://www.census.gov/.

4. The only study of the entire refugee community is Nathalie Dessens, *From Saint Domingue to New Orleans: Migration and Influences* (Gainesville: University Press of Florida, 2007). The migration was rediscovered in the second half of the nineteenth century and such historians as Gabriel Debien, Paul Lachance or Alfred Hunt have started delineating their main areas of influence on the Louisiana society.

5. On the process of creolization, see Robert Chaudenson, *Des Iles, Des Hommes, Des Langues: Langues Créoles – Cultures Créoles* (Paris: L'Harmattan, 1992), or David Buisseret et al., *Creolization in the Americas* (Arlington: Texas A&M University Press, 2000).

6. Among the best sources on the Creole language in Louisiana are Alcée Fortier, "The French Language in Louisiana and the Negro-French Dialect", *Transactions of the Modern Language Association of America* 1 (1886): 96–101; Morris F. Goodman, *A Comparative Study of Creole French Dialects* (London: Mouton and Co., 1964); Albert Valdman, *Le créole: structure, statut et origine* (Paris: Editions Klincksieck, 1978); and John Holm, *Pidgins and Creoles: Theory and Structure*, 2 vols. (Cambridge: Cambridge University Press, 1988).

7. On Congo Square, see Jerah Johnson, *Congo Square in New Orleans* (New Orleans: Louisiana Landmarks Society, 1995).

8. See, for instance, John Michael Vlach, "Plantation Landscapes of the Antebellum South", in *Before Freedom Came: African-American Life in the Antebellum South*, ed. D.C. Campbell, Jr. (Charlottesville: University Press of Virginia, 1991), 21–50.

9. Alfred P. Hunt, *Haiti's Influence on Antebellum America. Slumbering Volcano in the Caribbean* (Baton Rouge: Louisiana State University Press, 1988), 50–51. This is confirmed by the marriage contracts of the New Orleans Notarial Archives, as well as by all the indenture contracts and other sources also indicating the occupational pattern of the free refugees of colour.

10. On the main free authors of refugee descent, see Caryn Cossé Bell, "Haitian Immigration to Louisiana in the Eighteenth and Nineteenth Centuries", *African American Migration Experiences* (New York: Schomburg Center for Research in Black Culture, New York Public Library Digital Library Collection, forthcoming), http://digital.nypl.org.

11. The best document on the most influential persons of colour of nineteenth-century Louisiana remains the 1911 *Nos hommes et notre histoire* by Rodolphe Desdunes. It was published in English as *Our People and Our History: Fifty Creole Portraits*, trans. and ed. Sister Dorothea Olga McCants (Baton Rouge: Louisiana State University Press, 1971).

12. The *Plessy v. Ferguson* case was organized by a group of New Orleans men of colour of refugee descent. This episode, which is too often thought to have been spontaneous, is quite well described in Desdunes, 142–44. Also see Joseph Logsdon and Lawrence Powell, "Rodolphe Lucien Desdunes: Forgotten Organizer of the *Plessy* Protest", in *Sunbelt*

St Domingue Refugees in New Orleans

Revolution: The Historical Progression of the Civil Rights Struggle in the Gulf South, 1866–2000, ed. Samuel C. Hyde, Jr. (Gainesville: University Press of Florida, 2003): 42–70.

13. Moreau de St Méry, an inhabitant of St Domingue, was probably the best chronicler of life in the island in the pre-revolutionary years. For a detailed description of St Domingue's society, see his *Description Topographique, Physique, Civile, Politique et historique de la Partie Française de l'Isle de Saint-Domingue*, 3 vols. (Paris: Société de l'Histoire des Colonies Françaises et Librairie Larose, 1958).

14. On the French Louisiana press in the nineteenth century, see Samuel J. Marino, "Early French Newspapers in New Orleans", *Louisiana History* 7, no. 4 (Fall 1966): 309–22. The links between the Louisiana press and the refugee community are best traced by Hunt, *Haiti's Influence*, 53–54.

15. On education in Louisiana, see Stuart G. Noble and Arthur G. Nuhrah, "Education in Colonial Louisiana", *Louisiana Historical Quarterly* 32 (1949): 759–76. The link with the refugees is very well established by Hunt, *Haiti's Influence*, 54–57.

16. See, for instance, René J. Le Gardeur, *The First New Orleans Theatre, 1792–1803* (New Orleans: Leeward Books, 1963).

17. All the ballrooms that were opened in early-nineteenth-century New Orleans were opened by refugees, among whom was John Davis. To quote George W. Cable's 1884 *Creoles of Louisiana* (repr., Gretna, La: Pelican, 2000), "the West Indian was a leader in licentiousness, gambling and duelling" (218).

18. See Cossé Bell, *Revolution, Romanticism*, 145–86.

19. "Those responsible for introducing both the French opera and voodoo to the United States came to New Orleans . . . in the same refugee boats", Hunt, *Haiti's Influence*, 4.

20. Thomas Fiehrer writes that "they were drawn together by ties of blood, affinity and economic interdependence. They shared a lengthy, tumultuous experience and a common Creole sub-culture. Pressed close together by the spatial limits of New Orleans, forced upon each other by the shores of the lake and river, they congregated in the 'back of town' and in the Faubourg Marigny, where their building traditions are everywhere in evidence". Thomas Fiehrer, "An Unfathomed Legacy", in *The Road to Louisiana*, ed. Carl A. Brasseaux and Glenn R. Conrad (Lafayette: University of Southwestern Louisiana Press, 1992), 26. Alfred Hunt expresses the same thought when he writes that they "were bound together in a strange land by their Creole culture and by the harrowing violence in Saint-Domingue", *Haiti's Influence*, 41.

21. Caryn Cossé Bell, "Herman Grima House: A Window on Free Black Life and Urban Slavery in Creole New Orleans", *Louisiana Cultural Vistas* (Summer 2000): 74.

22. Paul Lachance, "The 1809 Immigration of Saint-Domingue Refugees to New Orleans: Reception, Integration and Impact", *Louisiana History* 29, no. 2 (Spring 1988): 128.

23. Desdunes, *Nos hommes*, 94.

24. Many tombstones in the New Orleans St Louis Cemeteries bear testimony to this habit. A tombstone in Charleston's St Mary of the Annunciation Cemetery bears the

following epitaph: "Firmin LE ROY, Né à Baugenci, France, Chirurgien et habitant de Saint-Domingue, Mort le 30/04/1819, Agé de 76 ans" [born at Baugency, France, Surgeon and inhabitant of St Domingue, died 30/04/1819, at the age of 76].

25. Lachance, "The 1809 Immigration", 128.

26. Gabriel Debien and René Le Gardeur, "The St Domingue Refugees in Louisiana", in Brasseaux and Conrad, *The Road to Louisiana* (Lafayette: University of Southwestern Louisiana Press, 1992), 114.

27. There are many examples. Among them, the very famous Couvent school or the school of the Sisters of the Holy Family co-founded with Henriette Delille by Juliette Gaudin, of St Domingue descent. This was a really essential move since, for lack of educational facilities in late-eighteenth-century Louisiana, the free people of colour had not had more opportunities to get educated than the white Louisianans.

28. When *L'Abeille* was founded in 1827 under the impulse of white refugees, the editors displayed a clear tendency towards progressive beliefs in matters of race and race relations. Several free blacks, using pen names, contributed to its columns. See Mary Gehman, *The Free People of Colour of New Orleans* (New Orleans: Margaret Media Inc., 1994), 54.

29. Cossé Bell, *Revolution, Romanticism*, 182.

30. The *Calinda*, the *Bamboula* and the *Chica* were imported to New Orleans from St Domingue by the refugee slaves. Among musical instruments, the *Banza*, the *Bamboula* (a small drum made of bamboo in St Domingue) and the *Marimba* (most certainly derived from St Domingue's *Marimbula*) became common in New Orleans in the early nineteenth century.

31. Louis Moreau Gottshalk, *Notes of a Pianist* (Philadelphia: J.B. Lippincott and Co., 1881), 27.

32. On the Creole cottage, see Patricia L. Duncan, "The French Creole Style", in *Louisiana Architecture: A Handbook on Styles*, ed. Jonathan Fricker, Donna Fricker and Patricia L. Duncan (Lafayette: Center for Louisiana Studies, 1998), 7. On the controversy concerning the shotgun house, see Andrew Gravette, *Architectural Heritage of the Caribbean* (Kingston: Ian Randle, 2000), 31. See also Hunt, *Haiti's Influence* (citing Vlach), 45.

33. Many sources mention the participation of all refugees in the spreading of new recipes in Louisiana. Many pastry cooks came among the refugees. Some famous refugees, such as John Davis, opened restaurants where Creole food was served. Jambalaya and mirliton are said to have Afro-Caribbean origins. The *filé*, made from ground sassafras, was "popularized by white and black St Domingans", Hunt, *Haiti's Influence*, 70.

34. The anterior marker "te", the prospective marker "ava", and a continuous form "apé" are among those introductions into the Louisiana Creole.

35. Robert Tallant, *Voodoo in New Orleans* (1946; repr., Gretna: Pelican, 1998), 16, 44 and 112.

36. Paul Lachance, "The Foreign French", in *Creole New Orleans, Race and Americanization*, ed. Arnold R. Hirsh and Joseph Logsdon (Baton Rouge: Louisiana State University Press, 1992), 130.

37. The Books of Wills of New Orleans may be consulted at the New Orleans Public Library.

38. The 1845 collection of poems was reprinted in its original language in 2003 by Les Cahiers du Tintamarre (Shreveport, La.).

39. On the concept of "symbolic ethnicity" see Herbert Gans, "Symbolic Ethnicity: The Future of Ethnic Groups and Cultures in America", first published in 1979 and reprinted (with author's comments) in *Theories of Ethnicity: A Classical Reader*, ed. Werner Sollors (New York: New York University Press, 1996), 425–59.

CHAPTER 3

Arguing around Toussaint
The Revolutionary in a Postcolonial Frame

Charles Forsdick

> *What is the story about Toussaint that we ought to tell out of the present we ourselves inhabit? . . . Part of the astonishing brilliance and enduring value of* The Black Jacobins . . . *is that James provides us with significant clues about the kind of story we might usefully tell – through Toussaint Louverture – about the relation between our past, our presents, and our possible futures.*
>
> – David Scott, *Conscripts of Modernity*

> *The evidence, it must be admitted, will support the most diverse interpretations; hence the many guises of the historiographical Toussaint, from the flawed radical hero of James's* Black Jacobins *to the self-aggrandizing and racist "Ancien Regime revolutionary" of Pierre Pluchon; from Ralph Korngold's altruistic* Citizen Toussaint *to the ruthlessly calculating Führer of Erwin Rüsch.*
>
> – David Geggus, *Haitian Revolutionary Studies*

Critics of postcolonial studies have commented – often with some justification – on the tendency of those working in the field to privilege certain individuals to the point of fetishization. This process is particularly true in relation to the key thinkers dubbed the "Holy Trinity" – Bhabha, Said and Spivak – the anthologization and exegesis of whose work risked, especially in the late 1990s, leading the postcolonial project into an analytical *impasse*. The aim of this chapter is to suggest the ways in which a subsequent widening of reference – to encompass non-anglophone zones and to expand the range of focused examples from which more general reflections might be extrapolated – has been central to the reinvigoration of the field.

In *Le Discours antillais*, Édouard Glissant suggests that there is a need to "argumenter autour de Toussaint" [argue around Toussaint][1] and in the following essay I reflect on the means whereby such a complex and often contradictory reflection on what the Haitian revolutionary leader meant in his colonial context (and now means in the postcolonial present) has contributed to ongoing processes of critical diversification in the postcolonial area. This essay also considers the ways in which "arguing around Toussaint" has contributed to the clarification of issues of gender and ethnicity, permitted further elaboration of concepts such as mimicry and hybridity, and at the same time encouraged a more general critique of the postcolonial project. The critics and thinkers discussed have emerged from a variety of contexts, both American (in the hemispheric sense of that term) and European. What links them is their connection, however loose and however unwitting, to a series of wider critical and even epistemological shifts often gathered under the term "postcolonialism". The chapter's critical approach is underpinned, as a result, by an awareness that the diverse interpretations explored – like all other representations or instrumentalizations of Toussaint – require thorough contextualization, both synchronic and diachronic. These interpretations are not only to be read in the light of the social construction of the critical field of which they form a part, but are also to be seen as a continuation of earlier debates addressing often similar questions. Discussions of Toussaint's ethnicity and hybridity cannot be fully understood, for instance, without an awareness of the contradictory versions of him – "mulatto" and "noiriste" – generated by the competing traditions of nineteenth-century Haitian historiography; and any materialist engagement with the heroic mythologization of Toussaint must be read in the light of the critique by Marxist historians in 1950s Haiti and of C.L.R. James's own questioning of the emphases of *The Black Jacobins* in his later career. Anthony Hurley has recently suggested that postcolonial engagements with Fanon are often characterized by an inevitable compromise of their subject's initial context, impact and meaning. The aim of this chapter's exploration of the shifting postcolonial interpretations of Toussaint himself is to highlight the ever-present risks of what Hurley dubs "presumptuousness" or "masked ideological assumptions",[2] while at the same time underlining the potential contribution of this complex Haitian exemplum to ongoing debates about colonialism and its legacies.

CHARLES FORSDICK

THE PERSISTENT REVOLUTIONARY

In a 2003 documentary entitled *Génération FLNC,* Matthieu Fillidori recalls the Corsican independence struggles of the 1970s: "We thought of ourselves as the new sons of Toussaint."[3] The claim does not lack a certain irony, especially given the origins of Napoleon Bonaparte, the man often presented as Toussaint Louverture's negative double and principal adversary. Moreover, the adoption by Corsican activists of the Caribbean revolutionary – whose associations with republican France, at certain points in his career, eclipsed any independentist desire on his part – creates an uneasy alliance, a situation highlighted when one considers the *modus operandi* of the activists in question, prone to combining Maoist ideology with practices more common among Fascist paramilitary groups. The association remains, however, a suggestive one: on the one hand, it illustrates the continuing usefulness of the Haitian revolutionary to those endeavouring to unpick, in a postcolonial period, the centralizing and monocultural logic of the French Republic; on the other, it reflects Toussaint's persistent flexibility, for the historical figure serving in the 1970s as an inspiration for Corsican autonomy would, by the end of the following decade, feature prominently in the decidedly pro-Republican celebrations of 1989.[4] The tensions inherent in this seemingly contradictory double appropriation are central to the web of narratives whereby postcolonial France has often attempted – successfully or otherwise – to manage (or even minimize) the legacies of colonialism while endeavouring to safeguard certain connections between the past and the present.

To a certain extent, the divergent uses identified above continue two centuries of apparently conflicting and often even opposing appropriations of Toussaint, who has been recruited to a variety of ideological and aesthetic causes. In Marcus Wood's terms: "Toussaint L'Ouverture never was a stable historical entity, and he is now a more Protean cultural phenomenon than ever before". My arguments in this chapter will echo Wood's contention that Toussaint's complex portability has in fact been accentuated in the postcolonial period.[5] Far from being reduced to the status of a static historical figure, fixed through the processes of monumentalization, Toussaint has continued to trigger reflection on the colonial past and the postcolonial present – and this not least in Haiti, where Jean-Bertrand Aristide's rhetoric was carefully interwoven with the contemporary memorialization of Louverture, and where the president's alleged removal from power, as Deborah Jenson demonstrates in an enlightening recent article, recalls Toussaint's own kidnapping two centuries before.⁶ What follows relates, therefore, to the question of those shifts in representational emphases that have occurred as Toussaint, no longer exclusively or even perhaps predominantly an exemplum of anti-colonial struggle, has emerged as a site of postcolonial anxieties. This chapter addresses the transformations witnessed in his mythologization or instrumentalization as these processes have evolved from a period of active decolonization to one of postcolonial reflection. There is a need, of course, to acknowledge the flawed nature of any such linear interpretation. The elasticity or versatility inherent in Toussaint's portability and translatability means that there is no monolithic, homogenized orthodox representation of him at any given moment: in the first epigraph chosen for this chapter, David Scott's plural ("the kind of story we might usefully tell – through Toussaint Louverture – about the relation between our past, our *presents*"; my emphasis) is a telling one. To give a specific earlier example from the period immediately following the Second World War, for instance, Neruda's *Canto General*, in which Toussaint figures among the "Liberators", will be juxtaposed with Jones's almost contemporary creation of Toussaint as embodiment of an obedient colonial society informed by muscular Christianity and marked self-restraint.⁷ At the same time, and especially in the context of the francophone Caribbean, it should be stressed that the term "postcolonial", with any chronological implications of a neat completion of decolonization, seems inappropriately premature. The chapter addresses these reservations, articulated for instance in Édouard Glissant's discussion of the "Toussaint complex" that affects the contemporary francophone Caribbean, by adopting Jeannie Suk's understanding of the term "postcolonial" – that is, as a "contractual indicator of a practice of reading that accentuates the commonality of the problems that arise from colonialism" – and also by addressing the ways in which Toussaint has been drawn into the theory and criticism that explores the "problems" to which Suk alludes.⁸

Toussaint's postcolonial persistence, two centuries after his death, may appear surprising. Whereas the success of the Haitian Revolution (and the abandonment that this necessitated of any plans to consolidate French holdings in North America) marked the end of the empire associated with France's Ancien Régime, Napoleon's strategic humiliation in 1802–3 may arguably be seen to have led him to an alternative expansionism that, a decade after his death, would lead to the further appropriation of colonial territories that formed the beginnings of the Republican Empire.⁹ In this context, the death of Toussaint Louverture, occurring at this transitional moment in French (overseas) history, was thus a solitary and even exceptional event.

Deprived – in what must surely be read as a symbolic reimposition of slavery – of rank, uniform, heat, light, food, money, writing materials and even human company, the Haitian revolutionary leader died locked in his prison cell while Amiot, the commander of the Château de Joux, spent several days away from his post. Not executed, but rather abandoned in the depths of the Jura, Toussaint experienced a final solitude that reflected his growing political isolation, even as the events of the revolution he had led themselves continued to unfold. Whether his arrest by Brunet at Ennery was a punishment for serious, even hubristic miscalculation, the result of naivety, or a catalytic strategy of self-sacrifice, there is no denying that by June 1802 – despite the loyalty of a close group of followers and the residual hopes of a wider cross-section of Haiti's black majority – Toussaint was distanced from his generals and playing an increasingly uncertain role in his country's history.

This chapter acknowledges that, despite the uncertainty over Toussaint's legacy that immediately followed his death, his representation in postcolonial literatures has nevertheless continued unabated, aided not least in recent years by the interest generated around the bicentenary of his death in 2003. Madison Smartt Bell has recently, with *The Stone the Builder Refused* (2004), completed his monumental trilogy of novels devoted to Toussaint, and a number of Haitian authors – based in France and Haiti – have produced equally important if less well known novels and plays that continue to interrogate this persistently present figure.[10] At the same time, the lack of cinematic representations of Toussaint is currently being rectified, in the documentary and epic genres, in *Toussaint* and *Spirit*, directed by Danny Glover and Art Jones respectively;[11] and Louverture continues to be represented in the visual arts, most notably in the work of Édouard Duval-Carrié.[12] In addition, the historiographic knowledge of Toussaint's biography has continued to progress with increasing attention being given to abundant archival traces that often contradict the received ideas underpinning the revolutionary leader's mythologization.[13] In part, this development is allied to the increasingly sustained attention that the Haitian Revolution attracts among historians, especially in the period leading up to and marking its bicentenary; yet at the same time, this work reflects the continued biographical fascination with Toussaint as an exemplary or exceptional figure.

It is important to note, however, that in the context of such postcolonial shifts (linked to a critique within anti-colonial historiography of the mythology of the hero) Toussaint's pre-eminence has itself been challenged. Such a destabilization was first mooted in two earlier texts that have tended to remain submerged in the history of the Haitian Revolution: Etienne Charlier's *Aperçu sur la Formation Historique de la Nation Haïtienne* (1954) and Michel-Rolph Trouillot's *Ti difé boulé sou istoua Ayiti* (1977).[14] Despite their divergence in form and inspiration, both constitute demystificatory attempts to analyse the relationship of the revolutionary leaders (and in particular Toussaint) to the Haitian people, restoring agency to the latter and demonstrating the ways in which the despotism and dictatorship that characterize certain periods of post-revolutionary history have their roots in the revolutionary period itself. The aim of such works is not to reimpose a francocentric reading of the Haitian struggle whereby French defeat is brought about by disease and climate (as opposed to a Haitian strategic advantage) – that is, not, in Glissant's terms, to "enfermer [Toussaint] dans un fort plus terrible que Joux" [shut Toussaint in a more terrible fort than Joux], by which Glissant means that of historical silence; instead, it is to relativize the role of the revolution's leaders and to reassess that of the people.[15] Carolyn Fick's work has recently done much to popularize such an endeavour, demystifying Toussaint's power and restoring agency to those traditionally granted a subaltern role:

> By seeing the embodiment of the St Domingue revolution in the figure of Toussaint Louverture, we may interpret that revolution as part of the modern age, and rightly so. But by doing so, we also risk reducing to a level of impertinence those vital social, economic and cultural realities of the ex-slaves whose independent relationship to the land, African in outlook, formed the foundation of their own vision of freedom, while it flew in the face of the modern state that Toussaint was trying to build.[16]

Continued representation of Toussaint – fictional and historiographic – is accordingly tempered by a growing awareness of the pitfalls of monumentalism, hagiography and hero creation, and of the construction of representativity or exceptionalism – as well as associated exclusions – that these imply.

Rereading Toussaint I: Identity, Gender, Ethnicity

The tensions inherent in these seemingly contradictory movements encapsulate the contemporary urgency of a need (in Glissant's terms, as discussed above) to "argumenter autour de Toussaint", a need apparent in the associated and sustained critical attention to which Toussaint – and the representational field via which he has travelled – have been subject. The "postcolonial turn" by which many fields of academic enquiry have recently been shaped has led to a variety of recent studies (some predictable, others less so), ranging from Marcus Wood's lively and illuminating reading of Harriet Martineau's fiction (in which a "whited" version of Louverture figures) to the postcolonial perspective implicit in the analysis by Prown et al. of the Toussaint pitchers originating in 1830s Massachussetts.[17] The attention to Toussaint – as an embodiment of the Haitian Revolution and its contradictions – is perhaps not surprising at a time when Haiti emerges somewhat belatedly as a foundational, exemplary case study in the postcolonial field. As Nick Nesbitt explains:

> Two of the processes that came to distinguish the twentieth century were invented in Haiti: decolonization and neocolonialism. Haiti was the first to demonstrate that the colonized can take hold of their own historical destiny and enter the stage of world history as autonomous actors, and not merely passive, enslaved subjects. Less happily, newly independent Haiti also demonstrated to the world the first instance of what would later be called neocolonialism, as ruling elites (both mulatto and black) united with the military and merchant class to create an instable balance of power.[18]

In this way, Haiti is seen as a premature or prophetic illustration of what Suk (see above) dubs the "problems that arise from colonialism", and Toussaint is seen as a key agent in those efforts to struggle with the paradoxes these problems generate. Commenting on these efforts, Henry Louis Gates Jr. pinpoints writing as a "crucial terrain of black struggles in the Age of Enlightenment", with former slaves "[meeting] the challenge of the Enlightenment by writing themselves into being".[19] As a result of this, postcolonial critics, with an interest in (self-)inscription as a form of agency, now recognize Toussaint as one of the first black memorialists and even as a foundational figure in a "francophone" literary tradition.[20]

This extrapolation, from the case of Toussaint, of a more abstract reflection on the postcolonial condition is not, of course, an exclusively contemporary phenomenon: for example, in the text presented by Rob Nixon as foundational in the postcolonial field, *The Pleasures of Exile*, George Lamming builds on C.L.R. James's reading of Toussaint in order to "get out from under this ancient mausoleum of [colonial] historic achievement";[21] in the much-cited appendix to *The Problem of Slavery*, David Brion Davis employs the relationship between Napoleon and Toussaint to explore, in an imaginary if historically grounded case study, the ramifications of Hegel's master-slave dialectic.[22] Lamming's work on *The Black Jacobins* has been developed by recent postcolonial reassessments and attenuations of James, one of Toussaint's principal interpreters. Indeed, *The Black Jacobins*, of which a new Penguin edition appeared in

2001, continues to be one of the most regularly cited studies of Louverture and the Haitian Revolution: in James Walvin's terms, it is even "*the* pre-eminent account".[23] The study's flaws have now been explored in some detail,[24] and C.L.R. James himself – whose lifelong fascination with the book's subject is revealed in his progressive textual and paratextual additions to his text – was among the first to discuss how he might have written the work with very different emphases had he come to it later in his life. In lectures given in 1971 to the Institute of the Black World, published only recently in *Small Axe*, James addressed not only the genesis of the book in 1930s England, but also the ways in which his thought had evolved in the intervening four decades.[25] The relationship of recent rereadings of *The Black Jacobins* to the original work is accordingly not a purely exegetical one. Instead, they use a critique of James and of his version of Toussaint as a means of reflecting, more heuristically, on a number of interlinked issues relating to postcolonial identity, such as gender, colonial mimicry, and hybridity and/or creolization.

Maryse Condé's critique of the dominance of Caribbean history by male heroes – and by what she dismisses as "conventional revolutionary bric à brac" – is part of a wider exploration of the role of gender in colonial and postcolonial identities.[26] Recent work by scholars such as Doris Kadish has gone some way towards unearthing the role of women in abolitionism as well as in the wider anti-colonial struggle associated with the Haitian Revolution, suggesting the ways in which certain discourses are constructed in the light not only of ethnicity but also of gender.[27] Commenting on Anna Julia Cooper's early-twentieth-century research, Henry Louis Gates Jr. points to the "fallacy of referring to 'the Black man' when speaking of black people", adding that "just as white men cannot speak through the consciousness of black men, neither can black *men* fully and adequately . . . reproduce the exact Voice of the Black Woman".[28] The gendering of the black Haitian hero receives further critical attention in Hazel Carby's *Race Men*, in which she addresses the 1930s forging, through the figure of Toussaint Louverture, of a "revolutionary black male consciousness" that permitted exploration of the circumstances in which "black male autonomy, self-government, and patriarchal black nationhood could be enacted".[29] Reading *The Black Jacobins* in relation to James's other writings on Trinidadian politics (*The Life of Captain Cipriani*, 1932) and cricket (*Beyond a Boundary*, 1963), Carby outlines a "direct, unmediated relation between the heroic male figure and the people",[30] identifying the ways in which "revolution is often represented as a homosocial act of reproduction: a social and political upheaval in which men confront each other to give birth to a new nation".[31]

Such a gender-oriented critique of the black hero figure has been accompanied by closer scrutiny of Toussaint's identity along the lines of ethnicity and class. Perhaps not surprisingly, Toussaint's social status has been the focus of a number of historians who, following the initial work of Debien, Fouchard and Menier, have sought to clarify further the role played by the future revolutionary leader in pre-1789 St Domingue.[32] It is, however, on questions of ethnicity that a number of postcolonial critics have focused, attempting to cast light on Toussaint's complex self-positioning as well as on the roles that subsequent interpreters have coerced him into playing. Following the production and publication of Glissant's *Monsieur Toussaint*, it has become a commonplace to present Louverture as a hybrid figure, a quintessentially Caribbean shape-shifter who exploited a range of ethno-cultural allegiances for his own strategic purposes. A clear example of this tendency may be seen in a reading of Duval-Carrié's recent portrait of *Le Général Toussaint enfumé*, playfully subtitled "Pretty in Pink". The picture is familiarly paradoxical, contradicting the artist's previous, more monumental portraits, and presenting its subject simultaneously as the subject of a romanticized, intimate image in a locket (hence the smoky, pink background) and as a revolutionary leader whose angular profile recalls that of Ogoun, the black deity of war. The commentary states: "Toussaint Louverture is a contradictory hero. Like Odysseus, he is a refined trickster or, as Haitians would say, 'Master of the Crossroads'. . . . He is a man of Africa who fought for Saint-Domingue and died in France: slave and freeman, child of the Enlightenment, and fervent Catholic who served the lwa of Vodou. In short Toussaint Louverture is the quintessential Haitian."[33]

"Cet homme", as Lamartine famously wrote along these same lines, "fut une nation" [This man was a nation], and it is clear that the pragmatic, strategic, diplomatic Toussaint possesses a representational capital that generates an impression of creolized unity in a way that Dessalines and Christophe do not. There is a risk, however, that such a refiguring occludes the troubled historical legacies of Louverture, who has been as subject to denigration (especially in the work of historians inspired by the "mulatto legend" of Haitian history) as he has been to uncritical adulation (in a reading of national history generated by those inspired by the competing "noiriste" version).[34]

It is precisely a continued recognition of these tensions, as opposed to their elision, that has generated some of the more challenging recent interpretations of Toussaint. Carby's analysis of Louverture as a black male hero – clearly illustrating the gendered dimensions of James's 1930s efforts to develop what Cedric J. Robinson dubs a specifically "black Marxism" – may therefore be read as one of a series of general engagements with the revolutionary's black identity and the (ab)uses to which its has been put.[35] Marcus Wood explores the representation of Toussaint in early-nineteenth-century English literature. His lively discussion engages in particular with Wordsworth's sonnet to Toussaint and Harriet Martineau's *The Hour and the Man*, analysing the ways in which literature that is often presented as abolitionist and philanthropic in fact illustrates the "limitless capacities of Anglo-American culture to absorb and possess its own fictions of enslavement".[36] Sympathetic to James's reading of Louverture, Wood suggests that this "compulsion to steal black pain"[37] evacuates the violence of a closely policed and "whitened" Toussaint, neutralizing the incendiary impact of his "hybridized and politicized black consciousness".[38] It is Martineau in particular who is seen to distort Toussaint into a "blancophile" Christian gentleman, reflecting what Wood sees as "desires and anxieties about the free slave".[39]

Rereading Toussaint II:
Mimicry, Hybridity, Creolization

Such an exploration of the (negative) construction of Toussaint's ethnicity, highlighting the containment of black agency it implies, reveals the revolutionary's ongoing instability, an aspect further revealed by a critical tendency to problematize – rather than celebrate – Toussaint's own hybrid status. This reading would in fact seem to resonate with Glissant's own theatrical interpretation, according to which the protagonist is constantly circled, like a Vodou "mitan", by the various aspects of Black Atlantic culture that constitute his character. The tension between these – "the dead who visit him" and "the living who are powerfully summoned to witness his final agony" – is maintained without the achievement of any concluding synthesis.[40] A central and original aspect of Nicole King's *C.L.R. James and Creolization* is her claim that in both the dramatic and prose versions of *The Black Jacobins*, the protagonist's flaw is not only (as James and Césaire both suggest) a tragic inability to communicate his project to the people, but also (despite his presentation as a "creolized paradigm for understanding Caribbean revolutions") a related suspicion of creolization.[41] The paradox that King identifies in James's refiguring – this tension between, on the one hand, his hybrid identity and, on the other, an apparently francophile tendency to suppress hybridized elements of indigenous culture – is central to two other critical engagements with Toussaint, distinct but interrelated, that revolve around his perceived "mulatto" identity and issues of colonial mimicry. José Buscaglia-Salgado has recently pushed discussions of Toussaint's ethnicity in a new direction, challenging the "mulatto legend" of Haitian history (see above) that tended to belittle the role of the revolutionary leader, in order to present Louverture himself as part of the "body politic of mulatto societies".[42] Countering an orthodox critique of mulatto politics (especially those in nineteenth-century Haiti), seen to pay lip-service to racial solidarity yet to rely for the perpetuation of power on the refigured ethnic and pigmentocratic hierarchies of the colonial system, Buscaglia-Salgado's *Undoing Empire* presents figures such as Toussaint as "sites of convergence of and resistance to precisely that which the coloniality of power aims to keep apart".[43] Drawing on the revolutionary leader's own status as a "slave driver" (a claim for which there is in reality little more than oblique archival evidence) and as a "free black", as well as on his perceived deference to the French, Buscaglia-Salgado argues that Toussaint was "a mulatto 'by vocation', both in terms of James's characterization of mulatto subjectivity and in terms of the traditional role of the mulatto in the plantation".[44] Louverture's multiple allegiances are thus presented in terms of the search for a suitable father figure, and his intermediary, ambivalent status – "prodigal son vis-à-vis the French governor and . . . messiah vis-à-vis the Africans"[45] – as evidence of his attempts to balance loyalties.

"He was," writes Buscaglia-Salgado, "a conciliator and translator, liberator and enforcer, father, brother, and son. Could anyone but the mulatto, in all his subjective disposition to metaphoricity, wear so many disguises?"[46] This is a bold and provocative thesis, illustrating the flexibility of Toussaint within postcolonial debate and challenging a number of received ideas on which many interpretations of him depend. It is to be welcomed not least because it provides a counterpoint both to James's Toussaint as black Marxist leader and to the more ruthless character perpetuated by proponents of the "mulatto legend". Yet the construction of this new "mulatto" Toussaint may ultimately be seen to take little account of its subject's adoption of the strategies of slave resistance, such as double-speak and the formation of strategic allegiances. It refuses at the same time to see the black revolutionary's politics (as does, for instance, Eugene Genovese) in the light of an emergent modernity in which he aims to see Haiti playing a full role.[47] Both phenomena, strategic and political, are privileged in competing postcolonial readings that foreground mimicry and imitation. As Jennifer Yee makes clear in her discussion of Hugo's *Bug-Jargal*, focus on mimicry played a role in a French neo-colonial critique of post-emancipation Haitian society.[48] Contemporary imagery of Toussaint presented as incongruous the perceived mismatch of the black body and a French republican general's uniform – a mismatch updated by more recent critics of Louverture for whom allegiance to Enlightenment ideas alienated the revolutionary from the masses he endeavoured to lead. Although the genuflecting black body – passive, vulnerable and mute – was a formulaic element in the representation of the black slave, used even in abolitionist images, the majority of Toussaint's images from the earlier nineteenth century present him instead before capture and humiliation, with the detail of his French officer's uniform exploited as a marker of the artists' admiration of, or of their indignation at, the perceived mismatch between black body and a French general's insignia. In Aravamudan's terms, Toussaint is portrayed "in vocabulary that the colonial power can understand, admire, and regret".[49]

More recent analysts have, however, challenged such a Manichean interpretation of mimicry, in order to explore the strategic or provisional aspects of Toussaint's alliances, postures and manoeuvrings; they suggest that any contradictoriness is more apparent than actual, for – as Mudimbe-Boyi explains – it "underscore[s] the behavior of a character who evolves as an ambiguous, elusive, and inscrutable subject enclosed in his unfathomableness". This is a state related, she suggests, to Louverture's performance of the ambiguities of abolitionist logic as well as to an awareness of the importance of disguise as a mode of anti-slavery resistance.[50] Such an interpretation counters a loosely Fanonian response to Toussaint, one that privileges Dessalines and presents Louverture as a type of subservient "évolué", who was incapable of breaking ties with France and moving towards independence. Instead, it follows Bhabha in seeing mimicry as a potential form of camouflage and even mockery, presenting "flawed colonial mimesis" as a site of resistance.[51] Although it is quite feasible that mimicry might feature among those strategies of resistance employed by Toussaint, such a reading ultimately skirts around those aspects of the revolutionary that constitute and encapsulate his revolutionary impact: whereas mimicry depends on – and simultaneously calls into question – the relationship of a copy to its original, Toussaint Louverture, in his appropriation, adaptation, hybridization and ultimate reformulation of metropolitan phenomena (ideas, military strategies, political imperatives), questions the validity of these very poles. Just as, in his relationship with Napoleon, Toussaint begs the question of who is the copy of whom, so, in his conduct of a revolutionary war, he asks searching questions about where, in the late eighteenth century, one might situate the hub of Atlantic revolutionary history.

In an extremely thoughtful article, Nick Nesbitt suggests in this vein that Louverture's actions represent an intervention in philosophical and ideological debates, serving to displace these debates' centres of gravity away from their traditional metropolitan sites: "Toussaint was not passively parroting ideas that had been imported from France and forced upon him. Before Toussaint, the Rights of Man were, with rare, tentative exceptions, not understood to extend to African slaves. In the face of this aggressive partiality, Toussaint used the public sphere of the Enlightenment with tactical genius to redefine the notion of universal right."[52]

Dismissing claims of passive mimicry or ventriloquism, Nesbitt's reading resonates with that of Srinivas Aravamudan, who – in *Tropicopolitans* – has suggested that Toussaint (as a reader of Raynal's *Histoire des Deux Indes*) confounded western assumptions about slavery and ethnicity. Forcing his way into restructured transnational dialogues in order to radicalize the debates of Parisian salons, Louverture reveals their blind spots and silences. "Catachrestically revivifying myth," writes Aravamudan, "postcolonial genealogies tropicalize the Enlightenment",[53] and his aim is to demonstrate the ways in which mimicry and parody may be seen as elements of agency – that is, as effective and empirical practices, and not simply the discursive effects into which Homi Bhabha has been accused of transforming them.[54] It is such a response to Toussaint that, in addition to attenuating certain notions that risk becoming commonplace in postcolonial criticism, has also permitted a more wholesale critique of the field. Elisabeth Mudimbe-Boyi describes the ways in which the revolutionary may be seen to "deconstruct some assumptions of the postcolonial, such as the ideological imperial gaze, the concern with cultural identity, the opposition between center and periphery, race as a locus of enunciation, and, in a cursory note, the predominance of the postcolonial in the Anglo-Saxon world".[55] In a discussion of C.L.R. James and Anna Julia Cooper, Donna Hunter goes on to prolong this list of possible points of contestation by exploring the ways in which Toussaint permitted those (crucially non-francophone) authors to think through the problematic concept of universalism in strategic, progressive and radical ways.[56]

Conclusion

David Scott has offered one of the most sustained recent explorations of Toussaint in *Conscripts of Modernity*, his study of *The Black Jacobins*, and I will conclude here with a consideration of this book's implications for the wider postcolonial field. Although

ARGUING AROUND TOUSSAINT

Scott acknowledges (and, in part at least, responds to) the need for a thorough examination of the historical genesis of James's text (that is, of the use of sources, the progressive textual accretions, the public statements regarding his reassessment of the text, the private correspondence in which its continued centrality to his reflections becomes apparent), the aim of *Conscripts* is not specifically related to the postcolonial history of the book. This follows the author's previous *Refashioning Futures*, in which he challenges orthodox understandings of postcoloniality and explores the rapidly changing postcolonial present (dislocating it accordingly from the teleological expectations of the colonial and decolonial past).[57] The more recent volume explores the implications, for tragic and romantic understandings of postcolonialism (as well as for the epistemological assumptions on which these are based), of James's 1963 additions to the opening of the thirteenth chapter of *The Black Jacobins* concerning post/colonial tragedy. Scott's aim is to use the representation of Toussaint to explore the nature of the tragic present, postcolonial yet at the same time neo-colonial, in the light of the collapse of an anti-colonial ideal. His claim is that the teleological assumptions of Romantic, emancipationist versions of history have become unwound – and were indeed already unwinding in James's 1960s rereading of Toussaint's dilemma, as he emphasized the revolutionary's location at the "crossroads of absolute choice between options to which he is equally committed (the freedom of the slaves on the once hand and the enlightenment of revolutionary France on the other)".[58]

Scott reads these shifts in the light of James's changing grasp – between the 1930s and the 1950s – of the postcolonial future his study of Toussaint projects, and takes this as a means of reimagining "our past, our presents, and our possible futures". In Scott's terms, Toussaint emerges not simply as an agent, but more as a conscript of modernity, striving to construct a postcolonial state, but "constrained to imagine and make the revolution he imagined and made within the conceptual and institutional terrain of modernity".[59] The focus, therefore, is not on Toussaint's struggle for emancipation, but on the ways in which this struggle embodies the constraints and ambiguities of the context of that emancipation. Whereas Dessalines is seen to focus on freedom at any cost, Toussaint is concerned more with "the project of imagining and constructing a sustainable freedom within new forms of life".[60] It is in this emphasis that there is a shift away from the anti-colonial romance and revolutionary heroism, both of which provide redemption for the Toussaint martyred at Joux, towards a remorselessly tragic narrative – shaped no doubt by his experience of the late 1950s Caribbean – in which individual agency is attenuated and even (at its most deterministic) denied by the impossible conditions through which it is shaped. For Scott, it is such a narrative – "focusing our attention on the paradoxical inscriptions of pasts within the present, on the persistence of contingencies within freedom, on the intransigence of failure within success" – and not its celebratory and vindicationist equivalent, that permits understanding of "so unyielding a postcolonial present as our own".[61]

Describing his methodology, Scott claims: "my aim is less to write about *The Black Jacobins* than to write *through* it",[62] and it is *through* James's Toussaint, granted in Scott's analysis a markedly metacritical status, that he proposes a challenging and ultimately pessimistic contribution to discussions of postcolonial paradigms. Ranging from Mudimbe-Boyi's radical unfathomability to Scott's tragic conscription, the postcolonial Toussaint may be seen to articulate a range of positions that illuminate his challenge to the postcolonial present, as much as they do his contribution to the revolutionary's own colonial past. Already, in the early nineteenth century, embodying certain dilemmas that would re-emerge in different forms and in the different context of the decolonial 1950s and 1960s, it is no surprise that key thinkers and writers of that period – Dadié, Glissant, James, Lamming – turned their attention to the Haitian revolutionary during a moment characterized by a mix of real hope and uncertainty. Postcolonial criticism, taking the work of these authors and their peers as its foundation and inspiration, continues to revisit Toussaint and to rehabilitate him in analyses of its own location. What Toussaint's recurrently spectral presence suggests is that any genealogy of postcolonialism that tracks the concept back to the 1950s remains no more than partial. Toussaint Louverture – whether black or mulatto, agent or conscript, romantic or tragic, mimic or original – embodied the dilemmas of the postcolonial long before these were articulated as such. In so doing, postcolonial interrogations of Toussaint, far from revealing what Anthony Hurley sees (in relation to Fanon, as discussed above) as the "presumptuousness of postcoloniality", offer particular insights into those ways in which the Haitian revolutionary continues to encapsulate the persistent imbrications of his pasts in our presents.[63]

Acknowledgements

This essay was written while its author was a British Academy senior research fellow; the support of the Academy in its preparation is acknowledged with gratitude.

Notes

1. See Édouard Glissant, *Le Discours antillais* (Paris: Seuil, 1981), 233.

2. E. Anthony Hurley, "Power, Purpose, the Presumptuousness of Postcoloniality, and Frantz Fanon's *Peau noire, masques blancs*", in *Postcolonial Theory and Francophone Literary Studies*, ed. H. Adlai Murdoch and Anne Donadey (Gainesville: University Press of Florida, 2005), 21.

3. Herman Lebovics, *Bringing the Empire Back Home: France in the Global Age* (Durham: Duke University Press, 2004), 18.

4. On this subject, see my article "The Black Jacobin in Paris", *Journal of Romance Studies* 5, no. 3 (2005): 9–24. The paradoxical dimensions of Toussaint's portability are made apparent by Raphaël Confiant's suggestion in *Eau de café* (Paris: Grasset, 1991) that General de Gaulle was hailed by those in the French Caribbean during the Second World War as a latter-day Louverture who would save them from the *békés*. See Michèle Praeger, *The Imaginary Caribbean and Caribbean Imaginary* (Lincoln: University of Nebraska Press, 2003), 189n3.

5. Marcus Wood, *Slavery, Empathy, and Pornography* (Oxford: Oxford University Press, 2002), 270.

6. For a fascinating discussion of parallels between Aristide and Louverture (with particular reference to their respective removals from Haiti), see Deborah Jenson, "From the Kidnapping(s) of the Louvertures to the Alleged Kidnapping of Aristide: Legacies of Slavery in the Post/Colonial World", *Yale French Studies*, 107 (2005): 162–86.

7. See Pablo Neruda, *Canto General*, trans. Jack Schmitt (1950; repr., Berkeley and Los Angeles: University of California Press, 1991), 116–17; and W.M.A. Jones, *Black Emperor: The Story of Toussaint Louverture* (London: Harrap, 1949).

8. Jeannie Suk, *Postcolonial Paradoxes in French Caribbean Writing: Césaire, Glissant, Condé* (Oxford: Clarendon Press, 2001), 19. E. Anthony Hurley's reading of Suk's definition suggests it is posited on an understanding of colonialism as a completed process: see Hurley, "Power, purpose", 25. I would suggest that Suk instead allows for an open-endedness essential for readings of the uses of Toussaint, in line with Chris Bongie's coinage "post/colonial", understood as an "intimate (dis)connection of the colonial and the postcolonial". See *Islands and Exiles: The Creole Identities of Post/Colonial Literature* (Stanford: Stanford University Press, 1998), 12.

9. For a discussion of these strategic issues, see Yves Benot, *La Révolution Française et la Fin des Colonies* (1987; repr., Paris: La Découverte, 2004), and "Une préhistoire de l'expédition d'Alger", in *Rétablissement de l'Esclavage dans les Colonies Françaises 1802: Ruptures et Continuités de la Politique Coloniale Française (1800–1830)*, ed. Yves Benot and Marcel Dorigny (Paris: Maisonneuve et Larose, 2003), 537–43.

10. See Madison Smartt Bell, *All Souls' Rising* (New York: Pantheon, 1995), *Master of the Crossroads* (New York: Pantheon, 2000) and *The Stone That the Builder Refused* (New

York: Pantheon, 2004). This new material has been supplemented by new editions and translations of earlier texts in which the representation of Toussaint plays a key role, such as Victor Hugo, *Bug-Jargal*, ed. and trans. Chris Bongie (Peterborough, Ont.: Broadview, 2004); and Édouard Glissant, *Monsieur Toussaint*, trans. J. Michael Dash and Édouard Glissant (Boulder: Lynne Riener, 2005). See also Madison Smartt Bell's life of the revolutionary leader, *Toussaint Louverture: A Biography* (New York: Pantheon, 2007).

11. Over two hundred biopics have been devoted to Napoleon Bonaparte (see Dan Glaister, "Big Battle Over Little General", *Manchester Guardian*, 1 April 2004, 13); however, apart from one recorded silent film, there is little evidence of filmed versions of Toussaint's life. Eisenstein's *Black Consul* project was added to a series of the director's films that never reached production stage, despite the visit of Paul Robeson – who was to have played the lead – to Moscow in 1934.

12. See Donald J. Cosentino, *Divine Revolution: The Art of Édouard Duval-Carrié* (Los Angeles: UCLA Fowler Museum of Cultural History, 2004).

13. On untapped archival resources relating to Toussaint and the Haitian Revolution, see David P. Geggus, *Haitian Revolutionary Studies* (Bloomington and Indianapolis: Indiana University Press, 2002), 43–54; and Nick Nesbitt, "The Idea of 1804", *Yale French Studies* 107 (2005): 35–38. For recent historical investigations, see Gordon S. Brown, *Toussaint's Clause: The Founding Fathers and the Haitian Revolution* (Jackson: University Press of Mississippi, 2005), a study of early US diplomatic history that outlines the shrewd manoeuvrings employed by Toussaint in his effort to reopen trade with North America; *Toussaint Louverture et l'Indépendance d'Haïti: Témoignages pour un Bicentenaire*, ed. Jacques de Cauna (Paris: Karthala; SFHOM, 2004), a rich collection of articles and other resources relating to Toussaint, the revolution and its aftermath; Sibylle Fischer, *Modernity Disavowed: Haiti and the Cultures of Slavery in the Age of Revolution* (Durham: Duke University Press, 2004), a study of the role of the (dissemination and suppression of the) revolution in the foundation of Western modernity; and David P. Geggus, *Haitian Revolutionary Studies*, a collection into a single volume of some of the author's most important recent essays, including "The 'Volte-Face' of Toussaint Louverture" (119–36). Also of note is *Dictionnaire Historique de la Révolution Haïtienne (1789–1804)*, ed. Claude Moïse (Montreal: Editions Images; Editions du Cidihca, 2003), which provides clear evidence that Haitian revolutionary historiography is slowly being allowed to catch up with its American and French counterparts.

14. Etienne Charlier, *Aperçu sur la Formation Historique de la Nation Haïtienne* (Port-au-Prince: Les Presses Libres, 1954); and Michel-Rolph Trouillot's *Ti difé boulé sou istoua Ayiti* (Brooklyn: Kolèksion Lakansièl, 1977). In a much-needed discussion of the latter, Mariana Past encapsulates the text's revisionist intentions: "it is essential to pause and ensure that hero-worship does not overshadow or jeopardize a true appreciation of the political, cultural and artistic power of the Haitian people and the human capital that they represent, both at home and abroad". See "Toussaint on Trial in *Ti difé boulé sou istoua Ayiti*, or the People's Role in the Haitian Revolution", *Journal of Haitian Studies* 10, no. 1 (2004): 87–102 (100–101).

15. See Édouard Glissant, *Monsieur Toussaint* (Paris: Seuil, 1986), 161. This relativization also involves the *rapprochement* of Toussaint and the other leaders of the revolution. Édouard Glissant writes, in the preface to the new translation of his *Monsieur Toussaint* (see above): "The 200th anniversary of the declaration of Haitian independence . . . will perhaps witness the revival of the debate between those who consider Emperor Dessalines the true founder of the new nation and those who consider Toussaint its initiator and indisputable prophet. . . . In truth, Toussaint and Dessalines, and all the actors in this epic, are inseparable. . . . The grandeur of Toussaint's vision and the decisive actions of Dessalines complete each other" (11–12).

16. Carolyn E. Fick, *The Making of Haiti: the Saint Domingue Revolution from Below* (Knoxville: University of Tennessee Press, 1990): 250.

17. See Wood, *Slavery, Empathy, and Pornography*, 255–94; and Jonathan Prown, Glenn Adamson, Katherine Hemple Prown, and Robert Hunter, "'The Very Man for the Hour': The Toussaint L'Ouverture Portrait Pitcher", in *Ceramics in America 2002*, ed. Robert Hunter (Hanover: Chipstone Foundation, 2002), 110–29.

18. Nesbitt, "The Idea of 1804", 6.

19. Quoted by Donna Hunter, "Historically Particular Uses of a Universal Subject", in *French Civilization and Its Discontents: Nationalism, Colonialism, Race*, ed. Tyler Stovall and Georges van den Abbeele (Lanham: Lexington Books, 2003), 129–45 (137).

20. On Toussaint's memoirs, dictated at Joux and published by Saint-Rémy in 1853, see Daniel Desormeaux, "The First of the (Black) Memorialists: Toussaint Louverture", *Yale French Studies* 107 (2005): 131–45. The first case for Toussaint as author was made by the Abbé Grégoire in *De la Littérature des Nègres* (Paris: Maradan, 1808).

21. See George Lamming, *The Pleasures of Exile* (1960; repr., London: Allison and Busby, 1984), 27. See also Rob Nixon, "Caribbean and African appropriations of *The Tempest*", *Critical Inquiry*, 13 (1987): 557–78.

22. See David Brion Davis, "Toussaint L'Ouverture and the Phenomenology of Mind", in *The Problem of Slavery in the Age of Revolution, 1770–1823* (Ithaca: Cornell University Press, 1975), 557–64.

23. See James Walvin, introduction to C.L.R. James, *The Black Jacobins* (repr., Harmondsworth: Penguin, 2001), viii (emphasis in the original).

24. See, for instance, Alex Dupuy, "Toussaint-Louverture and the Haitian Revolution: A Reassessment of C.L.R. James's Interpretation", in *C.L.R. James: His Intellectual Legacies*, ed. Selwyn R. Cudjoe and William E. Cain (Amherst: University of Massachusetts Press, 1995), 106–17.

25. See "The C.L.R. James Lectures", *Small Axe*, no. 8 (2000): 65–112.

26. See Maryse Condé, "Order, Disorder, Freedom and the West Indian Writer", *Yale French Studies* 83, no. 2 (1993): 121–35 (133).

27. See Doris Y. Kadish, "Guadeloupean Women Remember Slavery", *French Review* 77, no. 6 (2004): 1181–92, and "Haiti and Abolitionism in 1825: The Case of Sophie Doin", *Yale French Studies* 107 (2005): 108–30. See also Wood, *Slavery, Empathy, and Pornography*, 237.

28. Cited by Donna Hunter, "Historically particular uses of a universal subject" (138; emphasis in the original).

29. Hazel V. Carby, "Body Lines and Colour Lines", in *Race Men* (Cambridge, Mass.: Harvard University Press, 1998), 113.

30. Ibid., 116.

31. Ibid., 127.

32. See Gabriel Debien, Jean Fouchard and Marie-Antoinette Menier, "Toussaint Louverture avant 1789, légendes et réalités", *Conjonction: Revue Franco-Haïtienne* 134 (1977): 65–80; and Stewart King, "Toussaint L'Ouverture before 1791: free planter and slave-holder", *Journal of Haitian Studies* 3–4 (1997–98), 66–71. In a discussion that illuminates reflection in the present article on Toussaint's ability to shift between identities, David Geggus comments on his "free coloured" status as a manumitted slave, simultaneously dominant and subaltern, to explore Louverture's apparent social mobility in an otherwise highly stratified society. See "Slavery, War, and Revolution in the Greater Caribbean, 1789–1815", in *A Turbulent Time: The French Revolution and the Greater Caribbean*, ed. David Gaspar and David P. Geggus (Bloomington and Indianapolis: Indiana University Press, 1997), 12.

33. Cosentino, *Divine Revolution*, 60.

34. On these competing historiographic traditions, see David Nicholls, *From Dessalines to Duvalier: Race, Colour and National Independence in Haiti* (London and Basingstoke: Macmillan, 1988), 71–102.

35. See Cedric J. Robinson, *Black Marxism: The Making of the Black Radical Tradition* (London: Zed Press, 1983).

36. Wood, *Slavery, Empathy, and Pornography*, 294.

37. Ibid., 294.

38. Ibid., 235.

39. Ibid., 273.

40. Glissant, *Monsieur Toussaint*, 12.

41. Nicole King, "Double or Nothing: The Two *Black Jacobins*", in *C.L.R. James and Creolization: Circles of Influence* (Jackson: University Press of Mississippi, 2001), 35, 44.

42. José F. Buscaglia-Salgado, *Undoing Empire: Race and Nation in the Mulatto Caribbean* (Minneapolis: University of Minnesota Press, 2004), xiv.

43. Ibid.

44. Ibid., 205.

45. Ibid., 207.

46. Ibid.

47. See Eugene D. Genovese, *From Rebellion to Revolution: Afro-American Slave Revolts in the Making of the New World* (Baton Rouge: Louisiana State University Press, 1979).

48. See Jennifer Yee, *Other Voices: Subversion in Nineteenth-century French Exotic Fiction* (Leeds: Maney, 2008).

49. See Srinivas Aravamudan, *Tropicopolitans: Colonialism and Agency, 1688–1804* (Durham: Duke University Press, 1999), 303.

50. See Elisabeth Mudimbe-Boyi, "Unfathomable Toussaint", in Murdoch and Donadey, *Postcolonial Theory and Francophone Literary Studies*, 39.

51. See Homi Bhabha, *The Location of Culture* (London: Routledge, 1994), 86.

52. Nesbitt, "The Idea of 1804", 25.

53. See Aravamudan, *Tropicopolitans*, 292.

54. See Bhabha, *Location of Culture*, 85–92. On Toussaint's mimicry of Napoleon, especially as represented by Bernard Dadié in his *Iles de tempête*, see Mudimbe-Boyi, "Unfathomable Toussaint", 42–43.

55. See Mudimbe-Boyi, "Unfathomable Toussaint", 45.

56. On Haiti and questions of the "difficult construction of a universal freedom", see also Nick Nesbitt, "Troping Toussaint, Reading Revolution", *Research in African Literatures* 35, no. 2 (2004): 18–33.

57. See David Scott, *Refashioning Futures* (Princeton: Princeton University Press, 1999). Additional recent scholarship on C.L.R. James includes Christopher Gair (ed.), *Beyond Boundaries: C.L.R. James and Post-national Studies* (London: Pluto, 2006); Frank Rosengarten, *Urbane Revolutionary: C.L.R. James and the Struggle for a New Society* (Jackson: University Press of Mississippi, 2007); and Brett St Louis, *Rethinking Race, Politics, and Poetics: C.L.R. James' Critique of Modernity* (New York and London: Routledge, 2007).

58. Scott, *Refashioning Futures*, 13.

59. Ibid., 129.

60. Ibid., 133.

61. Ibid., 169.

62. Ibid., 15; emphasis in the original.

63. See Hurley, "Power, Purpose, the Presumptuousness of Postcoloniality".

CHAPTER 4

THE HAITIAN REVOLUTION AND A NORTH AMERICAN GRIOT
THE LIFE OF TOUSSAINT L'OUVERTURE BY JACOB LAWRENCE

CAROLYN WILLIAMS

In 1939, an exhibit of paintings entitled *The Life of Toussaint L'Ouverture* by Jacob Lawrence, an African-American artist, was shown at the De Porres Interracial Council headquarters in New York City.[1] In this masterful work, the artist went beyond merely telling the story of the life of the heroic Toussaint Louverture and constructed a visual history of Haiti from the arrival of Columbus to its birth as the first black republic in the world. While interpreting the revolution and the life of the complex founding father of Haiti, Lawrence found his vocation and devised his unique format, a series of images accompanied by word texts.

Lawrence received an early level of acknowledgement and commendation that eluded many other artists. He is considered one of the most important American artists of the twentieth century. In addition to his importance as a visual artist, Jacob Lawrence is heralded as a significant chronicler of the black historical experience in the New World.[2]

The particular circumstances of his life prepared the artist to be a visual griot. On the one hand, Jacob Lawrence shared the common experiences of twentieth-century African Americans, who lived in a separate world, apart from mainstream society. Looking back on his life he expounded: "My early beginnings, as most Negroes in the United States, has been the Negro experience. This is all I knew at one time, was the Negro experience. My whole background, Negro family, Negro community, everything was Negro. So, I think it was natural that I would use this symbol for my expression, you see."[3]

Not only was this black universe the subject of his initial creative efforts, African-American artists provided virtually all of his formal training and mentoring.

Lawrence described the meaning and the significance of this:

> So I mention this [meeting African-American artist Romare Bearden] to say the importance of contact with artists or people in the arts is part of your education, part of your development. . . . I think it's significant that all of this happened in Harlem. When I say "Harlem" I mean in the broad sense; I don't just mean New York Harlem; but I imagine this was happening to many people and many Negroes throughout the country in their own Harlems. You see so many positive things came out of these communities. I know to me it was a very positive experience. So much that I still feel very much a part of the Negro community. I've never left the Negro community in spirit.[4]

THE FORMATIVE YEARS OF JACOB LAWRENCE AND THE HARLEM RENAISSANCE

Lawrence arrived in the world at a key stage of the African-American experience, nearly a half-century after emancipation. To escape the violence and poverty that followed the end of slavery, many African Americans began to leave the region where their ancestors had been held in bondage. This black exodus from the south is now called the Great Migration.[5]

Jacob Lawrence's parents – Jacob Lawrence, Sr, born in South Carolina and Rosa Lee Armstead Lawrence, a native of Virginia – were part of this grand shift of the Southern black American population to the urban areas of the north and Midwest. They met and married in Atlantic City, New Jersey, where their first child, Jacob, was born on 7 September 1917. Later, this son depicted the historical journey of his parents and scores of others in the series known as *The Migrants*.[6]

The Lawrence family moved to Philadelphia, where two other children – William and Rosa – were born. Soon after the birth of the younger children, the family fell apart. Jacob and Rosa Lee Lawrence separated. Rosa left the children in foster care to seek a livelihood in New York City. Mother and children later reunited and relocated to the New York community of Harlem.

The year was 1930, a pivotal time for the Lawrence family and for Americans generally. The decade of the Great Depression had begun. Concurrently, the flowering of the arts and political activism of black people in America that became known as the Harlem Renaissance continued.[7]

Due in part to the Great Migration – the social and psychological upheaval of the post–First World War era and the meeting of talented and adventurous people of African descent from different parts of the world – a new wave of black artistic creativity and political energy was unleashed during the Jazz Age of the 1920s. Many migrating black Southerners, like the waves of European immigrants that preceded them, were attracted to New York City and settled in the district of Harlem.

The increasing population and accompanying social problems influenced the growth of the community and the rise of civil rights organizations. The National Association for the Advancement of Colored People (NAACP), founded in 1909, was a chief beneficiary of this demographic and political surge. A number of black journals – including *Crisis*, the literary organ of the NAACP, and *Messenger* and *New York Age*, edited by talented African-American intellectuals like W.E.B. Du Bois, A. Philip Randolph and James Weldon Johnson – reported and disseminated information about the African-American and the pan-African experience.[8]

As African Americans arrived from the south and other parts of the United States, another stream of people from the Caribbean converged on Harlem. Among the most important was the Jamaican-born Marcus Garvey – the father of black nationalism in the twentieth century – who affected a birth of pride in blackness and renewed psychological ties to Africa. One result was the celebration of African heritage and ancestry.[9] Claude McKay – also Jamaican, and a gifted poet – added political militancy to the arts.[10]

Other black intellectuals and artists contributed to the politicization of the arts during this period. Alain Locke, the first African-American Rhodes scholar, articulated a new black aesthetic. Locke – a philosophy professor and art critic at the prestigious black institution Howard University – urged African Americans to seek an authentic black identity, based on their African heritage and their particular experience in America. He introduced African art to the United States and promoted awareness of its impact on celebrated European artists Pablo Picasso and Henri Matisse.[11]

In 1925, Locke published an anthology, *The New Negro*, in which he argued that art would serve the political function of elevating black people in American society and the world.[12] The "New Negro" concept conveyed a renewed sense of personal and cultural worth and was expressed by writers, musicians, theatrical performers and a wave of visual artists, including Hale Woodruff, Aaron Douglas and Augusta Savage.

New resources supported black creativity. One of the most important was the Harmon Foundation, the product of white philanthropist William E. Harmon, a real estate investor from Iowa. Lawrence explained that the Harmon Foundation "gave awards in all the arts, poetry, music writing, and the plastic arts". He felt that Locke and Harmon were chief among the people: "responsible in making it possible by encouraging us to paint up to the point or up to the time when the art establishment was ready to take notice of what was going on" in Harlem and other black communities.[13]

Soon after arriving in New York, Lawrence began receiving art instruction in an after-school programme at the settlement establishment, Utopia House. Lawrence met his first role model, the painter Charles Alston, who ran the arts and crafts programme at Utopia House.[14] Alston, who later became an artist of note, proved to be a fortunate teacher for the teenage Lawrence. He understood how to help the aspiring artist. Alston explained: "It would have been a mistake to try to teach Jake. He was teaching himself, finding his own way. All he needed was encouragement and information."[15] Lawrence was naturally drawn to art:

> [Art] was something I just liked to do. . . . I didn't even known what it was about . . . it was beyond my experience. I never saw an art gallery until I was about eighteen years of age. . . . So my experience was almost like something I liked to do. I liked to colour. And that was it. This was my exposure and going to the settlement house I was exposed to arts and crafts; soap carving, leather work, woodwork and painting. It was an arts and crafts thing. And I went into painting. I did the painting with poster colour and things of that sort. That was my first real exposure.[16]

The instruction and support from Alston and other artists were important to Lawrence because he was not encouraged at home. Consumed by the struggle to support her family, Rosa Lawrence had little time or appreciation for the importance of the arts. Lawrence provides insight into their difficult relationship: "We always had problems and frictions. We couldn't communicate, and because of that we weren't very close. . . . My mother had no experience in the visual arts; the creative experience was not part of her experience. She encouraged me to go into the civil service because of the security it offered; she didn't see art as affording that type of security."[17]

Not just security but basic survival was an immediate challenge for the Lawrence family. In 1936, after his mother lost her job, Jacob Lawrence dropped out of high school and worked in the newly created federal jobs programme, the Civilian Conservation Corps. He planted trees, drained swamps and built dams in upstate New York for six months. He then returned to Harlem and became associated with the Harlem Community Art Center directed by Augusta Savage.

Augusta Savage, a native of Green Cove Springs, Florida, was an important figure in Harlem, as the community became a major recipient of new federal employment programmes for artists in the 1930s. Lawrence indicated Savage's role in his life: "She was very influential . . . in making me a professional really in that she liked my work. . . . She was the professional person in that area at the time in the Harlem area."[18]

In the 1930s, Lawrence lived near Savage's storefront studio in Harlem. She encouraged all to enter. Artist Romare Bearden described Savage at this time as a "talented woman artist who had studied in Europe and come back to Harlem [and] poured out warmth and enthusiasm to the young people".[19] Lawrence did not take classes at Savage's gallery, but he became acquainted with a number of her students, including Gwendolyn Knight, who later became his wife.[20]

Federal funding for the arts played a role in the evolution of Lawrence as a professional artist. One such programme was the Works Progress Administration (WPA) Federal Art Project set up to create jobs in the areas of the visual arts, writing and theatre. The WPA supported community cultural centres and art workshops in Harlem, where Lawrence was able to take classes with professional artists free of charge.[21] During this period Lawrence again came under the tutelage of his first art instructor, Charles Alston, who directed the Harlem Arts Workshop. The workshop was sponsored by the College Art Association and had facilities at the 135th Street Public Library, later named the Schomburg Library.[22] While studying with Alston, Lawrence also worked with painter and sculptor Henry Bannarn at a WPA workshop established in Alston's studio at 306 West 131st Street.[23]

The studio at 306 became a central gathering place for many of the Harlem Renaissance artists, intellectuals and political activists. Lawrence later recalled: "At 306 I came into contact with so many older people in other fields of art . . . like Claude McKay [the poet], Countee Cullen, dancers . . . musicians. Although I was much younger than they, they would talk about . . . what they thought about their art. . . . It was like a school. . . . Socially, that was my whole life at that time, the '306' studio."[24]

The contacts with artists at 306 were important as both a source of artistic inspiration and creativity. These associations also had a deeper personal impact. Lawrence explained: "I had acceptance at a very early age from the community and that does a lot. . . . I got my encouragement from Charles Alston and Augusta Savage. And you just have to believe that what you're doing has value and that's it."[25]

Lawrence developed strong lifelong ties with his more immediate contemporaries. Among these were Robert Blackburn, who later founded the internationally known Printmaking Workshop in New York City, Ronald Joseph, described as "the most promising young artist" in the New York school system in 1929, and the previously mentioned Gwendolyn Knight, all natives of the West Indies. When he met Lawrence, Joseph was working on a WPA mural project.[26]

Gwendolyn Knight, four years older than Lawrence, was also a painter. The close and mutually supportive relationship with Knight was an important and constant factor in Lawrence's life and career. He stated: "She's been a big help to me in my work as a critic whom I respect. It's been a good relationship. Surely artistically it's been excellent. And she's a person who I respect."[27] As the 1930s drew to a close, Lawrence began to produce significant paintings of everyday life in Harlem. Also during that period, the young artist's horizons were expanded and his work was introduced to the public.[28] In 1937 his paintings were in two exhibits sponsored by the Harlem Artists Guild at the 115th Street Library.[29] Both exhibitions included art works by his instructors, Alston and Bannarn, who continued to be key influences on their student and *protégé*.

In addition, in 1937 Alston created a large pair of WPA murals entitled *Magic and Medicine* that explored the differences between African and American approaches to medicine in a historical context. Bannarn, a painter and a sculptor, shared with Savage the ability to illuminate the beauty of the commonplace African-American experience, as well as the grand historical aspects of this experience.[30]

Despite the parallels between his art and that of his mentors, Lawrence did not feel that they directly influenced his style.

> Their professional example was more important: I must attribute my motivation and my desire to be an artist to . . . the black community . . . and certain people within it, like Augusta Savage and Claude McKay, whom I knew as a young man. Of course, [McKay] wasn't a visual artist but was a writer who had a very strong sense of the human condition. I talked with him and knew him. It was quite an experience for me.[31]

He observed that Mckay, like Savage ascribed to a black nationalist outlook. "[Savage] was very nationalistic in that she was of the period, she was of the same kind of thinking of a Claude McKay, people [like] that – Garvey."[32] Part of Savage's nationalism was her recognition of African-American political activists. In addition to her busts of Marcus Garvey, Savage also sculpted the heads of James Weldon

Johnson and W.E.B. Du Bois. The content of her work – rather than the medium and technique – influenced Lawrence, who later chose influential black figures for his first major works.

Black nationalism was reinforced by the general interest of Harlem artists and intellectuals in African art, culture and identity. Harlem residents were able to view works from Alain Locke's collection of African art and African sculpture in the 115th Street Public Library.[33] Lawrence was also affected by other sources. One was a self-made educator who earned a living as a carpenter, "Professor" Charles Christopher Seifert. The artist described Seifert:

> [He was] a black nationalist who gave lectures in black history to any interested groups. . . . One of his projects [besides the collecting of books pertaining to black history] was to get black artists and young people such as myself who were interested in art . . . to select as our content black history. . . . For me, and for a few others, Seyfert was a most inspiring man, in that he helped give us something that we needed at the time.[34]

Lawrence was part of an excursion, organized by Seifert in 1935, to an exhibition at the Museum of Modern Art. This exhibit, *African Negro Art*, featured West African sculpture. Lawrence remarked later: "The show made a great impression on me."[35] Another Museum of Modern Art exhibit that was important to Lawrence was a show featuring the work of William Edmondson, a self-trained artist. At the age of sixty, the Tennessee native began carving gravestones from limestone.[36] Edmondson directly carved from materials rather than having the pieces cast in another medium. Lawrence recollected the 1937 show, sponsored by *Harper's Bazaar*:[37] "I remember a great deal of talk about Edmonson, a Negro sculptor. He was given a big show. I think in content it meant a lot to me. . . . He had this big show at the Museum of Modern Art. I was just a kid at the time. . . . But I remember this had a great influence on me. I don't know how this was translated in my painting, if it was at all. But I remember it had a great impact."[38]

Trips to the Metropolitan Museum of Art introduced him to art history.[39] He also spoke of having read numerous books at the Harlem Art Workshops he attended. In addition to what he read, Lawrence was affected by the conversations he heard:

> I do remember a discussion once, which I didn't participate in because these people were older than myself; they spoke of one painting with snow and a string of birds moving across in a straight line [Pieter Brueghel's *Hunters in the Snow*, 1565]. They used to talk of these things and respond

to my composition and picture structure because they thought I had a feel for it, and my work was hard-edge[d] and rather flat.

Lawrence recalled that other artists "mentioned there at that time were the Mexican muralists (Diego Rivera, Jose Clemente Orozco and David Siqueiros), the Chinese woodcut artists and Käthe Kollwitz, William Gropper, and George Grosz. We were interested in these artists because of their social commentary."[40] Jacob Lawrence stated that he "liked the Mexican school of painting . . . pure bold colour, the big forms . . . the content – dealing with people".[41] The Mexican muralists introduced a new political artistic genre, Social Realism, generated by the Mexican Revolution. Rivera and Orozco were among the post-revolutionary artists who issued a manifesto declaring their commitment to social concerns. This resulted in a national programme of monumental paintings emphasizing the Indian, rather than the European, heritage of Mexico. In the 1920s, the Mexican artists made a profound impression on artists in the United States when they were invited to paint large murals in New York, Detroit and other large American cities.[42] Artistic and political forces from Europe had an effect on American artists during this period as well. Rising political repression and the subsequent threat of war caused a number of European artists to come to the United States in the 1930s, and many of them settled in New York City. The vitality of this European wave virtually overwhelmed the indigenous American art world. The works of European artists figured prominently in major museums and galleries in the Depression era United States. A plethora of styles, including German expressionism, Surrealism and Dadaism, appeared and transformed the American art scene.

The fusion of art and politics helped shape Lawrence as an artist. He explains: "This was the way that all artists in every area were thinking; the writers, the artists, the people in the theater. . . . It wasn't a selection on my part. It was that this was the trend, this was it. . . . And therefore any youngster involved in that period of art, this was the all he would get, because his teachers were oriented in this way."[43]

Because of the circumstances of his life and the era, Lawrence could not merely copy the examples he observed in the museums outside of Harlem. He had been formed by a virtually exclusive black world. "I was all my life confined to the Harlem community. This is where I lived. This is where I grew up. This is where I got the material of my painting, the content of my painting and so on."[44]

He articulated how this environment and experience affected his work as an artist. "My first contact was with the Negro painter and teacher and the people from the neighborhood."⁴⁵ Lawrence went on to explain that he came on the art scene at a pivotal moment. That is, when "the white art community was beginning to see that . . . the Negro artist was a source which had never been tapped nationally".⁴⁶

Jacob Lawrence and the *Toussaint L'Ouverture* Series

Jacob Lawrence was the first black artist to achieve prominence in what was still a largely segregated art world and society as a whole. This experience led to the topic of his first major work. "I was very involved with Negro history at the time. I think my first involvement came about from hearing someone at the Harlem YMCA tell the story of Toussaint Louverture, the Haitian liberator who is often referred to as the George Washington of Haiti."⁴⁷

Lawrence was also inspired by the play *Haiti*, a melodrama written by W.E.B. Du Bois. The play was based on the lives of Toussaint Louverture and Henri Christophe. The Federal Theatre Project, a New Deal programme, provided funding for the production of the work. The art historian Ellen Harkins Wheat credits the Du Bois play with inspiring Lawrence to do a painting on the Haitian epic.⁴⁸

Lawrence's original intention in creating the *Toussaint L'Ouverture* series was to provide African Americans with a sense of pride, accomplishment and hope.

> I've always been interested in history, but they never taught Negro history in the public schools. . . . It was never studied seriously like regular subjects. My first real introduction to Negro history was when I was very young – thirteen; I imagine when a Mr. Allen spoke of it at Utopia House. He spoke of Toussaint Louverture. . . . Having no Negro history makes the Negro people feel inferior to the rest of the world. . . . I had several reasons for doing this work, and these are some of them. Someone had to do it. Another reason is that I have great admiration for the life of such a man as Toussaint Louverture.⁴⁹

Jacob Lawrence expressed a common desire of African Americans in the Harlems of the early twentieth century to tell their story, to articulate the tragic dimensions but ultimate triumph of the African diaspora. One person who contributed the resources to accomplish this was Arturo A. Schomburg. Schomburg – a Puerto Rican of African, Indian and German descent – spent over thirty years collecting materials documenting the experiences of Africans and their dispersed descendants. His archival collection was eventually acquired by the New York Public Library and housed in the Harlem branch, the 135th Street Library. Schomburg served as the curator of this collection until his death in 1938.[50]

Lawrence expressed the significance of the Schomberg collection. "The Schomburg Library is one of the most extensive libraries dealing with Negro – not necessarily just American Negro history in the world. . . . This became a favorite place of mine to go and do research."[51] After considerable investigation of Haiti had helped him to grasp the magnitude of the topic, Lawrence decided to do multiple images, rather than one picture. He chose the series format.

The forty-one paintings of the *Toussaint L'Ouverture* series constitute a narrative, each picture depicting an important episode in Haiti's history, culminating with the successful fight for independence. The works are in tempera on white paper. The dimensions of the paintings are relatively small size (11½ x 19 inches).[52] In composing the *L'Ouverture* series, Lawrence designed the form that is now part of his signature as an artist.

Lawrence refined his method in subsequent works. He began by laying out hardboard panels of the same size on the floor of his workspace. The panels were organized in vertical and horizontal patterns. This allowed the artist to see the pieces together and paint them at the same time.

To ensure consistency of the colours for the series, he systematically applied one colour at a time to each panel. He began with black and moved on to lighter colours. He often used his colours unmixed so that they would not vary from one panel to the next. Common colours used in the *L'Ouverture* series were black, white, gray and shades of red, yellow, blue, green, orange and brown. He added white to make lighter shades of a colour. He then carefully constructed captions and drew images. By repeating the shapes, colours and words throughout the narrative for each work, Lawrence produced a coherent chronicle.[53]

Decades after the creation of the *L'Ouverture* series, when asked about where he obtained the information used, Lawrence responded by citing some of the main sources. "Most of my information came from Charles Beard's book *Toussaint L'Ouverture*. I read other books – there were more novels than anything else. One book I don't remember its name – told me of the conditions of the islands, and its sources. It gave a short sketch of the history of the Haitian Revolution. From that I got the appearance of the island."[54]

Lawrence is probably referring to Reverend John R. Beard's *Toussaint L'Ouverture: A Biography and Autobiography*, first published in London in 1853.

Beard, a Unitarian minister, relied heavily on translations of Toussaint's correspondence with military figures and on official reports. Beard's account is replete with references to the impact of Christianity in shaping the character and explaining the actions of the revolutionary leader. For example, he reports that at a crucial stage of the Haitian war for independence, Louverture "preached a religion which, acknowledging all men as brothers, disclaimed and condemned slavery, and made his soldiers feel that fighting for freedom they fought on the side of God and Christ".[55] A chapter of the biography is devoted to "Toussaint's presumed scriptural studies", in which Christianity figures prominently.

Beard's sympathetic treatment of Louverture and the revolution reflects a common nineteenth-century English view. This interpretation was formed by two major factors. One was the residual resentment many British people had for France, whose rivalry with England culminated in the Napoleonic wars. In addition, Beard and other English sympathizers were strong supporters of the anti-slavery struggle during this period.

Britain had been a pioneer in the global abolitionist campaign. After ending slavery in the British Empire, the English government launched a campaign to stop the African slave trade. Many individual citizens, particularly those from Quaker, Unitarian and evangelical Protestant backgrounds, continued to lobby for the abolition of slavery. Thus, in fundamental respects, Beard's biography of Toussaint Louverture was a grand anti-slavery treatise. His opening remarks reflect this position:

> The life which is described in the following pages has both a permanent interest and a permanent value. But the efforts which are now made to effect the abolition of slavery in the United States of America, seem to render the present moment specially fit for the appearance of a memoir of Toussaint L'Ouverture. A hope of affording some aid to the sacred cause of freedom, specially as involved in the extinction of slavery, and in the removal of the prejudices on which servitude mainly depends, has induced the author to prepare the present work for the press.[56]

Beard regarded Louverture as an ideal subject to address these issues because of his untainted African blood: "The appearance of a hero of negro blood was ardently to be wished as affording the best proof of Negro capability. . . . Toussaint was a Negro. We wish emphatically to mark the fact that he was wholly without white blood. Whatever he was, and whatever he did, he achieved all in virtue of qualities which in kind are common to the African race."[57]

The Haitian Revolution and a North American Griot

Celebration of the African ancestry of Louverture and the commitment to demonstrating the "negro capability" surely had a tremendous appeal to the young Lawrence, as would have a statement made by Beard at the end of this study: "Toussaint Louverture commands our respect and admiration. But the race at large cannot be accounted equal to some others, if only because as yet it has no history"[58] anticipates the sentiment expressed by Lawrence: "Having no Negro history makes the Negro people feel inferior to the rest of the world."

Lawrence extrapolates many of the heroic dimensions of Louverture and the extraordinary exploits of this chapter of the African diaspora presented by Beard and combines this with his own unique telling of the story. Consequently, *The Life of Toussaint L'Ouverture* marks the creation of "a new theme for the twentieth century – an imaginative, yet didactic, pictorial narrative"[59] of the African diaspora. This work launches Lawrence as one of the twentieth-century American griots, "a praise singer", who used the experiences of the dispersed descendants of Africans to illuminate the universal struggle against oppression and for recognition of human dignity.

In constructing his tale, Lawrence both introduced a form, the series, and reflected a technique, storytelling, that was becoming a growing aspect of the visual arts in the 1920s and 1930s. Previous artists, particularly early-twentieth-century African-American painters, Lawrence's mentor Charles Alston for example, chose the mural. Other important examples are Aaron Douglas's paintings depicting the African-American experience, and Hale Woodruff's *Amistad*.[60]

An important source of storytelling as a medium was provided by the relatively new visual arts of photography and motion pictures. In the 1930s, Americans were introduced to photographic essays in magazines like *Life* and *Time*. The works of major photographers Margaret Bourke-White and Dorothea Lange – who possessed a keen eye for and interest in social concerns – were becoming part of the cultural landscape of the United States. Documentary films recorded the plight of people in crisis. Works of the new visual media wove "together images and words, which at times enhance one another's messages".[61] Lawrence's paintings combined the narrative quality of the mural with the detail of the photograph. Each picture of his various serials captured a moment that "literally tells a story".

A particular feature of his work that illustrates this unique phenomenon is his ability to create an air of spontaneity and infuse the still image with motion. Elizabeth Steele and Susana Halpine attribute Lawrence's "success in obtaining . . . charged depiction" to "his individualistic use of materials and his unique approach to technique, both of which he manipulates to suit the series format". His paintings are well thought out, but the final images appear "full of movement and spontaneous". The paint he used, fast-drying casein tempera, allowed Lawrence to "capture the essence of movement", resulting in "a narrative that is both expressive and forceful".[62]

Citing his "command of aqueous media", Steele and Halpine explain that he used the water based tempera in a unique way. That is, he painted "in one layer, and achieved a sense of movement and space in his strong sense of line and by varying his brushwork and juxtaposing flat, opaque passages next to more transparent ones in which his brushwork is expressive".[63] Lawrence described his method as a "mechanical process". He rejected the notion of complexity and implied an innate sense of composition: "You have a feeling for space. You have the feeling for design. I think people do the same things in their homes. If you decorate a room you don't put everything on one side, even if you've never gone to art school. Without even knowing the term design, you have a feeling for space, colour, texture."[64]

Lawrence combined his intuitive sense of composition with careful planning of the dimensions, shapes and selection of colours. He envisioned exhibiting the multiple paintings as one work. Therefore he plotted the alternating horizontal and vertical formats that would give the work of art "a certain interest, a certain rhythm".[65] The *L'Ouverture* series is a vivid illustration of this calculated display.

Weaving pictures with words, Lawrence reconstructs the odyssey of African people who have been struggling against European colonization and oppression for the past half-millennium. Similar to James Beard, Lawrence's account of Haiti begins with the first defining encounter between the indigenous people of the area Europeans called the "New World" that was an extension of the field of European rivalry for global domination.

The first four panel texts of the *L'Ouverture* series depict this chronological progression from Columbus until the conclusion of the first round of the European contest for the region. The image of the first panel conveys the brutal suppression of the original inhabitants accompanied by the planting of Christianity. Panel text one states "Columbus discovered Haiti on December 6, 1492. The discovery was on Columbus's first trip to the New World. He is shown planting the official Spanish flag, under which he sailed. The priest shows the influence of the Church upon the people."[66]

In the text of the second panel Lawrence articulates the experience of the indigenous people. "Mistreatment by the Spanish soldiers caused much trouble on the island and caused the death of Anacanca, a native queen, 1503. Columbus left soldiers in charge, who began making slaves of the people. The queen was one of the leaders of the insurrection which followed." Panel text three states, "Spain and France fought for Haiti constantly, 1665–1691." Panels one, two and three are horizontal. This allows the viewer the illusion of "reading" the opening sequences like a book.

The written text of panel four states: "Spain and France agree to divide Haiti, 1691." The vertical arrangement of this text underscores the conclusive nature of the first major stage of the European contest for Haiti. The opening four panels set the tone of the series with regard to the arrangement of shapes and colours. Vertical paintings are often used to call attention to the significance of events, for example, pivotal historical moments and the stages of Toussaint's life. The same colours appear in scenes addressing similar issues and themes.

The bodies of the indigenous people, who were the first slaves of Europeans in the New World, are painted black, conveying their kinship to the enslaved African people who will replace them. The sky is coloured ultramarine (to reflect the dismal plight of the first inhabitants and the warfare between the Europeans). At the conclusion of their battles, as they stand over the map of Haiti and draw the blueprint for the division of the region (which is painted black), the French and Spanish conquerors are cloaked in black headdresses that resemble the hood of the Grim Reaper. Lawrence then turned to the odyssey of the Africans and their descendants.

Elizabeth Catlett, another major twentieth-century visual griot of the African diaspora, provides insight into the particular ability of Lawrence the storyteller. Catlett praised Lawrence's style of painting with the use of "almost elemental colour and design". She felt the artist "strips his material to the bone". Lawrence's approach and his unique use of colour were regarded by Catlett as "a perfect means for the expression of the fundamental needs of the Negro". Others cited his "splendid gift of colour and design" and how in his work "form is simplified in order to articulate the essentials". Patricia Hills summarized the elements and utility of Lawrence's style: "These critics recognized that Lawrence forged a modernism – clarity of form, reductive colour range, absence of tonal variations, and simplified spatial relations – that expressed deeply felt social concern."[67]

In the fifth painting, the last panel created before he embarks on the odyssey of the life of Louverture, Lawrence portrays the African slave trade that was introduced by the early eighteenth century. The Africans are sitting in a heap against the tropical nightmare (the terrain is painted in green and black, a common colour pattern extensively used in the series) of the Haiti they are experiencing. The blacks watch with anxious eyes as the whites (a female and several males), dressed in elegant attire (painted white, black and grey), make selections of the people who will be delegated chattel. The panel text reads, "Slave trade reaches its heights in Haiti, 1730."

In the texts of panels six to nine, Lawrence tells the story of the future Haitian leader. He begins with the vertical panel six, which reads, "The birth of Toussaint L'Ouverture, May 20, 1743. Both of Toussaint's parents were slaves." Panel seven, which follows this, illustrates what the young Toussaint observed of slavery: "As a child, Toussaint heard the twang of the planter's whip and saw the blood stream from the bodies of slaves." This panel is horizontal and contains a brutal image of a planter (again dressed all in white) whipping a prostrate slave. The panel and a similar one (number ten, depicting the ongoing violent suppression of the slave) contain parallel images of a slave lying on a vermilion coloured ground with a planter dressed in white. The tenth painting also contains slaves in chains. The emphasis on the white garments of the slaveholders serves as an indictment of the Europeans.

Lawrence describes the future Haitian leader's education. The text of the vertical panel eight states: "In early manhood his seemingly good nature won for him the coachmanship for Bayor de Libertas, 1763. His job as coachman gave him time to think about how to fight slavery. During this period, he taught himself to read and to write." The text for panel nine (also a vertical painting) introduces an important chapter in the history of slavery, that is, the rise of the movement against the heinous institution. "[Louverture] read Rynol's Anti-Slavery Book that predicted a Black Emancipator, which language spirited him, 1763–1776."[68] This panel, like the one preceding it, is horizontal. The tenth painting reads, "The cruelty of the planters towards the slaves drove the slaves to revolt, 1776. Those revolts, which kept cropping up from time to time, finally came to a head in the rebellion." This panel, and the following one (painting eleven, the text of which states, "Jean Francois, first Black to rebel") are horizontal. As with the first three paintings, these panels give the viewer the sensation of reading a book.

Lawrence continues the narrative by referring to the English debate over emancipation in Parliament. The text for the eleventh panel states: "The society of the Friends of the Blacks was formed in England in 1778, the leading members being Price, Priestly, Sharp, Clarkson and Wilberforce."[69]

As the slave rebellion escalated "Toussaint led his master and mistress to safety" (Lawrence's written text for panel thirteen, a vertical painting). This episode was an expression of the fundamental attitude of Toussaint toward whites. Although Louverture never wavered in his commitment to the emancipation of the enslaved black people of Haiti, he refused to succumb to revenge.

After introducing these outstanding dimensions to Toussaint's character, Lawrence turned to his first appearance in the revolution. Initially Toussaint played a secondary role. The text for panel fourteen reads, "The blacks were led by the three chiefs, Jean-Francois, Biassou, and Jeannoc; Toussaint serving as aide-de-camp to Biassou."[70]

In the next twenty-two panels, that is, paintings fifteen through thirty-six, Lawrence illustrates the brilliant spectacle of Toussaint's rise and fall, the various individuals and groups, and the dynamics both in Haiti and abroad that drive them. He demonstrates the tri-racial (involving blacks, whites and mulattoes) nature of the struggle within the country, as well as the international forces that Toussaint had to negotiate as he led his people to independence.

Louverture was small in stature, but had enormous reserves of energy and inner strength. He was an inspiring and intrepid military leader who conducted his campaigns on horseback. Lawrence used this insight in many of the scenes – for example, panels sixteen, seventeen, twenty-one, twenty-nine, thirty-three and thirty-four – in which the leader is portrayed on horseback. Apparently he was a superb horseman. Beard described Louverture as being at one with the horse. Lawrence captures this merger of man and beast in panel twenty-one (its text reads "General Toussaint L'Ouverture attacked the English at Artibonite and there captured two towns"). In this painting Toussaint is dressed in white jodhpurs and a black jacket, set off by a red sash. The red is carried through in the hat, accented by a white plume. He is mounted on a galloping white horse that exhibits the same exhilaration and determination as the rider who leans forward with a cadmium yellow sword in his raised hand.

A particular challenge for Toussaint was that the people of colour of in Haiti were not united. The mulatto population, created over the years by the rape and seduction by European men of African slave women and their female descendants, generally disdained blacks and aspired to rise to a position of equality with the whites. Consequently, mulattoes aided the Europeans in putting down the black revolution. Lawrence depicted their position in panel fifteen ("The Mulattoes, enemies of both the Blacks and the Whites, but tolerated more by the Whites, joined them in battle forces against the Blacks, 1793").

Concurrently, the ongoing European rivalry erupted into formal warfare between France and England. Fortunately this facilitated Louverture's campaign.

This is conveyed in panel nineteen: "The Mulattoes had no organization, the English held only a point or two on the island, while the Blacks formed into large bands, and slaughtered every Mulatto and White they encountered. The Blacks learned the secret of their power. The Haitians now controlled half the island."

Toussaint consolidated the power and determination of the blacks. This was most vividly conveyed in the powerful painting of panel twenty-three ("General L'Ouverture collected forces at Marmelade, and on October the 9th, 1794, left with 500 men to capture San Miguel"). Here Lawrence uses the technique described by Steele and Halpine. The scene is of many soldiers marching through the green- and black-coloured terrain, their rifles held in military precision. The juxtaposition of opaque and transparent shapes gives the picture a strong sense of motion and power. Grey and white are used for the pants and hats of the soldiers. Their jackets are brown and orange. The weapons are orange and black. These colours pick up a similar pattern used in the scenes of the panels immediately preceding and following it.

With determined troops and committee military leaders, Toussaint Louverture was victorious. He achieved his goal of making Haiti into a French republic. Lawrence demonstrated these accomplishments in panels twenty-seven ("Returning to private life as the commander and chief of the army, he saw to it that the country was well taken care of, and Haiti returned to prosperity. During this important period, slavery was abolished, and attention focused upon agricultural pursuits") and twenty-eight ("The constitution was prepared and presented to Toussaint on the 19th day of May, 1800, by nine men he had chosen, eight of whom were white proprietors and one mulatto. Toussaint's liberalism led him to choose such a group to draw up the constitution. He was much criticized for his choice, but the constitution proved workable").

Lawrence illustrates the results in panel twenty-nine ("L'Ouverture made a triumphant march into San Domingo on the 2nd of January 1801, at the head of 10,000 men, and hoisted the flag of the French Republic. Toussaint did not wish to break with the French, the largest group of Haitian inhabitants. The Blacks themselves spoke patois"). To illustrate Toussaint's triumph, Lawrence depicts the Haitian hero in full uniform of red with raised white-gloved hand firmly grasping a Bocour yellow sword on a prancing white horse.

Following this scene of the victorious leader is a painting of the man who would engineer the downfall and the eventual demise of the Father of Haiti. Panel thirty states, "Napoleon Bonaparte begins to look on Haiti as a new land to conquer. Conquest inevitably meant further slavery." Napoleon is painted against a cadmium yellow background. He clutches a piece of parchment, presumably the new Haitian constitution. His arrogance and ambition are evident.

Like Washington, who retired to private life following the military victory that liberated his country – but returned to public life when his services were required – Toussaint rose to the occasion. Unlike Washington, who was able to lead his country to a stable new beginning after the creation of the constitution, Toussaint's re-emergence into the public arena involved a return to the field of battle. He was removed by treachery and ended his life in the prison cell of the former colonial power.

Lawrence records the poignant final chapter in the life of the great leader in paintings thirty-seven and thirty-nine (both vertical panels). They are powerful images of the bleak last days of the heroic leader. The black backgrounds are relieved only by gray squares of the single window. In panel thirty-seven, the text of which reads, "Toussaint is taken to Paris and imprisoned in the dungeon of the Castle Joux – August 17, 1802", the artist painted the figure of Toussaint holding on to the window frame as he looks out in desperation. A yellow octagon is used to depict the cot that is his bed. In the last scene depicted in panel thirty-nine, the defeated leader is shown sprawled face down with his head cushioned on his bent right arm and his left arm dangling over the edge of the cot that served as his deathbed. (This final rendering of Louverture has disturbing parallels to the prostrate slave being punished by his masters depicted in panel seven of the series). The text to the latter painting reads, "The Death of Toussaint L'Ouverture in the Prison of Le Joux, April 1803. Imprisoned a year, Toussaint died of a broken heart."

A combination of the tenacity of Toussaint's troops and yellow-fever epidemics eventually forced the French to relinquish their hold on Haiti. New, more ruthless and less competent men led the Haitian people to their final victory of liberation and independence. Sadly, instead of a prosperous republic, Haiti ended up as a dictatorship. Lawrence concludes the tale. The text for the final painting, the vertical panel forty-one, reads "Dessalines was crowned Emperor October 4, 1804, thus; Jean Jacques the First of Haiti. Dessalines, standing beside a broken chain, has the powers of dictator, as opposed to Toussaint's more liberal leadership." From the perspective of Jacob Lawrence, the central tragedy of the Haitian Revolution was that instead of the "George Washington of Haiti", the newly liberated West Indian nation was first ruled by a black Napoleon.

This tale had been virtually omitted from the national and international historical narratives. In the 1960s, when African Americans were engaged in a sustained and, in some fundamental respects, successful political movement for enfranchisement and empowerment, and as Africans were overthrowing European colonialism, Lawrence shed light on the motivation for this work:

> I didn't do it just as a historical thing, but because I believe these things tie up with the Negro today. We don't have a physical slavery, but an economic slavery. If these people, who were so much worse off than the people today, could conquer slavery, we certainly can do the same thing. They had to liberate themselves without any education. Today we can't do it in the same way. . . . How will it come about? I don't know. I'm not a politician. I'm an artist, just trying to do my part to bring this part about.[71]

A 1939 review of the work that appeared in the *Baltimore Sun* summarizes the impact of this powerful first serial work of Jacob Lawrence:

> These small sketches, with their economy of flat, sharply defined forms and their . . . variations in consistent colour pattern, are charged with feeling and movement. The designs are full of swift, racing vigor, and the notable mingling of realistic and symbolic elements of simplified abstract form with the quality of illustration give them a powerful impact. The theme, moreover, is well developed and the mood finely sustained and, both individually and as a series, they constitute a striking and original work.[72]

Through the various exhibitions and studies of this work, critics have debated the specific technical artistic influences on Lawrence manifested in the *L'Ouverture* series.[73] Most important, this collective work signalled an important new figure on the American art scene, one with an original style and technique who had much to say. Art critic Paul Karlstrom echoes the sentiments of the artist: "Lawrence's art may be viewed as a quest for a different modernist essentialism, one that embodies African American universal, humanistic ideals and values . . . [and] . . . a simultaneously held conception of art as an autonomous form of knowledge. As a means to uplift and restore his people, Lawrence's art seems purposely to embrace and integrate both of these modernist ideals."

Karlstrom goes on to define the astounding accomplishment of Lawrence in articulating the epic of the African diaspora in the New World through the medium of art: "Never entirely absent, however, nor far beneath the flat surfaces, is the African [diasporic] historical saga and contemporary experience. For Lawrence, the challenge was to fuse these concerns: modernist pictorial theory and form and group identity. This was admirably achieved in *The Life of Toussaint L'Ouverture* and the series that followed immediately thereafter."[74]

The Haitian Revolution and a North American Griot

In 1986, Lawrence and silkscreen artist Lou Stovall decided to recast the *L'Ouverture* series in a silkscreen edition. The images of the latter edition are larger than the original paintings. The dimensions of the silkscreen portraits are twenty-two inches by eleven inches. Lawrence retained the words that he created in the 1930s for the latter, limited edition of the series.

The fifteen images Lawrence selected for this series illuminate his essential view of Louverture as the "George Washington of Haiti" and the success of the liberation campaign. The heroic Louverture continues to occupy centre stage and is a compelling figure. The image, entitled *General Toussaint L'Ouverture,* that was captured in panel twenty of the original series is the first painting of the silkscreen edition. In both paintings, Louverture is depicted resplendent in a venetian red uniform and hat, accented with white plumage. His profile is ivory black. The figure is painted against a Bocour green background. It is the most famous painting of the series and the most magnificent. (The caption states, "General Toussaint L'Ouverture, Statesman and military genius, esteemed by the Spaniards, feared by the English, dreaded by the French, hated by the planters, and reverenced by the Blacks.") The Haitian hero is featured in eight of the other images.

The final appearance of Toussaint Louverture in the revised silkscreen edition ends with the deception that removed him from the arena of the Revolution. In fundamental ways this was Lawrence's last word and definitive interpretation of Toussaint, as well as reminder to the world and the dispersed descendants of Africa that, like their ancestors, they must continue to fight to "preserve their freedom".

Notes

1. The De Porres Council was a Catholic centre on Vesey Street in New York. The exhibit was Lawrence's first one-man show outside of Harlem. The poet Claude McKay helped make the arrangements for the exhibit. Ellen Harkins Wheat, *Jacob Lawrence American Painter* (Seattle: University of Washington Press, 1986), 43. Peter Nesbett and Michelle DuBois report that the *L'Ouverture* series was first exhibited at the Baltimore Museum of Art. This information is contained in *Over the Line: The Art of Jacob Lawrence*, ed. Peter T. Nesbett and Michelle DuBois (Seattle: University of Washington Press, in association with Jacob Lawrence Catalogue Raisonne Project, 2000), 26.

2. For information about Lawrence see Wheat, *Jacob Lawrence*, and Nesbett and DuBois, *Over the Line.*

3. Jacob Lawrence Oral History Interview, conducted by Carroll Greene for the Smithsonian Archives of American Art (26 October 1968), 18. (http://www.aaa.si.edu/collections/oralhistories/transcripts/lawren68.htm)

4. Ibid.

5. For a discussion of the dynamics involved and the impact of this relocation see Alferdteen Harrison, ed., *Black Exodus: The Great Migration from the American South* (Jackson: University Press of Mississippi, 1991).

6. See the discussions of various scholars in Elizabeth Hutton Turner, *Jacob Lawrence: The Migration Series* (Washington, DC: Rappahannock Press in association with the Phillips Collection, 1993).

7. Important studies of the Harlem Renaissance include David Levering Lewis, *When Harlem Was in Vogue* (New York: Oxford University Press, 1989); and Nathan Irvin Huggins, *Harlem Renaissance* (New York: Oxford University Press, 1973). For a discussion of the visual art and artists of the Harlem Renaissance, see Mary Smith Campbell, comp., *Harlem Renaissance: Art of Black America* (New York: Studio Museum of Harlem, 1987).

8. Bruce Kellner provides brief descriptions of the journals cited in *The Harlem Renaissance: A Historical Dictionary of the Era* (Westport, Conn.: Greenwood Press, 1984), 6, 76, 86, 239.

9. Information about Caribbean immigrants to Harlem is presented by Irma Watkins-Owens, *Bold Relations: Caribbean Immigrants and the Harlem Community* (Bloomington and Indianapolis: Indiana University Press, 1961). Also see Heather Hathaway, *Caribbean Waves: Relocating Claude McKay and Paule Marshall* (Bloomington and Indianapolis: Indiana University Press, 1990), 12–28; and Joyce Turner Moore, *Caribbean Crusaders and the Harlem Renaissance* (Urbana: University of Illinois Press, 2005). The following studies of Garvey should also be consulted: Rupert Lewis, *Marcus Garvey: Anti-Colonial Champions* (Trenton, NJ: African World Press, 1988); and Tony Martin, *Literary Garveyism: Garvey, Black Arts and the Harlem Renaissance* (Dover, Mass.: Majority Press, 1983).

10. The following studies are excellent sources of information about Claude McKay and the political dimensions of his poetry and other works: Hathaway, *Caribbean Waves*, 29–85; Wayne Cooper, *Claude McKay: Rebel Sojourner in the Harlem Renaissance* (Baton Rouge: Louisiana State University Press, 1987); and Tyrone Tilley, *Claude McKay: A Black Poet's Struggle for Identity* (Amherst: University of Massachusetts Press, 2002).

11. For discussions of how Picasso and Matisse were affected by the art of Africa see Elizabeth Cowling, *Picasso: Style and Meaning* (London: Phaidon Press, 2002); Jack Flam, *Matisse: The Man and His Art, 1869–1918* (Ithaca: Cornell University Press, 1986), 180–194; Jack Cowart et al., *Matisse and Morocco, The Paintings and Drawings, 1912–1913* (New York: Harry N. Abrams Publishers, 1990), 325–75; and Elizabeth Cowling et al., *Matisse Picasso* (New York: Museum of Modern Art, 2002).

12. See the anthology edited by Locke, *The New Negro: An Interpretation* (New York: Albert and Charles Boni, 1925). For information on Locke, see Leonard Harris, *The Philosophy*

of *Alain Locke: Harlem and Beyond* (Philadelphia: Temple University Press, 1989); Manning Marable, "Toward an Aesthetic of Black Folk Expression: George Hall, Alain Locke and the Sense of the African Legacy"; and Russell J. Linneman, "Alain Locke and Black Folk Music", in *Alain Locke: Reflections on a Modern Renaissance Man*, ed. Russell J. Linneman (Baton Rouge: Louisiana State University Press, 1982), 77–90, 100–108, 122–32.

13. See Gary A. Reynolds and Beryl J. Wright, eds., *Against the Odds: African-American Artists and the Harmon Foundation* (New Jersey: Newark Museum, 1989). The quote is from Lawrence, interview by Greene, in Reynolds and Wright, *Against the Odds*, 33.

14. Elizabeth Hutton Turner illuminated Alston's role in the education and early years of the professional life of Lawrence in "The Education of Jacob Lawrence". Also see Leslie King-Hammond, "Inside-Outside, Uptown-Downtown: Jacob Lawrence and the Aesthetic Ethos of the Harlem Working-Class Community". The Hutton Turner and King-Hammond essays are in Nesbett and DuBois, *Over the Line*, 70–71, 73, 97–120. Also see Sharon Patton, *African-American Art* (New York: Oxford University Press, 1998), 144–56.

15. Romare Bearden interviewed Alston in 1969. This quote is included in Romare Bearden and Harry Henderson, *A History of African-American Artists from 1792 to the Present* (New York: Pantheon Books, 1993), 294.

16. Lawrence, interview by Greene, in Reynolds and Wright, *Against the Odds*, 5.

17. Wheat included these quotes in her interviews with Lawrence on 24 February 1982, 7 April 1983, 21 April 1983 and 24 July 1984 in *Jacob Lawrence*, 31.

18. Lawrence, interview by Greene, in Reynolds and Wright, *Against the Odds*, 5.

19. This quote was included in Wheat, *Jacob Lawrence*. The original quote is from Jervis Anderson's essay about Harlem in the *New Yorker* "Harlem, Hard Times and Beyond", 20 July 1981, 60–61.

20. Wheat presents information about Knight and the other young artists that Lawrence met at Savage's studio during this period in *Jacob Lawrence*, 31. Also see King-Hammond, "Inside-Outside, Uptown-Downtown", 73; Richard Powell and Jock Reynolds, *To Conserve a Legacy: American Art from Historically Black Colleges and Universities* (Andover, Mass.: Addison Gallery of American Art and New York: Studio Museum of Harlem, 1999), 171–72; and the exhibition catalogue *African-American Artists, 1929–1945: Prints. Drawings and Paintings in the Metropolitan Museum of Art*, ed. Lisa Mintz Messinger, Lisa Gail Collins and Rachel Mustalish (New York: Metropolitan Museum of Art, and New Haven: Yale University Press, 2003), 40.

21. For information about the federal government and artists during the New Deal see Milton Meltzer, *Violins and Shovels: WPA Art Projects* (New York: Delacorte Press, 1976).

22. Patton provides information about the Harlem Art Center in *African-American Art*, 144–45.

23. Information about Bannarn and the 306 Studio is included in Powell and Reynolds, *To Conserve a Legacy*, 173–74.

24. Wheat, *Jacob Lawrence*, 30 (quotation); the remarks first appeared in Jacqueline Rocker Brown, Jr. (MA thesis, Howard University, 1974), 109.

25. These remarks are from Wheat's interviews with Lawrence, 24 February 1983, 21 April 1983 and 14 July 1984 and were included in *Jacob Lawrence*.

26. Information about Blackburn and Ronald Joseph and the remarks quoted are in Messinger, Collins and Mustalish, *African-American Artists*, 31 and 72. For additional information about Blackburn, see Powell and Reynolds, *To Conserve a Legacy*, 178.

27. King-Hammond, "Inside-Outside, Uptown-Downtown", 71; and Reynolds and Wright, *Against the Odds*, 10.

28. See Wheat, *Jacob Lawrence*, 32–34; and King-Hammond, "Inside-Outside, Uptown-Downtown", 67–95.

29. See the discussion of the Harlem Artists' Guild in Patton, *African-American Art*, 144–45.

30. Wheat and Patton discuss Alston's 1937 mural in *Jacob Lawrence*, 34, and *African-American Art*, 145, respectively. James A. Porter, who was an artist, art historian and art critic, stated that "Bannarn's finest work appeals to the most discriminating taste of the art world; and whether it be such a lowly theme as 'scrubwoman' or epic themes such as John Brown, the boundless strength of the primitive wells up in the work". This quote is included in Powell and Reynolds, *To Conserve a Legacy*.

31. Wheat, *Jacob Lawrence*, 34. The quote first appeared in Clarence Major, "Jacob Lawrence, Expressionist", *Black Scholar* (November 1977): 23–24.

32. Lawrence, interview by Greene, in Reynolds and Wright, *Against the Odds*, 23–24.

33. Wheat reported on the widespread interest in African art in Harlem during the 1920s in *Jacob Lawrence*, 35.

34. Wheat included this excerpt from a letter for Lawrence to Charles Alan, dated 29 December 1972, in *Jacob Lawrence*, 35. For a discussion of Seifert, see Bearden and Henderson, *A History of African-American Art*, 247–50.

35. Wheat, *Jacob Lawrence*, 35; and King-Hammond, "Inside-Outside, Uptown-Downtown", 26, 77–78.

36. For information about Edmundson, see Patton, *African-American Art*, 132.

37. Nesbett and DuBois, *Over the Line*, 28.

38. Lawrence, interview by Greene, in Reynolds and Wright, *Against the Odds*, 15.

39. According to Wheat, Lawrence gained knowledge of early European masters including Giotto, Breughel and Goya, as well as later artists like Van Gogh and Matisse, from his visits to the Metropolitan Museum of Art. He also learned about African art and abstract art and was exposed to the narrative serial tradition of Egyptian and medieval wall paintings. *Jacob Lawrence*, 36.

40. Wheat included remarks from conversation with Lawrence on 2 July 1984 and 24 July 1984 in *Jacob Lawrence*, 36.

41. Lawrence, interview by Greene, in Reynolds and Wright, *Against the Odds*.

42. For information about these artists see Leonard Folgarait, *Mural Painting and Social Revolution in Mexico, 1920–1940: Art of the New Order* (Cambridge: Cambridge

University Press, 1998); and Desmond Rochfort, *Mexican Muralists: Orozco, Rivera and Siqueiros* (New York: Universe, 1994).

43. Lawrence, interview by Greene, in Reynolds and Wright, *Against the Odds*, 10–11.

44. Ibid., 33.

45. Wheat, *Jacob Lawrence*, 39. The original quote is in Elizabeth McCausland, "Jacob Lawrence", *Magazine of Art* 59 (November 1945): 16.

46. Lawrence, interview by Greene, in Reynolds and Wright, *Against the Odds*, 12–13.

47. Ibid., 14.

48. For information about Christophe, see Hubert Cole, *Christophe: King of Haiti* (New York: the Viking Press, 1967). Wheat discusses the impact of the Du Bois play about Haiti in *Jacob Lawrence: American Painter* (Seattle: University of Washington Press, 1986).

49. Wheat, *Jacob Lawrence*, 40. The original quote appears in Harmon Foundation 5 (55/590), Archives of American Art, Smithsonian Institution, Washington, DC.

50. Schomburg's original collection has been augmented over the years by numerous other relevant sources. The library is now called the Schomburg Center for Research in Black Culture. The Schomburg Center remains the most important archive of its kind in existence. Also see Elinor Des Verney Sinnette, *Arthur Alfonso Schomburg: Black Bibliophile and Collector* (Detroit: New York Public Library, 1989).

51. Lawrence, interview by Greene, in Reynolds and Wright, *Against the Odds*, 34. Also see Deborah Williams, "The Schomburg: A Rich Resource for Jacob Lawrence", in Hutton Turner, *Jacob Lawrence*, 27.

52. Nesbett and DuBois, *Over the Line*, 27.

53. Elizabeth Steele presents an important discussion of the materials and method of Lawrence in "The Materials and Techniques of Jacob Lawrence", in Nesbett and DuBois, *Over the Line*, 247–65.

54. Wheat, *Jacob Lawrence*, 39. The remarks were first included in the Harmon Foundation, "Jacob Lawrence Biographical Sketch", 12 November 1940, Downtown Gallery Papers, Roll NDS, Archives of American Art, Smithsonian Institution.

55. John R. Beard, *The Life of Toussaint L'Ouverture: The Negro Patriot of Hayti* (1853; repr., Westport, Conn.: Negro Universities Press, 1970), 202.

56. Ibid., 1.

57. Ibid., 23.

58. Ibid., 318.

59. Patricia Hills, "Jacob Lawrence's *Migration Series*: Weavings of Pictures and Texts", in Hutton Turner, *Jacob Lawrence*, 147–48.

60. Early-twentieth-century Mexican muralists also reinforced the significance and the power of the mural as a visual narrative recounting the experience of the common people.

61. Hills, "Jacob Lawrence's *Migration Series*", 147–48.

62. Elizabeth Steele and Susanna M. Halpine, "Precision and Spontaneity: Jacob Lawrence's Materials and Techniques", in Hutton Turner, *Jacob Lawrence*, 155.

63. Ibid., 157.

64. Ibid. Steele and Halpine include this quote from their interview with Lawrence. Others present were Elizabeth Chew and Shelly Wischhusen-Treece, The Phillips Collection, Washington, DC, 4 June 1992.

65. Ibid.

66. Reproduction of the forty-one images and texts of Lawrence's *L'Ouverture* series are included in Peter T. Nesbett and Michelle DuBois, *Jacob Lawrence: Paintings, Drawings, and Murals (1935–1999) A Catalogue Raisonné* (Seattle: University of Washington Press in association with Jacob Lawrence Catalogue Rasionné Project, 2000), 28–36. The pictures and words of the first four panels are presented on page 28 of this study. The original paintings are located in the Amistad Research Center in the Aaron Douglas Collection of Tulane University in New Orleans.

67. Hills, "Jacob Lawrence's *Migration Series*",142.

68. This is a reference to the pioneer eighteenth-century French anti-slavery advocate Abbé Raynal.

69. For a comprehensive study of the English anti-slavery activists, see David Brion Davis, *The Problem of Slavery in the Age of Revolution 1770–1823* (Ithaca: Cornell University Press, 1975), 343–522.

70. See C.L.R. James, *The Black Jacobins* (New York: Random House, 1976), 85–144.

71. Patricia Hills includes this quote in "Jacob Lawrence's Expressive Cubism", in Wheat, *Jacob Lawrence*, 18. The source of the quote is the Harmon Foundation's "Jacob Lawrence Biographical Sketch".

72. Wheat, *Jacob Lawrence*, 43. The review was by A.D. Emmart and appeared in the *Baltimore Sun*, 5 February 1939.

73. For a comprehensive list of the exhibitions of the *L'Ouverture* series see Nesbett and DuBois, *Jacob Lawrence*, 27.

74. Paul J. Karlstom, "Modernism, Race and Community", in Nesbett and DuBois, *Over the Line*, 238.

Chapter 5

Reading in the Dark?
Racial Hierarchy and Miscegenation in Heinrich von Kleist's *Die Verlobung in San Domingo* (1811)

Wendy Sutherland

Heinrich von Kleist began writing *The Engagement in Santo Domingo*[1] in 1801 and had it published in 1811. Kleist sets his novella in 1803 during the final stages of the revolution on the island of Santo Domingo where chaos reigns: blacks are murdering whites, and whites are on the march seeking refuge or a swift escape from the island. Toussaint Louverture is dead, and General Dessalines and his army of thirty thousand blacks have already advanced on Port-au-Prince, the last stronghold of French power on the island. Kleist chooses this backdrop to stage a peculiar, interracial engagement between two unlikely characters: Toni, the yellow-skinned mestiza, and Gustav von der Ried, a white Swiss army officer fighting on the side of the French. Interestingly, in introducing the characters, the narrator presents a racial hierarchy beginning with the figure of Congo Hoango, the African from the Gold Coast, his companion Babekan, a mulatta woman, her daughter Toni, a mestiza, and Gustav von der Ried, the white Swiss soldier. In other words, a racial hierarchy from pure black to brown to yellow to white is established through the appearance and order of the characters presented.

The novella's plot is as follows: Gustav von der Ried, the Swiss soldier, has left his family in hiding in search of a safe haven. He unknowingly comes upon the house of Congo Hoango, the leader of the revolution, and receives refuge from Babekan, a mulatta, and her mestiza daughter Toni. Unknown to him, Congo Hoango has left orders with Babekan and Toni to lure white fugitives to the house so that he might kill them. During the night, Gustav and Toni fall in love, spend the night together and become "engaged". The next morning, Toni's allegiance to the cause of the revolution wanes, and she vows to save the life of her white lover. In an attempt to save Gustav's life, Toni sends one of Congo's sons to deliver a letter written by Gustav so that his family will arrive in time to rescue him. As fate would have it, Congo arrives earlier than expected. Recognizing the urgency of the situation, Toni ties up Gustav so that it will *appear* that she has not betrayed Congo. She then races with urgency to meet Gustav's family who are already on their way. After some gunfire, the Strömlis free Gustav and take Congo's two young sons hostage until they find safety. It seems that all will be well until Gustav reaches for a gun and shoots Toni in the chest, believing that she has betrayed him. Herr Strömli explains to Gustav that it was Toni who saved his life by alerting the family to his predicament. Realizing the gravity of his actions, Gustav turns the gun on himself and shoots himself in the mouth (an act similar to Kleist's own suicide). On their way to escape the island, the Strömlis bury Gustav and Toni, then flee on a British ship headed for Europe.

Given the historical context of the engagement, that of the revolution, it appears that Kleist's novella is a statement against the intolerance engendered by slavery and colonialism in the Caribbean. However, on closer inspection, we see that the colour hierarchy he sets up not only points out the dangers of miscegenation or racial mixing; it also shows the tragic outcome of miscegenation at the dawn of the foundation of a new state. Is Kleist simply trying to show the difficulties inherent in the relationship between the master and slave, the colonizer and colonized, or is there a deeper message here concerning the relationship between miscegenation and nation formation? Before I begin the analysis of the novella, I would first like to present Immanuel Kant's ideas on race and miscegenation within the context of late-eighteenth-century German perceptions of this topic.

In his 1775 essay, "On the Different Human Races" ("Von den verschiedenen Rassen der Menschen"), German Enlightenment philosopher Immanuel Kant[2] (1724–1804) defines race as "deviations that are constantly preserved over many generations and come about as a consequence of migration or through interbreeding with other deviations of the same line of descent, which always produces half-breed offspring".[3] Later in his 1785 essay, "Determination of the Concept of a Human Race" ("Bestimmung des Begriffs einer Menschenrasse"), Kant defines race as the "difference in category of animals and their stock as far as this difference is unavoidably inherited".[4] Fundamental to Kant's definition of race and the differences among races is *skin colour*, which is an inherited trait. The difference in skin colour, according to Kant, is based on a difference in blood. Not unlike anatomists and philosophers Johann Friedrich Blumenbach, Johann Gottfried Herder, Christoph Meiners and others, Kant was an opponent of racial mixing, deeming it contrary to nature, *widernatürlich*, and a means of degrading the white race without uplifting darker races.[5] In his article, "Kant as an Unfamiliar Source of Racism", Robert Bernasconi writes: "Kant's definition of race, which proved influential for Blumenbach and others, strengthened the resistance against what later came to be called miscegenation by providing a scientific or pseudo-scientific justification for the already widespread view that race mixing was contrary to nature."[6] Simultaneously, Kant sets up a hierarchy of races, which Kleist seems to mirror in his novella by the use of colour and racial imagery. Kant, a monogenist, believed that all human species come from the same origin, the white brunette, or stem genus, from which all races "degenerate".[7] At the top of the hierarchy is the white race, followed by the yellow Indian, the Negro and the copper-red American (native American). Implicit in this hierarchy is the assumption that the closer the approximation to whiteness, the closer a link to intellectual, aesthetic and moral perfection. In other words, for Kant, whiteness does not only represent an outward, racial signifier, it also marks aesthetic, intellectual and moral traits of the individual. Specifically relevant for Kleist's novella are Kant's views on race and skin colour as an indicator of a moral state of development or a moral scale of feeling.[8] According to Kant, racial mixing was unnatural, therefore the products of miscegenation were unnatural because racial mixing leads to the extinction of characteristics, which distinguish races from each other. This, according to Kant, is contrary to nature. Diversity, therefore, represents the natural order of things. The amalgamation of races or racial mixing and its product therefore result in chaos.[9]

For Kleist, whiteness, embodied in the figure of Gustav, therefore signifies the positive traits of moral purity and innocence, while blackness, represented in the figure of Congo Hoango, symbolizes treachery, moral decay or simply a lack of morality. Babekan, the brown mulatta, and Toni, the yellow mestiza, possess traits of blackness, which apparently enable them to commit acts of treachery against the white population. Simultaneously, Toni's apparent whiteness, which can be equated with innocence, is the appropriate tool used by Congo to deceive and mislead the whites. Apparently fashioning the revolutionary slave on Toussaint Louverture and Jean-Jacques Dessalines, the narrator presents Congo Hoango, a native of the Gold Coast, as *ein fürchterlicher alter Neger*, "a terrible old Negro"[10] who, because he had saved the life of his master, received his freedom, a house and property. However, Congo ultimately betrays his white master when he joins the revolution and kills the master despite the kindness he received from him. The narrator goes on to depict Congo's savagery by recounting his destruction of his former master's plantation and his role as leader of the blacks, whose sole purpose is to attack and kill whites. His thirst for revenge is described as *unmenschlich*, "inhuman". Congo's main character trait is that of deceitfulness, which represents blackness and links all the characters of black blood. Black blood therefore signifies deceit because black skin cannot be read, or turn red when emotions heighten. Deceit and the ability to deceive that link Congo to Babekan and Toni, for each contains this seed (*Keim*) of vice, and this causes them to mislead. Why is Toni an appropriate lure for the whites? Because she herself, due to her high-yellow complexion, comes closest to whiteness and most represents white virtue and purity, and therefore trust. Her approximation to whiteness is also revealed in the fact that she turns red when she blushes. This sign also functions as a marker of Toni's racial ambiguity: Toni's yellow colour is also deceptive since she can look black as well as white, depending on the lighting (pp. 169, 172).

Toni is the central figure in the racial drama in that, because of her birth in Paris to a wealthy Frenchman, she is connected to Europe in a way that Babekan is not. This connection, and her skin colour, link her more closely to Gustav, who will seek to claim her. Toni's ambiguity is compounded by the fact that she incorporates the colour spectrum of black, yellow, red and white in her being and therefore functions as a link to the other characters. A product of colonialism and miscegenation, she has no fixed racial or cultural location. As a product of racial mixing, she is racially ambiguous and therefore hard to read: is she moral or is she treacherous? Kleist's use of *Schein* and *Sein*, "appearance" and "being", serve to complicate Toni's ambiguity, when Gustav tells two stories of women, one representing Toni's foil, and the other, her double. Both stories are told under the cover of darkness, which symbolizes a cloak that seems to cover the racial tensions of the revolution, at least until dawn. The first story is that of a black girl, a yellow-fever victim and former slave of a white planter who tried to force his attentions on her. After she refused him, the planter had her severely punished and sold. During the slave rebellion, the girl, now a yellow-fever victim, sends for her former master to spend the night with her. Thinking that she would save him from the rebelling blacks, the former master accepts her offer. At the end of the lovemaking, the girl utters: "You have been kissing someone with the plague, someone with death in her breast – that's what you have been kissing!

Now go and give the fever to all those who are like you!" (p. 173). The colour yellow, represented by yellow fever, links Toni to this disease, which was rampant during the revolution and killed many British and French soldiers in St Domingue. The colour yellow also serves as a metaphor of distrust, for it is this colour which embodies Toni's racial ambiguity and allows for the seduction of the white male by the black woman, a seduction that ends in tragedy. Interesting parallels can be made to Gustav's connection to Toni, whose function it is to mislead him through her ambiguous skin colour and thereby lead him to his death; simultaneously though, Toni's apparent "whiteness" makes her incapable of such a treacherous deed, which, according to Gustav, is not quite as diabolical as white treachery during the days of slavery and colonialism. Implicit in the colour symbolism is the association of whiteness with goodness and purity and blackness with treachery. Also implicit in Gustav's comments is the view that white treachery is an oxymoron.

Gustav relates the second story about his former fiancée. After Gustav had made remarks against the French revolutionary tribunal, he was hunted down to be killed. His fiancée sacrificed her life for his after his arrest and was beheaded. Because of his fiancée's physical resemblance to Toni, this narrative functions as a foreshadowing of events to come. *Schein und Sein*, "appearance and being", play a role here as well: is Toni, the yellow-fever victim, wanting to seduce Gustav to his death or is she his loyal fiancée, the martyr willing to sacrifice her life for his? The colour yellow therefore symbolizes both possibilities, embodying Toni's ambiguous position: a person of colour in the revolution and a woman in love.

The climax of the action is marked by the "engagement" and the ensuing intimacy between Gustav and Toni. At night, he sees her, her physical beauty and ugliness defined by her racial traits, which arouse both desire and disgust in him: "Her hair, rippling in dark curls, had tumbled over her young breast as she knelt down; an expression of extraordinary charm played around her lips and over the long lashes that jutted out from her downcast eyes; if not for her colour, which repelled him, he would have sworn that he had never seen anything prettier" (p. 174). Simultaneously, Toni's ability to blush erases Gustav's doubts, which in turn leads to his ultimate doom, because his senses in fact are seduced by her charm: "when the stranger jokingly whispered in her ear to ask whether it took a white man to win her favour, she hesitated dreamily for a moment and then, as a charming blush flamed in her sunburned face, suddenly pressed herself against his breast" (p. 175). The larger context of the revolution is set aside, allowing for Gustav's seduction: "He swore he would never stop loving her, and that it was only in the delirium of his strangely disordered senses that the mixture of desire and fear she inspired in him could have seduced him into doing such a thing" (p. 176). The intimacy, ensuing engagement and seduction take place under the cloak of darkness. Reading in the dark, so to speak, could possibly be deceptive: has Gustav broken the laws of nature that govern racial mixing; are his senses seduced into loving a mestiza; does the darkness of night make possible the seduction of the white man's senses away from reason?

The falling action occurs when, on the following morning, Toni's loyalty shifts. When Babekan explains to her that Gustav must be kept in the house until Congo returns, Toni's physical reaction is "an angry flush reddening her face", which symbolizes the claim that Europe has on her both genetically and morally, if whiteness is equated with loyalty. Simultaneously, because Toni betrays her "blackness" and the revolution by siding with Gustav, her ambiguous position becomes even more pronounced and her yellow skin begins to take on a new meaning in the context of the revolution. Babekan now intepretes Toni's whiteness as a source of disloyalty and begins to mistrust her. Toni's ambiguity is further depicted when she realizes that her actions mark her as disloyal to the race: "The girl stopped in front of the door and read the proclamation nailed up there that forbade all black people, on pain of death, to give aid and comfort to a white man; and as if panic-stricken at realizing the crime she had been about to commit, she spun around and fell at her mother's feet who, as she well knew, had been watching her from the back" (p. 178).

The separation from the mother, which marks any coming-of-age story of a young adult, takes a tragic turn here because in severing her ties to the mother, Toni also abandons her connection to home and family and her association to blackness. Her loss of home through her "engagement" to Gustav casts her into an ambivalent space where she has no footing or foundation. Ultimately, it is the appearance (*Schein*) of her actions, and not the actions themselves, that condemn her to death. Babekan's ultimate loss of trust in her leads to the final catastrophe: her need to *appear* to be loyal to her family and the revolution as well as to Gustav. Toni's ambivalent position is further complicated when Congo Hoango unexpectedly returns home a day early. The concept of *Schein und Sein*, "appearance and being", also plays a role here. Circumstances now force Toni to prove her loyalty to the black rebellion by tying up Gustav so that she might still appear to be on the side of the blacks. At the same time, tying him up appears to be the only way to save his life. When Gustav recognizes his predicament he can only judge the situation based on what it appears to be: Toni has misled him with her affection and has all along planned on betraying him.

When Gustav's family arrives to rescue him, Toni's racial context changes. Toni, because she alerts the family to Gustav's predicament, gains their trust. The arrival of the Strömli family also allows Toni to cross over, so to speak, to the side of the whites, whose physical presence provides her the footing and foundation she lacked by allowing her to claim fully her European legacy of whiteness. After Herr Strömli ties up Congo and Babekan and takes Congo's sons as hostage, Babekan curses Toni for having betrayed the blacks. In a symbolic statement, which marks her new racial alliance, Toni replies: "I did not betray you; I am white and engaged to the young man you are holding prisoner; I belong to the race of those you are waging open war against, and shall know how to account to the Lord for my having sided with them" (p. 185). Toni therefore loses a mother and homeland by siding with the whites, and claims Europe as her real and actual home, the place where she belongs; apparently acknowledging that Europe will accept the complexity of her racial identity.

The tragic moment occurs, however, when Gustav, after having been rescued by his family, takes a pistol and shoots Toni in the chest, calling her a whore and a monster. To him she appears to be like the yellow-fever victim who used her sexuality to lure the white man to his death but, in reality, Toni functions more like her double, Gustav's deceased fiancée, who sacrifices herself, parents and homeland in order to save him. Toni's last words to Gustav, "You shouldn't have distrusted me!" (p. 187), echo the tragedy of her ambivalent racial position, which, in Kleistian fashion, marks her doom from the beginning. When Gustav realizes his mistake, he shoots himself in the head. In the final scene, Gustav's family buries the tragic lovers in the same grave on the island, which symbolizes that this interracial and therefore tragic couple does not in fact belong to Europe, but to the New World created by colonization, hybridization and racial mixing.

In conclusion, it seems that Kleist's choice of conflict – an interracial engagement set during the revolution – serves to show the tragic results of racial mixing on various levels. First, Toni's ambiguous racial identity brings about her conflict of allegiance when confronted with the dilemma of choosing between the blacks and the revolution, on the one hand, and Gustav, her white lover, on the other. Kleist seems to suggest that such a conflict results from unnatural unions: Babekan and Bertrand, her white French lover and father of Toni, Toni and Gustav, and, ultimately, Europe and the Caribbean. Second, perhaps Kleist is also expressing a disguised critique of colonialism and its inherent mixing, fusion or hybridization of cultures, reflecting perhaps the anxiety Kleist felt toward Napoleon and the French occupation of Prussia. Third, early-nineteenth-century Germany was a collection of German states lacking a central government but possessing strong regional identities. Simultaneously, notions of German national identity emerged that were grounded in unifying ideas of culture, language, blood and common soil or common locality as prerequisites for belonging to the German cultural group. Perhaps Kleist, in his depiction of a tragic end to an interracial relationship hints at the cultural contradictions implicit in early-nineteenth-century Germany's contemplation of its future definition of its own national identity and of those who would belong or not belong to this new and future nation.

Notes

1. The German author Heinrich von Kleist, known for his dramas and novellas, was born in Frankfurt an der Oder in 1777 and died in Berlin-Wannsee in 1811. Kleist's sources for this novella are: Rainsford's "Geschichte der Insel Hayti" ["History of the Island of Haiti"] published in Hamburg in 1806 and Dubroca's "Geschichte der Empörung auf St Domingo" ["History of the Uprising on St Domingo"], which appeared in *Minerva* in 1805.

The more appropriate designation is "mulatta", however Kleist chose the term "mestiza", which was used in eighteenth-century German discussions on race. In *Unterhaltungen ueber den Menschen. Erster Theil: Ueber die Kultur und aesserliche Bildung desselben*, Ernst Christian Wuensch defines the "mulattoes" as "produced by brown and black, and 'mestizos', if produced by white and brown parents" (378–79). See also Susanne Zantop's "'*Die Verlobung in St Domingo*' and the Discourses of Miscegenation", in *A Companion to the Works of Heinrich Von Kleist*, ed. Bernd Fischer (Woodbridge, UK: Boydell and Brewer, 2003), 198.

After several emotional and creative crises, Heinrich von Kleist committed suicide by shooting himself in the head at Wannsee near Berlin on 21 November 1811.

2. In March 1801, Kleist experienced the so-called *Kantkrise*, a crisis which ensued after reading Kant's *Kritik der reinen Vernunft* [*Critique of Pure Reason*] and *Kritik der Urteilskraft* [*Critique of Judgment*], from which he gleaned that man can never know absolute truth.

3. See Robert Bernasconi, "Kant as an Unfamiliar Source of Racism", in *Philosophers on Race*, ed. Julie K. Ward and Tommy L. Lott (Malden, Mass.: Blackwell, 2002), 146. Also see Immanuel Kant, "On the Different Human Races", trans. Jon Mark Mikkelsen, in *The Idea of Race*, ed. Tommy L. Lott and Robert Bernasconi (Indianapolis: Hacket, 2000), 9. See Immanuel Kant, "Von den verschiedenen Rassen der Menschen", in *Schriften zur Anthropologie, Geschichsphilosophie, Politik und Pädagogik I,* ed. Wilhelm Weischedel (Frankfurt: Suhrkamp,

1977), 12. "Abartungen, . . . welche sich sowohl bei allen Verpflanzungen (Versetzungen in andre Landstriche) in langen Zeugungen unter sich beständig erhalten, als auch, der Vermischung mit andern Abartungen desselbigen Stamms, jederzeit halbschlächtige Junge zeugen."

4. "Der Klassenunterschied der Tiere eines und desselben Stammes, so fern er unausbleiblich erblich ist." See Immanuel Kant, "Bestimmung einer Menschenrasse", in Weischedel, *Schriften zur Anthropologie*, 75.

5. Bernasconi, "Kant", 155.

6. Ibid.

7. The word *degenerate* comes from the Latin *de*, "from" or "down from", and *genus, generis*, "race" or "kind".

8. See Immanuel Kant, *Observations on the Feeling of the Beautiful and Sublime*, trans. John T. Goldthwait (Berkeley and Los Angeles: University of California Press, 1960), 97–116. Also Emmanuel Eze, *Race and the Enlightenment* (Malden, Mass.: Blackwell, 1997), 48–57.

9. Bernasconi, "Kant", 157.

10. Heinrich von Kleist, "The Engagement in Santo Domingo", trans. Martin Greenberg, in *Interracial Literature: Black-White Contacts in the Old World and the New*, Werner Sollors (New York: New York University Press, 2004), 167. Subsequent references to this novella appear parenthetically in the text.

The falling action represents the events that follow the climax and lead to the resolution, in this case, to the catastrophe or tragic end.

Chapter 6

"Les Créoles Galantes?"
White Women and the Haitian Revolution

Kathleen Gyssels

> *Women have the right to mount the scaffold. They should have the right to mount to the tribune too.*
> – Olympe de Gouges, *Declaration of the Rights of the French Woman and Citizen*, 1791

> *The only true word [about] the Caribbean is . . . schizophrenia.*
> – Fignolé

"White Women, Slaves, and Oxen"

In her book *Colonialism and Gender Relations*, Moira Ferguson underlines the subordinate position of women in general in the colonies of the New World: "white women, slaves, and oxen become part of a metonymic chain of the tyrannized; this association of colonial slavery with female subjugation opens up new political possibilities, despite its ethnocentric dimension".[1] A feminist *avant la lettre*, Mary Wollstonecraft (1759–97) put forward her claims for equal rights at the time of the French Revolution, while contemporaries such as Olympe de Gouges (1755–93), Mme de Staël (1766–1817) and Mme de Duras (1778–1828, author of *Ourika*, 1811) similarly protested against the cruelty of paternalism and the subordination of women, independently of questions of colour. Needless to say, women in France remained far from emancipated at the time of the French Revolution. Olympe de Gouges referred to the oppression suffered by blacks in the French Caribbean as demonstrated in her dramatic work *De l'esclavage des Noirs ou l'heureux naufrage*.[2] She died on the scaffold for being the first to defend the rights of French women, and women of colour and slaves in the French colonies. Although their situation was immeasurably better than that of slaves, white and Creole women in the colonies were considered largely the "property" of their husbands, faced neglect and cruelty, and had to find ways to resist the biases of a hypocritical masculine world.

As in other European colonies, French women lived in the shadow of their husbands and were deprived of social and political roles. The male-defined world of colonialism and the plantation society not only reproduced a model of the broader patriarchal world, but also rendered white women invisible. When referred to in accounts written by white men, the white woman is portrayed as a victim of the white male's colonizing adventure. The historian Moreau de Saint-Méry, in his *Topographic Description of the Island of Saint-Domingue* briefly summarizes French women's destiny in the French colony of St Domingue: the *Française* or the Creole born lady (of European descent) is said to rapidly lose her charms and youth in France's richest colony.[3] Worse, the wife of the planter was seen as a difficult creature, frustrated about her repressed artistic and emotional aspirations, the subject of all kinds of fantasies, and capable of the worst deeds of jealousy. Not only does she rapidly lose her beauty and youth, her freshness and charms, very often, like her sister in the Deep South, she becomes "the green-eyed monster of slavocracy" taking revenge for the inferior place and minor role that society has defined for her.[4] Because both the circumstances and the status of the white and Creole women remain largely undocumented in colonial and postcolonial literature, white women have remained as invisible and unheard as the illiterate slave. Moreover, in Haiti, most of the planters who survived the slave uprising left the island after the events of 1793–1804, a mass departure of St Domingue's whites and free persons of colour that interrupted the creolization process so characteristic of all Caribbean colonies. Most of the French families fled to America (New Orleans), travelled back to France, or went to other Caribbean islands (Trinidad, Cuba, Jamaica). As a consequence of that historical turmoil, the white presence in Haiti is even more marginal than it already is on the Dutch, British, Spanish and French Caribbean islands. Subsequently, the Creole language of Haiti uses the word *blanc* (white) to designate every non-Haitian, every individual coming from abroad, whether coloured or not. At the same time, the word *nègre* has lost in Haiti its racial signification to mean simply "man". Except for the notorious Marie Chauvet (*Amour, Colère, Folie* [1968]), who could pass for white but belonged to the coloured elite, and in contrast to writing from other Caribbean islands, white women writers and white protagonists are generally absent in Haitian literature.[5] It will therefore be the aim of what Hayden White calls "historiographic metafiction" – the counter-narrative generated by overall scepticism and suspicion about the "truth" of history to uncover the Creole lady, silenced and excluded by historians and storytellers alike. In these counter-narratives, dominant versions of particular epochs, struggles and historical figures are revisited, often through a polyphonic lens, with much parody and dense intertextual play. Historiographic metafiction, as Linda Hutcheon similarly observes, is a specific postmodern version of the novel, in that it questions the underlying assumptions of female inferiority, the ideologies of paternalism and the narrative of history as a particular discourse.[6]

While the white woman is a marginal character in most of the novels of the Caribbean and more specifically of the Haitian Revolution, two recent novelists – the American Madison Smartt Bell and the Haitian Jean-Claude Fignolé – have presented French and white Creole women in detail, bringing them out of the shadows of history. Not only do these authors fill in this historical gap, revising previous portraits of white Caribbean femininity offered by Victor Hugo in *Bug-Jargal* (1846) or by Alejo Carpentier in *The Kingdom of this World* (1949), but they also seek out the reasons – and not the excuses – for the terrible deeds and wrongdoings some mistresses inflicted on the "livestock" of the plantations. However touching and beautiful Carpentier's *The Kingdom of this World* is, neither the slaves nor the white women in that novel speak for themselves; the narrative is conducted by a dominant (white) male omniscient writer who speaks and thinks for the Other (the reader reads Ti Noël's and the planter's wife's thoughts through the mediation of the narrator). Bell and Fignolé recuperate the place and voice of these neglected characters, the white women living in France's richest colony on the eve of the revolution. Both authors turn to Haiti's past and some of its most obliterated aspects, notably the white female's contribution to the war on race, filling in the gaps on "proceedings too terrible to relate", to quote Toni Morrison.[7] For Bell, an established, prolific writer born in Tennessee, *All Souls' Rising* is a new and important step in a successful career: famous for his focus on violence (*Doctor Sleep; Save Me, Joe Louis*) and for his forays into the underside of America's society, Bell holds a "messianic fascination" for Toussaint Louverture. In planning his work on Toussaint and the Haitian Revolution, Bell discovered that there existed no single historical novel nor a fictional biography of the "master of the crossroad", he who opened all the barriers so that his troops called him "L'Ouverture", or "The Opening". This lack of a fictional biography of Toussaint brought Bell to conceive a three volume encyclopaedic novel of which the final tome was published in 2004.[8] The second novelist, Fignolé, remains somewhat on the margins of the Haitian canon.[9] Fignolé is not as widely read as René Depestre, Émile Ollivier and Edwidge Danticat (the latter's books having been reviewed by Bell). Fignolé portrays black and white women (*La dernière goutte d'homme*, 1999), and like Bell he published symbolically in the year of Haiti's bicentenary, an avatar of the slave narrative with his *Moi, Toussaint Louverture, avec la plume complice de l'auteur*.[10] It is, however, his second novel, *Aube tranquille* (1990), in which Toussaint is a minor character, that interests me here, because in this work he presents the condition of European and Creole mistresses in a way which is strikingly similar to Bell's presentation of French ladies.[11]

Both novelists clearly distance themselves from the classic novels of race and sex set in St Domingue on the eve of the revolution. Instead of race melodramas and colonial romance, subgenres in which the attraction between male and female individuals from different ethnicities has generally been the frame to alter the (presumably white) reader's perception of the black slaves or the coloured subordinates, thereby enhancing empathy and compassion with the slave's condition and consequently suggesting the moral damnation of the enslaver. Neither white women nor coloured slaves have a voice in Hugo's *Bug-Jargal* or, as mentioned earlier, Carpentier's *Kingdom of this World*, classics which without doubt are well known to Bell and Fignolé. In these works white women cannot speak for themselves. Moreover, where Hugo[12] and Carpentier[13] pass over the (sexual) violence between white and black, the modern authors explicitly present scenes of interracial violation, sexual abuse, torture and murder. In *Aube tranquille*, it is the white female character Sonja Biemme, recently married to the Swiss Wolf von Schpeerbach, who will be feared by everyone because of her merciless punishments and stifling cruelty. In *All Souls' Rising*, Claudine Arnaud, married to the Creole Michel Arnaud, commits the most terrible acts of torture and murder. The two novels can be read as historiographic metafictions in that they unveil the century of Enlightenment, deliberately setting the tragedies and turmoil, the inequalities between men and women, the total incomprehension and even annihilation of the women as subjects, and their insanity and self-destructive behaviour against the putative gallantry, "refinement" and "delicacy" of that period. Through many intertextual references to the music, literature and philosophy of that time, the writers show how women in the colonies were rarely considered as reasonable beings, gifted with intelligence, deep emotions and feelings.

The ideals of romantic marriage and equal partnership were incompatible with the daily brutalities of managing a Caribbean plantation.

For instance, the concept of *marivaudage* – sophisticated banter in the style of the French dramatist and novelist Marivaux, and an invention of the eighteenth century – is mentioned in *Aube tranquille*, but appears hopelessly out of place in the context of slavery and colonization. While Wolf Schpeerbach expresses his admiration for Marivaux, his spouse lives their marriage not at all as a light-hearted *badinage*, but as a life-threatening war. Although her partner withdraws into his own world of fantasy (baroque art and libertine lifestyle) accorded to him by the privilege of birth and origin, she becomes increasingly sour, sad and sadistic, resorting to the most irrational behaviour, and eventually descending into madness. Their love is not at all subject to romance, and as one of Wolf's mistresses remarks, his substitute passions with women of colour – the affairs between master and slave – can never be innocent: they are literally "dangerous liaisons" (Choderlos de Laclos's epistolary novel being alluded to in the intrigues between Wolf and his white concubine Cécile).

A further example of the disjuncture between cultural productions of the European Enlightenment and the brutal lived reality of the colony is suggested in the reference made by Sonja to the famous opera by Rameau, *Les Indes galantes* (1735), which is said to encounter huge success in Paris, encouraging Parisians to dream about the gallantry and preciousness of the far away Indies and their inhabitants. Wolf, Sonja's self-professed philantropic humanist realizes that he has to give up his enlightened spirit and ideals of European democracy and gallant lifestyle if he wants to maintain authority over an increasingly large number of slaves. Similarly, in *All Souls' Rising*, the French doctor Antoine Hébert discusses the bestial cruelty that is all around him, and which takes place in "an age of reason" (p. 185). Wolf von Schpeerbach is forced to face the dilemmas of the Enlightenment: the promises of the French Revolution, of Romanticism – Chateaubriand's success is mentioned (p. 185) – and the threefold ideals of liberty, equality and fraternity. The contradictions of the time are laid bare in the fact that, while he was raised with Salomon, his black nurse's son, he later uses total terror to rule his property, by refusing civil and political rights to people of colour "whom he praises otherwise for their loyal services and intelligence" (p. 148). As soon as she arrives in St Domingue, Sonja realizes that her husband literally and figuratively does not see her, and does not pay attention to her needs and desires.

Despite their shared focus on white women and their rich mixture of historical fact and creative fiction, neither of these novels has yet been analysed in depth, nor

"Les Créoles Galantes?"

have they ever been compared. There are many reasons for this critical neglect of both narratives. First, most obviously, *All Souls' Rising* is written by an American author, and inclusion of non-Haitian authors in the Haitian canon remains problematic, just as André Schwarz-Bart (Guadeloupe) and Jean Rhys (Dominica) have long been considered outsiders in Caribbean writing. But for an American from the South, the problems of race, class and gender are integral components of his vision of American society and identity. For Bell, the question of who has the right to deal with a narrative challenge as complex as the Haitian Revolution is irrelevant. He firmly defends his "appropriation of voice", reacting against what he calls "splintered thinking" and what another gifted American author, Russell Banks, similarly denounces as "literary ghettoization".

In addition, both novels are considered problematic because of their staggeringly violent scenes. The torture of the flesh and its demoralizing effect on the soul of the slave is described in scientific, surgical detail. Whipping and raping, torturing and castrating are pictured in graphic, at times cinematographic writing, which has a deliberately unpleasant and discomforting impact on the reader. One example of this will suffice, one that alludes in both novels to a canonical masterpiece, so to recall that in many senses nothing new happened in the New World, and that all there was a rehearsal of the Old World's barbaric rites and savage acts. Re-enactments of Gloucester's torture from Shakespeare's *King Lear* feature in *All Souls' Rising*, as well as in *Aube tranquille*, where Fignolé presents the Biemme dynasty as a family of cruel and sadistic planters, forever cursed because one of the ancestors is said to have stolen Lord Gloucester's diamond. In *All Souls' Rising*, the mulatto nicknamed Choufleur, the son of Maltrot, a particularly cruel white planter, forces Michel Arnaud to watch an anonymous white man have his eye removed with a corkscrew:

> with a slow precision [he] began to turn [the screw] in. The white man went rigid against the chair back, and from behind the gag came a strangulated retching out. Arnaud's eyes squeezed shut and he bit into his lip. He heard Choufleur's voice in the dark, rapturously tonguing an English phrase.
>
> "*Out, vile jelly*", and in French again, "Does it remind you of the blinding of Gloucester?" He noticed Arnaud then, and slapped him so that his eyes popped open. "Watch, or you will take his place. You must see."
>
> Arnaud obeyed, his lids pinned back. He was having difficulty with his breathing.
>
> "Take out the gag," Candi said, and one of the others quickly did so. What came from the white man's mouth was a kind of sigh, an *aaahhhhh*. . . . There

was a sucking *plop*, followed by a shout of appreciation all around the room. The eyeball was larger than Arnaud would have thought possible, and pudgy, like a dumpling. It depended from a number of white twisting tentacle-like cords, till someone reached with a knife to cut it completely free. (p. 199)

Not only are eyes taken out, legs cut off, prisoners skinned and crucified in Bell's novel, but first whites and then blacks will raise heads and even infants' unborn bodies on spears as terrible prizes of war (p. 185).

It comes as no surprise, than, that the few reviews in the French and francophone realm of *All Souls' Rising* have been negative. The violence of sex scenes in particular reviled critics like Léon-François Hoffmann, who judges Bell's work to be pornographic literature.[14] Hoffmann's disapproval, however, obliges me to think about the "acceptable" representation of the suffering body of the slave, in its relation to its effect, be it voyeurism and sadistic pleasure or empathy and compassion. Clearly there is no "easy" way to present this kind of extreme suffering, mutilation and killing, but as Bell recalls, it is part of the historical truth of the Caribbean's past.

Another reason for the critical neglect of both novels is their complex structure and rich tapestry of historical facts and figures; fictional elements as well as unconscious fantasies are interwoven so as to blur the realm of the real and the imaginary. The dense fabric of the narratives might dissuade even the most skilled reader or scholar of Caribbean writing; the multiplicity of narrative perspectives and the presence of various historical and spatial worlds, especially in Fignolé's narrative, do not make for straightforward reading. The historical scope of both works is monumental. *All Souls' Rising* is an exceptionally long novel at more than five hundred pages long, whereas *Aube tranquille* narrates in two hundred and seventeen pages five centuries of Haitian history in a narrative that is without ordering principle, punctuation or chapters. Bell's linear historical novel is encyclopaedic in its accurate details, and yet it also reconstructs imaginatively the perspective of a voiceless slave, Riau, inventing a stilted, though eloquent, type of speech for the maroon figure. On the other hand, Fignolé is (like Glissant and other Caribbean writers) deliberately hermetic and opaque. As a co-founder of the "spiralist movement", a loosely defined literary movement breaking with indigenism in a reaction to Duvalierism, Fignolé, together with the late René Philoctète and Frankétienne, dismantles literary conventions and promotes chaos as a narrative principle. His novels are puzzles of meaning and demand a "participative" effort on the part of the reader. Fignolé brings into focus Haiti's "nightmare of History", to rephrase Joyce, and he denounces the "Caribbean ailment", the fact that all Caribbean communities developed what he calls a "pathology of expectations". Haitians in particular, says Fignolé, have not come to terms with the foundational madness, the violent beginnings of their country. Consequently, Haiti spirals downwards, as Fignolé states in an article in a special issue of *La Revue Noire*:

> Whichever way we look, the Caribbean is outburst. Of sweat and blood. Posted from the finite of the earth to the infinite of the heaven.
> Brought up from the South to the North, if it's not the other way round, sailing, indefinitely turned towards the West. . . . Imagination thus binds us to references which trap reality: chains of islands scattered into as many archipelagos. Chains? As if to plot out in advance for the Caribbean a destiny other than of suffering fits of tectonic Anger. CRUCIFIED!
> The only true word [about] the Caribbean is . . . schizophrenia.[15]

Both *Aube tranquille* and *All Souls' Rising* are particularly challenging because their women characters are capable and culpable of the most unthinkable and staggering atrocities. Claudine Arnaud (and, to a lesser extent, other Creole ladies, like Isabelle Cigny and Elise Thibodet, Hébert's sister) in *All Souls' Rising* and Sonja Valembrun Lebrun in *Aube tranquille* are monsters who display sadistic behaviour, pitiless creatures who slaughter their husband's concubines. But as the narratives unfold, the reader learns how, prior to these bestialities, they repeatedly had to deal with the infidelity and betrayal by their husband, with excesses of interracial sex and violence in the household and plantation. *All Souls' Rising* and *Aube Tranquille* both focus on the black body as the most important site in the racial and gender wars. The skin and the womb were the eminent sites of power and counter-power in the hellish life of the plantations, as Françoise Vergès aptly shows in her essay on literature from the Indian Ocean.[16]

The Womb, the Unbearable "Métissage"

Claudine and Sonja are driven to take revenge on what is the most precious "possession" on the plantation: their husbands' lovers. Both women understand clearly the dreadful law of atrocious tyranny and bloody rituals perpetrated by the master in order to guarantee his "safety" over the oppressed majority. Claudine formulates these "sacraments" in *All Souls' Rising*: "All over the island masters and slaves were expressing their relation in similar ways, and it was nothing to lop an ear or gouge an eye, even to cut off a hand, thrust a burning stake up a rectum, roast a slave in an oven alive, or roll one down a hill in a barrel studded with nails. All these were as sacraments, body and blood" (p. 89).

Driven insane by loneliness, boredom, but most of all by the repetitive scenes of adultery committed in her own home, Claudine withdraws into alcoholism and loneliness. When her husband leaves her for business in the city, she seeks solace in alcohol, a common refuge for alienated white women (think of the second woman of Lenormand de Mézy in *The Kingdom of this World*). Claudine whips Mouche, the pregnant slave, but loses control over the situation when she hears the young rebellious slave sing in her native language. All of a sudden, her hands cut out the foetus – her husband's child – from the womb:

> Mouche's body opened down the plumb line to the center and beyond, like a banana peel splitting down its seam. The blade furrowed through a whitish layer of fat; there was no blood, oddly, until the viscera slithered and slapped down tangling over Claudine's feet, and then she bled. . . .
> She stepped back and looked down, inexorably, at the snarl of vitals on the dirt floor. Something else was among them, pulsing inside its membranous sac; it was not exactly independent life, but it still lived a little, as her organs were still slightly living, though Mouche was certainly dead. (pp. 91–92)

Examples of this kind of unbearable butchery, described in clinical detail, are recurrent in the novel and naturally have a traumatizing effect on the slaves as well as on the colonizer. Witnessing the scene, some of the slaves escape from this madwoman and plan a rebellion which will be, as a consequence, just as "inhuman" and bestial. The author deliberately and provocatively confronts us with dreadful deeds such as these that have to be recalled, since Haiti and France have to come to terms with the origins and ongoing turmoil and torments of the Republic, in order to avoid their insane repetition and the "addiction to death", which more than one anthropologist has observed in modern-day Haiti.[17] Forever haunted by her own inhuman acts, Claudine feels trapped in a spiral of never-ending violence. Like Sonja in *Aube tranquille*, who realizes that slavery degrades both master and slave (p. 104), that it has created a barbaric, insane world for which they will have to pay one day (p. 85), Claudine becomes acutely aware of the haunting character of her insane acts of violence, which subsequently cuts her off from reality and makes her slip into the realm of the zombie-like priestess:

"Les Créoles Galantes?"

> But always [the foetus] returned, and when she least expected it – she never learned to expect it, but she might wake to find it settled on her navel, wiggling in a puddle of afterbirth and staring down at her with a dolphin's black eye, or, during her solitary ramblings through the house, it might come on suddenly from out of the other rooms. It had a metamorphic power and it showed her all its changes from a dot of plasma to a fish into a being like herself, but it let her know that her own being was as futile as some ancient extinct beast. (p. 93)

As in *Aube tranquille*, the generations that follow long after this savagery have to "account for", not pass over such facts in order to mourn the dead and not surrender to amnesia. However much the perpetrators of these deeds try to forget and erase this history, their offspring are doomed to come back to it.

The Skin, the Unbearable Mask of Difference

Claudine dreams of the harsh violations that marriage and her husband Michel Arnaud have inflicted on her; as he lies fatigued in the adjoining room with Mouche, she recalls her wedding bed, "the great carved wooden monstrosity where he had murdered her virginity, left her stabbed and bleeding in her tenderest recess while he amused himself with the better-experienced whores of the town" (p. 85). Not much later, the young married woman discovers the harsh laws of Creole marriage, which oblige both master and slave to hide their feelings, to wear a mask. What Sala-Molins has aptly called "the underside of Enlightenment", the hidden realities of an age of reasoning by fine and delicate philosophers, by gallant elites and rich aristocrats, is demonstrated in both novels, situated as they are at the birth of modernity.[18] Every reference to the Enlightenment becomes highly ironic, if not pathetic; the authors prove how the spirit of that time was incompatible on all levels with the daily reality of the plantation household. In other words, how hypocritical France was and how long after the decline of this colonial empire, France still hesitates before admitting the manifold wrongdoings and damages, preferring to celebrate the conquests and national heroes of the nation. As is shown through the interior monologue and conversations of the female characters, French colonialism in St Domingue involved insensitive masters mistreating their "livestock" and implied a constant and terrible masquerade. Hence the motif of the mask in both novels as a symbol of the master-slave dialectic.[19]

In *Aube tranquille*, Sonja's husband symbolizes the colonial moral dilemma in the age of Enlightenment. Born in the Jura and having Calvinist origins, Wolf initially takes a righteous, neutral stand on the French debate over slaves' rights. While aspiring to free the slaves and to improve their miserable and inhuman condition, Wolf confesses that he is too weak to take such a measure and admits that he failed, being totally passive to intervene in the insane society based on terror and inhumanity (p. 89). Yet, he does not undertake any measure to better their desperate lives or to intervene in the slaughter of his commandeur's concubine, Carmen, whom Sonja literally skins:

> Boto made an incision in the skin at the base of the neck, introduced in the narrow orifice a previously hollowed-out thin stem of *palma Christi*, he blew into it, the skin swelled up immediately, the disjoining was first like a hissing sound, almost imperceptible, then the veins cracked, fixed the throbbing torn skin in Carmen's throat. Behind the shutters of my office, I witnessed the slow agony of the flesh, I did not intervene. (p. 20)

An unbearable rift later tears Sonja and Wolf apart. In both novels, the married couples are set apart, as their husbands betray them and make bastard children with their coloured concubines: "She, Claudine, had conceived no child; Arnaud, however, had been sure to prove that this was in no way his fault; her husband's face grinned back at her from every yellow brat in the yard" (p.85). The two planters are completely blind to their wives' frustrations and disappointments. Upon arrival at the plantation, Sonja is immediately treated as an unwelcome intruder:

> I had wanted your weakness, I discovered it in her most primitive substance, the most bestial, infamous, cries of joys for your homecoming, you come out of the barouche that we hired in Jérémie, the hysterical clan of women around you, their gibberish, their childish talk, the sensitive words of which I only remember *bonjou mèt, mèt, retou nou kontan*, that little black talk assailed me, repelled me, even before they knew me. (p. 80)

Judged as an outsider by the black slaves and domestics, the French lady is considered an intruder. Consequently Sonja immediately hates the black domestic servants and slaves. Much later in the novel, another reason for her racism becomes clear: "a certain Biemme de Valembrun Lebrun . . . gave justification to the rabble who opposed us, demeaned, degraded his own family" (p. 134); her ancestor, having brought "negroes" to France and therefore publicly scandalized his family, had his hands cut off by order of Louis XIV, who had forbidden entrance to blacks in France (p. 80). It is suggested that these stories of her family being cast out because of her great-great-grandfather's involvement with the "inferior race" are in part responsible for Sonja's turbulent character:

> when I was a little girl, I listened to the memory of the storms of Brittany, terrified by the whistling of the wind through the ramparts of the castle, the roaring of the waves breaking against the cliffs.... In Saint Domingue, it's not the same thing, as in a hallucination, hallucinating, the night snaps its fingers, then a tree collapses in a great din, which is preceded by an immobile silence, but immediately taken over by the apocalyptic wailing of noices, . . . I open myself to all those unknown noises . . . they are stormily sensitive, mortally perverse, madly exciting, they liberate in me a chaos of barbaric blood of the Valembrun Lebrun dynasty, I cried out and frenetically, I was no more but a hurricane. (p. 134)

This incursion into Sonja's youth reveals how her senses were influenced by nature's tempestuousness, and how her transfer to the Caribbean island intensified this disposition, culminating in an untamed, "savage" frame of mind. The violent nature of the island echoes the violent, apocalyptic events that take place on their plantation. Femininity in those times was clearly defined by maternity, the need to provide an heir for the plantation. In the colonies, a white woman had no other task or responsibility than to raise the future commanders and rulers of slaves. Whereas Claudine Arnaud is rejected by her husband because of her infertility, Sonja will give birth to the heir but will show no maternal affection, as a reaction to Wolf's weakness and unfaithfulness, which creates a gap between them that only deepens as time passes. Sonja will try several times to convince her husband of the inhumanity of the system and to leave the colony before it is too late. She even suggests that Salomon, the gifted and beautiful mulatto, who reminds the reader of Soliman in Carpentier's novel and is the overseer of the plantation and her husband's *frère de lait* ("milk brother"), should take over the management of their plantation so that they could return to France. This *nègre à talents* inspires more than just profound admiration in Sonja's head and heart; she nourishes secret feelings for the slave. Sonja argues with her husband about the constant tension between rules and rights, between reason and emotion; she tries to save them both from the downward spiral of slavery. Altered by the discovery of her forbidden love, confused by her feelings but determined to punish the man who dared to resist her seduction, she informs her husband, who ignores her. To prove that she can stay and maintain her place as the wife of a white planter who looks down on all coloured people, she will go so far as to destroy the very object of her sincere love by mutilating and castrating him herself, in front of Saintmilla, the Vodou-like character of Fignolé's novel. This kind of slaughter counters the interracial romanticism offered in some novels dealing with slavery in the Caribbean, and at this point of the narrative, the reader is left wondering about the reasons for such an act. At the moment of her most extreme agony, Sonja still finds Salomon's body beautiful, and it is this precise, distorted emotion that clearly underscores her total loss of reason: "I'm troubled, to change my vision, his naked beauty, virile, an impression of serene force as if misfortune has made him more mature, a force, I would like to share his pain, feel the same joy of being unhappy together" (p. 168). Total chaos and madness seem to have taken over.

The novel ends with the complete ruin of the Valembruns: Sonja will be decapitated in a kind of "souls' rising" by a mob of armed zombies led by Toukouma, a woman warrior who was brought to St Domingue and violated several times at age thirteen to the point where she could not walk nor conceive children. With the approval of Saintmilla, mother of Salomon, wet nurse of Wolf, and magical healer of Toukouma, the white sorceress now suffers the same painful death as the one inflicted upon her son, who was chastised and castrated by Sonja.

Creole Ladies and Their Hearts of Darkness

Both *All Souls' Rising* and *Aube tranquille* bring to the forefront white women at the time of the uprisings in St Domingue; in each novel, the behaviour and despotism of the white and Creole women bring the colony into the spiral of violence, which will in turn bring St Domingue to its fall. Have Bell and Fignolé exaggerated the female ferocity and the "abnormal" behaviour of Claudine Arnaud and Sonja Biemme de Valembrun Lebrun? Revising Moreau de Saint-Méry's stereotype of the white lady in the colonies, both authors, through their historiographic metafictions, show how race hatred of white women developed as a kind of indirect revenge against their betraying husbands, how the worst of their behaviour was generated by their own miserable condition as women, and how they gradually shifted from contesting and rebelling wives to overt outrage and destructive, criminal deeds committed on both the slaves and themselves. The extremes of racial hatred are coldly programmed acts of revenge for being "othered" by the plantation universe. White women, as portrayed in Bell's and Fignolé's novels, bear chains of slavery, which, if not identical to those of the blacks, are similar in that they generate the same dehumanising, compulsive acts.

"Les Créoles Galantes?"

Bell and Fignolé offer chilling evocations of what some white women became in the Caribbean as a consequence of neglect and frustrations. If they suggest explanations for the white women's behaviour, the authors avoid excusing them. Without moralizing or being apologetic, the novels shed light on the marginal, invisible, subaltern white female in such a brutal, racist and inhuman society. They remind us how this violence existed at the origin of the Republic, and that this violent birth of Haitian society has to be memorized, just as the heroes of the revolution are remembered.

Notes

1. Moira Ferguson, *Colonial and Gender Relations from Mary Wollstonecraft to Jamaica Kincaid* (New York: Columbia University Press, 1993), 22.

2. Olympe de Gouges, *De l'esclavage des Noirs ou l'heureux naufrage* (1793; repr., Paris: Ed. Côté-Femmes, 1989).

3. Moreau de Saint-Méry, *Description topographique, physique, civile, politique et historique de la partie française de l'Isle de Saint-Domingue (1784–1790)*, 3 vols., 3rd ed. (Paris: Publication de la Société française d'histoire d'outre-mer, 2004), 39.

4. Minrose Gwin, "Green-Eyed Monsters of the Slavocracy: Jealous Mistresses in Two Slave Narratives", in *Conjuring Black Women: Fiction and Literary Tradition*, ed. Marjorie Pryse and Hortensia Spillers (Bloomington and Indianapolis: Indiana University Press, 1985), 39–45.

5. Evelyn O'Callaghan, contesting Braithwaite, observes that white women did contribute to a Creole culture in Barbados, Antigua and Jamaica. Evelyn O'Callaghan, "Politically Correct: Marginalisation and Early Narratives of the West Indies by White Women", in *Centre of Remembrance: Memory and Caribbean's Women Literature*, ed. Joan Anim Addo (London: Mango Press, 2002), 235–53.

6. Linda Hutcheon, "Historiographic Metafiction: The Pastime of Past Time", in *A Poetics of Postmodernism: History, Theory, Fiction* (New York: Routledge, 1988).

7. Toni Morrison, "Unspeakable Thoughts Unspoken: The Afro-American Presence in American Literature", *Michigan Quarterly Review* 28, no. 1 (1989): 1–34.

8. Madison Smartt Bell, *All Souls' Rising* (New York: Pantheon, 1995). All references are to this edition. The two other tomes are *Master of the Crossroads* (New York: Penguin, 1996), and *The Stone That the Builder Refused* (New York: Pantheon, 2004). The last title refers to the French rejection of Toussaint's idea of a free nation, ruled by democratic principles and resulting in a successful plantation economy. See also Kathleen Gyssels, "Un crapaud transpercé à une lance: La révolution haïtienne revue par M. Smartt Bell dans *Le Soulèvement des ames*, in *Mémoires et cultures: Haïti, 1804–2004*, ed. Michel Beniamino and Arielle Thauvin-Capot (Limoges: Pulim, 2006), 85–106.

9. Apart from Yves Chemla's insightful comments on the predominance of the female and the multi-layered narrative in *Aube tranquille* ("Entrée dans une spirale" on his personal website, http://homepage.mac.com/chemla/fic_doc/aub_tranq.html), this novel has been excluded from essays on spiralist writing. Cf. Philippe Bertrand, *Rêve et littérature romanesque en Haïti: De Jacques Roumain au mouvement spiraliste* (Paris: Karthala, 2003), as well as from comparative studies on the Gothic and marvellous real, Colette Maximin, *Littératures caribéennes comparées* (Paris: Karthala, 1996). Maximin studies at length Fignolé's first novel, *Les possédés de la pleine lune*, and she interprets the lunacy of descendants of slaves as the protest of the author against a violent past and the ongoing repression in modern Haiti.

10. Reviews of *Moi, Toussaint Louverture, avec la plume complice de l'auteur* (Montreal: Ed. Plume et Encre, 2004) are rare. One is available online: http://www.biblio-select.com/librairie/catalogue/product_info.php?products_id=319.

11. The first one is *Les possédés de la pleine lune* (Paris: Seuil, 1987) which encountered some critical attention and was said to be "promising". Three years later Fignolé published a second volume of what he announces as a trilogy, *Aube tranquille* (Paris: Seuil, 1990). All references are to this edition.

12. Also, in *Bug-Jargal*, the narrator spares us from the most upsetting effects that some evocations might have on our sensitive (and civilized) minds: "Numerous others have portrayed the first disasters of Le Cap, consequently, I pass rapidly over memories full of blood and fire; I will limit myself to tell you that the slave rebels were in possession of, as was told, of Dondon, Terrier-Rouge, the city of Ouanaminte, and even of the unfortunate states of Limbé, which made me very upset given its proximity to Acul." In *Bug-Jargal*, trans. K. Gyssels (Paris: Press Pocket, 1985), 72–73.

13. As subtle as Carpentier's baroque prose might be, *The Kingdom of This World* shows us Lenormand de Mézy, who can have all the servants he desires, while the white and Creole lady has to keep the "terrible secret" of racial mixing. Take, for instance, chapter 3, "L'Appel des Buccins": the insurrection is about to take place. We have the omniscient narrator describing how the master is extremely bothered by the turmoil in the colony, meditating on what he should undertake (or not) to prevent a slave insurrection. Looking for some distraction, Lenormand de Mézy is on his way to the tobacco house with an intention that the narrator presents as only "natural", inherent to the habits and customs of the planters at that given time: "It must have been ten o'clock in the evening when Monsieur Lenormand de Mézy, under the weight of his meditations, went into the tobacco entrepôt with the intention of raping one of the young slaves who came at that hour to steal tobacco leaves." *Le Royaume de ce monde* (Paris: Gallimard, 1954), 70.

On his way to rape one of his slaves, the master witnesses how the main buildings were invaded by rebellious blacks. As the slaves take all they can, some profit from the situation to finally realize their racial fantasies and forbidden dreams, and Ti Noël's thoughts are again rendered indirectly: "Afterwards he went upstairs, followed by his eldest sons, since he dreamed since a long time of raping Miss Floridor, who in the nights of theatre still showed beautiful breasts which have not been altered by the years under a dress with Greek motifs" (p. 72). It is clear that the narrator does not actually confirm if the rape takes place, but only suggests it. In any case, Carpentier always portrays male characters as lustful and "instinctively" possessive, while female characters remain voiceless.

14. Léon-François Hoffmann, "Prolégomènes à l'étude de la représentation de la Révolution haïtienne en Occident", *Anales del Caribe* 9, no. 20 (1999–2000): 364. I can think immediately of one particular scene which indeed calls for the terms "voyeuristic" and "pornographic". When Riau and his fellow runaways invade the Lambert plantation, they rape both Mme Lambert and her daughters, forcing the master to watch the scene. Riau, the illiterate "maroon", who in Bell's novel is a major voice, gives us his report on the gruesome details of this scene: "Then the Noé *commandeur* had a new idea and got himself behind the master and throttled him slowly with a lace from one of the whitewoman's dresses, holding him so he was forced to watch [the rape of a younger whitewoman, her bared body flopping on the floor like a skinned fish, crooked elbows working like fins in water]. Each time he tightened the master's eyes went white, and his tongue stuck out of his blackening face while the commandeur cried out in a loud voice, 'See! I am making a new nigger here!' . . . Under the strangulation the master's member rose and pointed and the commandeur called out thunderously, 'See how the whiteman is ready to take his pleasure!' . . . But he held the lace too long so that the whiteman died. . . . Riau finished and got up, scrambling for the knife he'd dropped when he began" (p. 172).

15. Jean-Claude Fignolé, "A Poetics of Schizophrenia", *Revue noire* 6, "Afrique, Caraïbe, Haïti: Schizophrénie, Art", http://www.revuenoire.com/anglais/essay/TH5.html

16. Françoise Vergès, *Monsters and Revolutionaries: Colonial Family Romance and Métissage* (Durham: Duke University Press, 1999).

17. Laënnec Hurbon, "Violence et raison dans la Caraïbe: le cas d'Haïti", *Notre Librairie* 148 (July–September 2002): 117.

18. Louis Sala-Molins, *Les misères des Lumières: Sous la raison, l'outrage* (Paris: Laffont, 1992).

19. Both novels draw on the (iron) mask to denounce the false appearance of colonial society with its rigid rules and hypocrisy. This is most notably the case with *Aube tranquille*, in which one of France's most famous legends, which has inspired numerous books and movies, is introduced: "the man with the iron mask". One of Sonja's ancestor's having stolen an iron mask which has haunted the castle since then. By taking the idea of the mask in the Biemme de Valembrun's castle, Fignolé not only sets his novel in the Gothic tradition to make tangible the haunting of the past of wrongdoings which will have to be paid back by subsequent generations, but he also reflects upon insanity as a consequence of oppression and subalternity. It is highly significant that his protagonist is a nun, Soeur Thérèse, who embarks on the Air France Millennium flight to Port-au-Prince. The "iron mask" fascinated Alexandre Dumas-père, himself son of a Haitian slave, in *L'homme au masque de fer* (1839–41) as well as Voltaire, in his *Le Siècle de Louis XIV* (1751).

Chapter 7

Revolutionary Acts of Translation
Language and Freedom in Guy Endore's *Babouk*

William Scott

Born in Brooklyn, New York, Samuel Guy Endore (1901–1970) is perhaps best known for his 1933 horror novel, *The Werewolf of Paris*, which was adapted to provide the screenplay for the 1961 film *The Curse of the Werewolf*. Shortly after he began publishing fiction in the early 1930s, Endore went to Hollywood to write screenplays for a variety of thrillers, historical dramas and horror films. Yet, throughout his career, his genre of choice remained the biographical novel, exemplified by works such as *The Sword of God: Jeanne d'Arc* (1931) and *King of Paris* (1956). In addition, Endore's close ties to the US Left were manifested in the pamphlets he wrote during the 1930s about the famous Scottsboro trials. Despite being blacklisted as a communist in the 1950s, Endore – who also read and translated French fluently – sustained a prolific writing career, publishing more than twenty novels, essays and translations (of, among others, Pierre Loti and Théophile Gautier).

In this essay, I will argue that Endore's 1934 biographical-historical novel about the Haitian Revolution presents this event in terms of a crisis of linguistic intelligibility. For the novel's main characters, the revolution itself must, initially at least, be disguised in and through acts of linguistic dissimulation. I propose that these acts of subversion or resistance can be fruitfully reread as acts of translation, which in turn point to the broader question of the cultural politics of translation in general. Moreover, as I will show, Endore's novel suggests the need for a critical recasting of the relation between translation and the discourse of so-called universal historiography.

Endore uses the example of the Haitian Revolution in order to outline a critique of US imperialist interests in 1934.[1] In spite of his occasional efforts to mask this critique by translating it into a Haitian idiom – a language employing Creole cultural signifiers and dialect to comment on the actual historical accounts of the event, which Endore scatters throughout the narrative – the message is clearly and repeatedly expressed through the narrative's structure and culminating moments. For this reason, the novel can be read as an attempt to adapt the events of 1790s Haiti to illustrate the need for a more inclusive revolutionary struggle in the United States during the mid-1930s. In other words, Endore's novel seeks to show how a revolutionary socialist response to the Great Depression would have to be, in addition, a struggle for the civil rights of African Americans and other groups of US subalterns; however, ironically, these same groups also perceived themselves as marginalized by the very discourse of universality that the Communist Party itself espoused at this time. Therefore, for Endore and the subaltern constituencies he was trying to represent, to be "free" in the terms that had already been spelled out by the Haitian Revolution amounted to becoming included – by acts of translation – in the historically specific discourse of freedom that had currency among the US Left's intelligentsia of the 1930s. For instance, at the end of *Babouk*, Endore's anonymous narrator asserts that there is only one authentic, universal truth in the world of 1934 – the universal class conflict between capital and labour: "For above such petty treacheries against this or that mapped country rises the greater treachery against that unmapped land, the land of property. What are the puny and intermittent wars between this or that mapped land, between this or that France or England compared with the perpetual war between the unmapped universal countries of those who have not and those who have?"[2]

Against the backdrop of this transnational, imperial-capitalist universalism, the narrator goes on to suggest that the slave rebellion in Haiti has created a truly universal class of world citizens:

> For the land of the bill of sale is the great mother-country of all. A thousand times more holy is our country of the bill of sale! Millionaires! You true internationalists who regiment your workers into countries, hoist aloft your flag: the bill of sale! You wretches out in the burning plain before Le Cap, where is your bill of sale? What! Have you taken your liberty and you have no bill of sale? . . .
>
> Some day the Negro's tomtom will truly be dreadful to hear. It will come out of the forest and beat down the streets of our cities. . . . And it will hunt us out among the girders of our dying skyscrapers as once we hunted them through their forests. . . .

This is the world of men and of women and of children.
This is THE world. The ONLY world. The WORLD of ALL. (pp. 179–80, 182)

Throughout *Babouk*, Endore describes the violence of the institution of slavery as being based, in part, on a suppression of the various African languages, the slaves' most immediate means of communicating with each other. From the opening pages of the novel, set in West Africa, where an African translator has to explain to the newly captured slaves what lies ahead for them, to the colonial plantation setting, where the power of language is used to terrorize and alienate them, the novel strongly underscores the idea of this linguistic slavery. This also implies, however, that the slaves can use language itself as a tool of resistance, as in the case of a veteran Ibo slave who refuses to "remember" his language when his master demands that he translate and issue work orders to the newly arrived Ibos (pp. 56–57).

As Michel-Rolph Trouillot reminds us, "Silences are inherent in history because any single event enters history with some of its constituting parts missing. Something is always left out while something else is recorded."[3] Endore's narrative closely examines how certain silences were produced in the context of transatlantic slavery; and yet some silences that surround the slave experience were not always produced simply by the omissions of later historians. Below decks during the tortures of the Middle Passage, some slaves "calmly put themselves to death": "In the midst of the general clamor they remained silent, until the moment when they chose to expire. Then they forced their tongues back into their throats and thus stopped up their air-passages" (pp. 29–30). The suggestion that suicide could be the result of a "tongue" producing a self-imposed silence is echoed later in the novel when Babouk is struggling to overcome the silence which afflicts him: "But Babouk could not speak to [his fellow slaves]. His mouth was still closed, his whole being was still shut up" (p. 83). A self-induced linguistic as well as corporeal silence, for these slaves, can be both oppressive and liberating at once. But significantly for Endore's narrative, the slaves' efforts to overcome such silences also work to establish the conditions for a transformation of consciousness. At one point, an older slave woman on Babouk's plantation:

> began to rack her brain in vain to remember the words of polite greeting she had once been taught to use. And try as she would, she could not remember a certain song. . . . She covered her face with her hand and meditated. Not a single word could she form. But the effort evidently brought back a flood of memories. . . . There was so much she would have liked to ask [Babouk].

> Embarrassed, sensing perhaps that her failure to remember her childhood speech was a matter of some shame, she began to mouth meaningless phrases into the palm of her hand and grin through the bars of her fingers. (p. 59)

In this passage, the woman's effort to speak her native tongue "brought back a flood of memories", which in turn produces a host of "meaningless phrases" and her unexpected grin. It is as if the failure of her memory is itself responsible for creating a new, meaningless, or as yet unheard-of language – a language that tells of the recuperation of memory and simultaneously of its constitutive failures. According to Endore, this new language, by taking the place of older, forgotten or suppressed languages, will prove instrumental in establishing a network of slave communication, a network that can lead to still greater collective accomplishments on the part of Babouk and his fellow slaves.[4]

The protagonist of the novel, Babouk (a fictionalized version of the famous rebel slave Boukman), is prized by the other slaves as a storyteller, and one of the stories disseminated among them is that of King Tleeka, a figure who was to buy all the slaves free. The slave masters of St Domingue waste no time in reacting to this perceived threat: "It was decreed that any Negro heard bearing this story should receive twenty-five lashes. . . . In addition, it was decided that an earnest effort should be made to trace this story to its source, for might not the author of it invent further disturbing tales?" (pp. 126–27). But like the old woman trying to recover her lost language, the slave masters encounter unforeseen obstacles to their plan to locate and suppress the source of the tale: "the finding of this original culprit proved difficult, for the Negroes do not sign their names to their stories, and by the time of the investigation King Tleeka in various versions had become part of the repertory of every Negro story-teller on the island" (pp. 126–27). Here, the uncontainable spread of the slaves' inventiveness and creativity has literally outflanked the designs of their masters; for, if it still makes sense to say that there is a uniquely identifiable "source" for this subversive tale, it is to be found in the mind and memory of "every Negro story-teller on the island".

But what interests me about Babouk's stories in particular is the context in which they are told – a setting where, as Endore typically describes it, translations need to occur among the slaves in order to convey the meanings of the stories. The reason I find this noteworthy is because at the moment that translations take place the slaves in the novel suddenly become aware of themselves in a radically new sense: namely, as a community forged around the creation of new, as yet unheard-of *collective* meanings to replace the gaps or silences left behind by the absent, forgotten or suppressed languages and memories of individuals. At one point early in the novel, while he was still on board the slave ship, Babouk begins to tell one of his many stories: " 'Yakuba and Djima were neighbors.' And he stopped, for, before he could continue, his words must be carried around the hold and the platform above the hold, and be repeated and translated a dozen times. Babouk did not mind the interruption. He sensed that he held his audience, and the longer he held them the prouder he was" (p. 31).

The interruption produced by the act of translation – a gap or caesura that constitutes the very continuity and meaningful coherence of his storytelling – also functions as a source of Babouk's personal pride. His pride here might be due to the fact that, in Babouk's eyes, the interruptions reveal the slaves' attempts to communicate to themselves a meaning that, even as it originates from him, now belongs to them, and in part defines them, as a collective of potential (and linguistically diverse) signifying agents. To tell and to translate a story, therefore, is to cultivate a community of storytellers; and yet, at the same time that this community comes into being, it interrupts, fragments and disseminates that original and originating story in unpredictable ways.

Translations, however, are not always a matter of decoding the words of one language and recoding them in the words of another. In *Babouk*, translations also take place between what conventionally would be considered totally disparate spheres of reality – for instance, between private psychic, physical or emotional experiences, such as the feeling of hunger or isolation, and openly discursive or performative acts, such as the offering of food: "Babouk spoke now, and the Indians answered, *without either of them understanding a single word*. But they offered him food, which he snatched at greedily, looking up now and then from his eating with an expression of gratitude" (p. 66; emphasis added). In this moment, the actual words used by Babouk and his Indian hosts are almost irrelevant, since they only serve to index a desire for communication without regard to its failure or success. And yet, here, the desire alone appears sufficient to establish the bond that, otherwise, each party would have sought to forge by way of a common language. In another scene, Babouk is organizing the slaves and teaching them about the more subtle ruses of the racial ideology of a slave society: "No doubt very few of the group understood Babouk's words, but some of the feeling with which he spoke communicated itself to them, and their hearts were opened to receive his final words" (p. 101). Endore distinguishes here between the meaning of words and the feeling that produces or conveys them, suggesting that it takes both of these together to constitute a communicative experience between people. But it is equally important to note that Babouk's feeling does *not* depend on the meaning of his words in order for him to successfully communicate it – along with some of its meaning – to his audience.

With these examples of unintelligible communication that nonetheless succeed in communicating something, Endore might be asking us to broaden our understanding of language to include, beyond words alone, a wider range of discursive acts, gestures and performances in the social constitution of meaning. If the Haitian Revolution, in Michel-Rolph Trouillot's words, "entered history with the peculiar characteristic of being unthinkable even as it happened",[5] then I want to suggest that Endore was well aware of this unthinkable character when he wrote his novel in 1934. Indeed, the constant appearance in the narrative of the figure of linguistic unintelligibility (and the translational acts that accompany it), or of the uncanny absence of language, could imply Endore's conviction that the events that took place in Haiti during the 1790s simply had no language – conceptual or otherwise – that would be commensurable to them. For example, take a scene early in the novel where two slave cargo ships, whose crews are both completely blinded by outbreaks of ophthalmia, attempt in vain to communicate with each other:

> The following day, though the weather was calm, the despair of all had risen. But it is in the lowest depths of our misery that salvation seeks us out, or at least so it appeared when the men of the *Prie-Dieu* were startled to hear a faint halloo come across the water. They listened, and the halloo was repeated several times, and each time louder.
> Then the blind second mate groped for the megaphone and shouted back in a hoarse voice: "Ahoy!"
> And now everyone heard plainly the response: "This is the *Sant' Iago* from Sierra Leone, bound for Havana with a cargo of blacks. As you love Christ send us over a pilot, for we are all blind here, man and mouse."
> The blind second mate put the megaphone to his lips, but he did not answer. What words do the blind say to the blind? (p. 41)

Trouillot himself describes the "unthinkable" in terms that recall the problem of translation, for instance when he states: "The unthinkable is that which one cannot conceive within the range of possible alternatives, that which perverts all answers because it defies the terms under which the questions were phrased."[6] Could it be that Endore, also deeply aware of the unheard-of or inconceivable character of the Haitian Revolution, has chosen to convey this impossible-to-convey meaning through the very figure of translation that Trouillot's thesis gestures toward but does not fully examine in its own right? For the anonymous narrator of Endore's novel, one thing at least is clear: the question of translation (and all its attendant problems) is linked in a crucial way to the fact that, in the enlightened year of 1791, "No, no one could explain this phenomenon: Negro slaves demanding their liberty" (p. 165).[7]

I want to propose that one aspect of a broader notion of language in *Babouk* is illustrated through what I call the writing of "biopower" (Michel Foucault's term) that repeatedly manifests itself in the novel through acts of violence. By this, I am referring to those moments, scattered throughout the narrative, when the institution of slavery leaves discursive traces of itself on and through the bodies of those subjects whom it simultaneously depends upon and constitutes as such. For instance, Endore's narrator explains how the island's slave owners judged the precise features of their slaves' bodies as "so many anatomical promissory notes of many years of hard work" (p. 56); Babouk himself must fix his teeth on stones in the ground when he is being whipped for trying to escape, because, the narrator notes, "That way, too, you avoided clamping your teeth down on your tongue which sometimes resulted in a tongue being severed in half" (p. 145). That the punishment for an escape attempt could lead to the destruction of one's "tongue" suggests that the silencing of language – itself linked to the (violently suppressed) functions of the body – is a tool for dealing with transgressions against the institution of slavery. Conversely, other slaves who try to escape are punished by having their ears nailed to a wooden post, after which "The releasing [of the slave] took place by the simple method of slicing off the ear that held the black to the post. And by this simple procedure was the law, that punished a first attempt at escape by the loss of an ear, satisfied" (p. 77).

In each of these instances, the conceptual and juridical difference between master and slave, white and black, is concretely manifested, inscribed or translated into the discursive figure of the law through acts of violence directed toward (and producing) the slave's body. In short, the narrator notes, "Through centuries [the whites] had maintained their feeling of superiority over the Negro race only by constant proof of it though whipping and torture" (p. 169).[8] Yet beyond this everyday practice of violence, a different, less concrete register of the writing of biopower is evident in historical accounts of the Haitian Revolution. In passing, Endore, through the voice of his narrator, observes how

> My history books preserve for me the tears of the queen [who cries at the thought of other white people being killed by the slaves]. They glitter on forever, cold, dry, imperishable, starring the pages of our heartless historians.
>
> But what of the tears of Babouk and the other Negroes? Who records them? Who preserves them? No one! . . .
>
> They are lost forever. Only the tears of queens are considered worthy of being embalmed. (p. 166)

Subjected to this more profound but less evident form of writing – or what I am here calling the writing of biopolitical power in and through human bodies – the slaves of Endore's novel work to produce a kind of counter-writing, or a revolutionary *rewriting* of that discourse of biopower that penetrates and dismembers both their lived experience and the subsequent historical accounts of their revolution. Beginning with the "meaningless phrases" and the "flood of memories" that the older slave woman experienced upon trying to remember her native tongue, Endore's novel gradually reveals a wholly new "tongue" that is the syncretic result of, on the one hand, the slaves' everyday experience of violence and, on the other hand, their subjective response to that violence. While Babouk struggles with the silence imposed on him from the slave regime, at one point he hears Creole (a mixture of French and West African idioms) being spoken by other slaves: "But already these French words pronounced with an African accent, these sentences constructed with an African syntax, made an almost familiar language to him. He felt that at any moment he might burst into speech himself" (p. 82). Soon after this incident, and just before he is to lead the initial slave insurrection of August 1791, Babouk is overcome by an uncontrollable linguistic faculty:

> He squirmed upon the ground, expelling the strangest sounds that ever were heard on earth.
>
> From his painfully strangled throat, from his torn, distorted lips, issued not simply sounds but great aggregates of words. All the silence of years was being driven from him by the rush of a vast throng of long-imprisoned words.
>
> He was aware that people had come running over from the bower and were now surrounding and staring at him. But he did not mind. His body continued to twitch and his mouth to pour forth a cataract of words and sentences, not merely in his native African language, not only in Creole, but in unknown tongues:

> *Eh! Eh!*
> Bomba!
> Heu! Heu!
> *Canga bafio té!*
> All that his ears had ever heard, all that his soul had ever wanted to say, was now suddenly released from him.
> All through the night his body kept pouring out its surcharge of words.
> (p. 86)

At this moment, a new, as yet unheard-of tongue is erupting uncontrollably from Babouk's body – a tongue made up of the fragments of other tongues, a "surcharge of words" that will usher in and accompany the unheard-of events of August 1791. When those revolutionary events actually do occur later in the novel, Endore's narrator describes them as the embodiment of the nexus of the possible and the real:

> Priests and sorcerers were already on hand . . . [and through their costumes they were] always striving to express their station, which was halfway between the seen and the unseen world, the link, as it were, between matter and force. . . .
> A wave of emotion swept through the congregation, as when in the cathedral the miracle of the transubstantiation takes place to the tinkle of a bell. (p. 149)

I want to propose that the reason why the insurrection of 1791 is portrayed here as a transubstantiation is not just because of the most obvious reason, namely that it brings into reality a hitherto unthinkable notion of freedom – the freedom of black slaves that was willed and executed by themselves alone. In addition to this, Babouk's excessive and uncontainable linguistic outburst, in conjunction with the stories he tells and the translations that these require, has already supplied the prior conditions that would make such an unheard-of event possible in the first place. For if we understand Endore's description of the slave regime as being founded upon the peculiarly violent writing of racial-colonial biopower, then this revelation from Babouk of an undefinable new tongue – a linguistic transgression in every sense of the term – seems to expose the limits of biopolitical significance in general: the violent writing/inscription of the meaning of power in and through human bodies. Such a critical recasting or rewriting of biopower's own inscribed violence would, it seems, necessarily have to take a bodily form, a position "halfway . . . between matter and force", but one which nevertheless confuses the distinction between these two terms. Similarly, from this point forward in the novel, the language of the slaves' speech – for example when they sing the song of vengeance that Babouk sang in an "unknown tongue" – will repeatedly confuse the distinction between force, feeling and meaning: "What the words meant not even the singers knew clearly, but the power was there nevertheless. Like the words that were written in letters of fire at Belshazzar's feast, the meaning may have been obscure but the portent was plain" (pp. 154–55).

In conclusion, in the course of his essay on the Haitian Revolution, Trouillot asks: "How does one write a history of the impossible?"[9] Guy Endore's novel, *Babouk*, suggests that such a history can indeed be written, but only as the narrative of its own (constitutive) impossibility. That is to say, the narrative unfolding of this novel, and especially the attention it pays to acts of translation between the various different registers of language, writing, memory, violence and experience, presents us with the birth of an entirely new tongue – a unique product of the historical experience of West Indian slavery – that only confuses those who try to translate it into a pre-existing idiom. Like any other, it is a tongue that must be translated, or meaningfully actualized as such in words and deeds, and yet it can never be fully commensurable to a "universal", formal linguistics if one assumes that this is the sole measure of successful communication. And this is because, in 1791, there was no pre-existing idiom of either words or concepts that was capable of accommodating the truth of African slaves demanding and bringing about the realization of their own freedom. But it is also and more precisely due to the fact that the silences of the slave experience, as Endore recognized, literally inhabit this new, unheard-of tongue as the very condition of its transmissibility – telling all of us, finally, of the impossibility of its final and ultimate telling.

Notes

1. Indeed, as Michel-Rolph Trouillot observes, since its actual occurrence, the Haitian Revolution has been used to advance a variety of different and even contradictory political agendas: "Thus [from 1791 to 1804] apologists and detractors alike, abolitionists and avowed racists, liberal intellectuals, economists, and slave owners used the events of St Domingue to make their case, without regard to Haitian history as such. Haiti mattered to all of them, but only as a pretext to talk about something else." Michel-Rolph Trouillot, *Silencing the Past: Power and the Production of History* (Boston: Beacon Press, 1995), 97.

2. Guy Endore, *Babouk* (1934; repr., New York: Monthly Review Press, 1991), 179. Subsequent references to this edition appear parenthetically in the text.

3. Trouillot, *Silencing*, 49.

4. On the significance of slave networks of communication, for the most part ignored by historians, Trouillot remarks that "many historians are more willing to accept the idea that

slaves could have been influenced by whites or free mulattoes, with whom we know they had limited contacts, than they are willing to accept the idea that slaves could have convinced other slaves that they had the right to revolt. The existence of extended communication networks among slaves, of which we have only a glimpse, has not been a 'serious' subject of historical research" (Trouillot, *Silencing*, 103).

5. Ibid., 73.

6. Ibid., 82.

7. I am suggesting here that Endore's novel anticipates a set of – now relatively widespread and accepted – revisionary assessments of the impact of the Revolution on Western thought. Trouillot introduces his thesis of the "unthinkable" as follows: "Indeed, the contention that enslaved Africans and their descendants could not envision freedom – let alone formulate strategies for gaining and securing such freedom – was based not so much on empirical evidence as on an ontology, an implicit organization of the world and its inhabitants. Although by no means monolithic, this worldview was widely shared by whites in Europe and the Americas and by many non-white plantation owners as well. Although it left room for variations, none of these variations included the possibility of a revolutionary uprising in the slave plantations, let alone a successful one leading to the creation of an independent state. . . . The Haitian Revolution did challenge the ontological and political assumptions of the most radical writers of the Enlightenment. *The events that shook up Saint-Domingue from 1791 to 1804 constituted a sequence for which not even the extreme political left in France or England had a conceptual frame of reference.* They were 'unthinkable' facts in the framework of Western thought. . . . In that sense, the Haitian Revolution was unthinkable in its time: it challenged the very framework within which proponents and opponents had examined race, colonialism, and slavery in the Americas" (Trouillot, *Silencing*, 73, 82–83; Trouillot's emphasis). For a closely related, but more philosophically oriented version of this thesis, see Susan Buck-Morss, "Hegel and Haiti", *Critical Inquiry* 26, no. 4 (Summer 2000): 821–65.

8. As an illustration of a classic biopolitical strategy, one that links acts of violence to the discursive production of difference, the following passage from the novel is worth quoting in full: "Through centuries they had maintained their feeling of superiority over the Negro race only by constant proof of it through whipping and torture. The fellows did look so damnably like human beings that one must keep perpetually insisting on those minute differences of black skin and heavy lips and wide nostrils and kinky hair, as must the white masters, for that matter, be continuously insisting on the bad grammar and unwashed hands of their peasants and workers. In fact, one must call upon the Church, upon God, upon nature, upon science for constant reassurance, and even then only by stepping on the Negro a dozen times a day can one be really positive" (p. 169). For Foucault's notion of "biopower", in the sense that I am using it here, see Michel Foucault, *The History of Sexuality, Volume I: An Introduction*, trans. Robert Hurley (New York: Vintage Books, 1990), 135–59; part 5, "Right of Death and Power over Life".

9. Trouillot, *Silencing*, 73.

CHAPTER 8

LETTERS LOST AT SEA
EDWIDGE DANTICAT AND ORALITY

BRENNA MUNRO

> *A man listening to a story is in the company of the storyteller. . . . The reader of a novel, however, is isolated, more so than any other reader.*
>
> – Walter Benjamin

> *I would write if there was no public. If there was nobody reading, I would still write.*
>
> – Edwidge Danticat

In *After the Dance: A Walk Through Carnival in Jacmel, Haiti*,[1] Edwidge Danticat describes how, as a young girl left in the care of relatives while her parents worked in the United States, she was not allowed to attend carnival. Her subsequent, moving family memoir, *Brother I'm Dying*, tells us more about her principled and tenacious uncle Joseph and the attachment between them; what we learn from this earlier piece is that in the Baptist minister's attempt to look after his brother's child, he instilled in her a fear of carnival crowds and their unruly sexuality.[2] Her subsequent sense of distance from Haitian popular culture was compounded by her eventual move to New York: "I avoided carnival, except as a distant observer, watching videotapes sold in Haitian music stores in Brooklyn, weeks after the festivities had ended, and marveling at the revelers' ability to surrender to the sway of so many others. . . I was aching for a baptism by crowd here, among my own people" (*After the Dance*, p. 15).

This image of video spectatorship vividly exemplifies the alienation that her adult experience of carnival in Haiti allows her to overcome: "I am one of those marchers and migrants, back from the purgatory of exile, expiating sins of coldness and distance. . . . The carnival offers all the paradoxical elements I am craving; anonymity, jubilant community, and belonging" (p. 147). Despite this temporary rite of possession, her travelogue-memoir concludes with a return to watching life onscreen:

> On one of the cafeteria-length tables is a television, which is replaying scenes from carnival the day before. . . . I spot myself briefly on the television screen. . . . Seeing myself . . . my head cocked back, arms draped around people I didn't even know, I had a strange feeling of detachment. Was that really me? So unencumbered, so lively, so free. So it did happen after all. . . . Even as others had been putting on their masks, just for one afternoon, I had allowed myself to remove my own. (p. 158)

These final lines remind the reader of the moment of Danticat's writing, post-carnival in America, when she has presumably put her "mask" back on, even as she reveals her thoughts and memories to her memoir's invisible audience. Writing, like television, becomes a technology of distance and solitude when compared with the noisy immediacy and physical presence of the crowd and its songs, but it is also a mode of connection across infinite distances.

Danticat's work engages, in an unusually sustained and nuanced fashion, with the relationship between written narratives and oral culture. She seems compelled by the border between orality and writing, and, appropriately enough as a transnational writer, attempts to reimagine that border. At times her writing of the disjunctures of migrant life summons up fusions of voice and the printed word, at others it explores what might be gained from textuality, and at others still her texts confront the impossibility of their being oral. Danticat thus mourns her texts' loss of the "jubilant community", or, more prosaically, the social capital that oral performances can build, but she also considers the arguably wider and more lasting mark that writing can leave on the world. Indeed, the solitude of writing can also be understood as a form of privacy in which women can create without the potential social restraints of more public forms of art. Danticat invokes a range of modes of communication and representation in her writing, from television to painting, in order to chart the complexities of this borderland. Chief among these tropes is the epistolary letter.

In much of her writing particularly in her collection of linked short stories *Kric? Krac!*[3] and her novel-in-short-stories, *The Dew Breaker*,[4] the letter is a recurrent motif, and a resonant sign for Haitian culture in an era of diaspora. As Keith Walker puts it in a discussion of Mariama Bâ's *So Long a Letter*, "as an artifact the letter is *in transit*, crisscrossing borders and barriers, negotiating the national and international in-between places".[5] Letters are, after all, literally writing in motion, bearing the stamp of their origin, while also marked by their journeys. A poignant synecdoche for migratory life, letters evoke both the attempt to maintain relationships, communities and identities across distance, and the struggle to attain the many different "papers" that might lead to citizenship in the new country. Along with scenes of letters being written, read and remembered, Danticat evokes the texture of immigrant experience by depicting people recording and listening to cassette tapes, sending telegrams, gleaning news of relatives over the radio, using the telephone, and, as at the very end of *The Dew Breaker*, hanging up abruptly – all the technologies of long-distance working-class families. The letter is part of a fragile repertoire of connection that moves back and forth between writing and speaking.

The very phrase "Krik? Krak!" invokes the ritualized beginning of oral narrative, and Danticat also uses the songs, rituals, word-games, sayings, cosmologies and stories of Haitian oral culture throughout her fictional work. In "Women Like Us", her autobiographical epilogue to *Krik? Krak!*, Danticat reveals how she was influenced by the "kitchen poets" she grew up around, "those whose fables and metaphors, whose similes, and soliloquies, whose diction and *je ne sais quoi* daily slip into your survival soup, by way of their fingers" (p. 220). Her writing is thus often seen as part of Haitian oral tradition, and this is certainly how the blurb on the back cover of *Krik? Krak!* presents her:

> "Steeped in the myths and lore that sustained generations of Haitians, *Krik? Krak!* demonstrates the healing power of storytelling." – *San Francisco Chronicle*.
>
> In *Krik? Krak!* Danticat establishes herself as the latest heir to that narrative tradition.
>
> "A silenced Haiti has once again found its literary voice." – Paule Marshall.

Implying that Danticat is resuscitating a tradition set in the past tense – "lore that sustained generations" – suggests that the orality she is "heir" to is dying, "silenced", or at least anachronistic; writing must take over where orality has fallen away. A written text is then in danger of becoming oral culture's museum, or even its funeral singer, entombing what it claims to revere, rather than constituting its "survival soup".

To imagine that a printed text can revive or continue orality is of course a contradiction in terms. While writing can describe oral culture, make use of its language, themes and structures, and even transcribe it directly, it cannot be oral in and of itself.

Even read out loud, a recitation still differs from an oral performance, because it must repeat the text, whereas oral performances tend to be different each time, shaped by specific moment and audience. In her discussion of African novels and their academic reception, Eileen Julien astutely suggests that the tendency in postcolonial criticism to overlook these kinds of gaps between orality and writing is produced by the politics of authenticity, so that a kind of essentialist romance of ethnicity or national belonging is produced through the idea of an unbroken connection between oral forms and printed literature.[6] References to these traditions in a text can be a form of cultural credentialing, masking the ways in which a novelist cannot be a griot. Writing inevitably shuts out those who cannot read; from land titles to novels, literacy has been used to colonize and to guard elite privilege, as the immigrant knows only too well. Try as the writer might to align themselves with an oral tradition, they have at least one foot on the other side of this border. To understand Danticat's writing as "giving voice" to Haitians – who after all speak another language entirely different from the English of her writing – is undoubtedly to gloss over a number of important discontinuities. On the other hand, a text's exploration of the relationship between literature and orality can powerfully represent the fractured terrain of postcolonial modernity.

In Haiti's modern history, for example, the relationship between orality, literacy and politics has been complicated. "Papa Doc" Duvalier, Haiti's dictator from 1957 until his death in 1971, when his son "Baby Doc" took over, gained the presidency partly through his populist appropriation of Vodou, the source of so much of Haitian folk culture, and his scorn for Catholicism, a religion "of the book". Duvalier recruited Vodou priests into his brutal apparatus and named his most feared militia after a well-known figure from Haitian legend, as Danticat elaborates in *Breath, Eyes, Memory*: "In the fairy tales, the *Tonton Macoute* was a bogeyman, a scarecrow with human flesh. . . . In his knapsack, he always had scraps of naughty children, whom he dismembered to eat as snacks. . . . Outside the fairy tales, they roamed the streets in broad daylight, parading their Uzi machine guns. *Who invented the Macoutes? The devil didn't do it and God didn't do it.*"[7] Duvalier, the "inventor" of these real-life monsters, was himself added to the pantheon of gods after his death. Oral cultures are not automatically weapons of the weak, and dissident writing may in fact offer an alternative, free space in this context.[8]

Changing the cultural politics of orality once again, young Haitians began in the 1990s to reclaim and transform folk culture in a very different spirit, as part of a *rasin* ("roots") movement that developed between Miami, New York and Haiti.

Elizabeth McAlister describes how Rara music, originating in a Vodou ritual in poor neighborhoods in Haiti, became a transnational cultural form, part of festivals and political rallies: "A song created in Leogane can be sung in Brooklyn a week later, creating a diasporic popular Haitian discourse" (p. 16).[9] Danticat is in many ways a part of this cultural-political moment, in which a self-conscious, loosely spiritual version of folk culture is the lingua franca of an informal pro-democracy movement developing in both cities and villages, both Haiti and North America. Danticat's acclaim as a writer has provided her with a kind of letter of introduction onto the stage of these protests and festivals, and her influential articles on Haitian politics have also expanded the reach of this movement into mainstream American discourse.[10]

Danticat's rendition of modern folk culture, unlike the rather male-dominated Rara bands' emphasis on the "drummer-hero" and the "classic man-of-words",[11] is also a specifically female-centred *rasin*. *Krik? Krak!* in particular can be read as an exploration of this feminist aesthetic practice. Like *The Dew Breaker*, these stories, set in both Haiti and America, follow one another in a not-quite chronological sequence, intersecting through recurring or related characters and echoing themes, in what could be called a diasporan narrative structure. A range of these disparate characters in *Krik? Krak!* turn out to be connected to a secret society of women who have lost loved ones in, or themselves survived, the 1937 massacre of Haitians in the Dominican Republic – an earlier tragic era of anti-immigrant feeling.[12] Some of these women claim to have flown over the river that separates the two countries. In the story "Nineteen Thirty Seven", one of these women has been cruelly imprisoned for being a *lougarou*, a "witch who can fly", and her daughter brings her a statue of the Virgin Mary that she hopes will cry miraculous tears for her mother.[13] Danticat's work thus offers a paradigm of folk belonging, a diasporan way of identifying as Haitian that is both resistant to Duvalierism and the more male-oriented aspects of the *rasin* movement.

In *The Dew Breaker*, the *lougarou* women appear to briefly return from *Krik? Krak!* when a character is forced to listen to an endless and intimidating speech by the country's then dictator, presumably one of the Duvaliers: "The president read what seemed like a hundred-page book, in perfect nasal French. . . . After the third, fourth, or fifth hour of the speech, he [the listener] found himself dreaming. He thought he saw a flock of winged women circling above the palace dome, angry sibyls ranging in hue from cinnamon, honey, bronze, sable to jet-black, hissing through the rest of the speech" (p. 193).

Danticat's feminist oral culture is embodied here in the "hissing", magical women of legend who interrupt the speech and thus the realm of public male politics with a colourful polyphony. Duvalier is cast as the producer of an oral performance that is a kind of punishment for the listeners, and is in itself a lifeless repetition. The oral performances of the *lougarous* – and all the other people we see storytelling and singing in Danticat's work – are presented in contrast as a democratic practice, a multiplication of counter-publics and an oppositional idiom, sometimes lyrical, sometimes biting, in which ordinary people are fluent.

These potentially subversive speech acts are also an antidote to the many scenes in her work of migrant people losing their voices; in *The Dew Breaker*, Danticat mentions Haitian children new to America whose parents bring them to the hospital because they have stopped speaking, and she also tells the story of a young Haitian-American man who killed his father and is "repatriated" to a country where he cannot speak a word of the language.[14] The women in *Krik? Krak!*'s secret society, on the other hand, belong to each other through a shared language, using complex verbal codes to recognize and greet one another: "You hear my mother who speaks through me. She is the shadow that follows my shadow. The flame at the tip of my candle. The ripple in the stream where I wash my face. Yes. I will eat my tongue if ever I whisper that name, the name of that place across the river that took my mother from me" (p. 45). The idea of the mother who speaks through the daughter is a central way in which Danticat presents her own writing as a kind of ancestral speaking in tongues, thus identifying her writing with this female oral culture and a Haiti she no longer inhabits.

This identification is, of course, riven with contradictions. In "Women Like Us", Danticat describes how she became a writer: "You remember thinking while braiding your hair that you look a lot like your mother and her mother before her. It was their whispers that pushed you, their murmurs over pots sizzling in your head. A thousand women urging you to speak through the blunt tip of your pencil" (p. 222).

The narrators of this epilogue turn out to be a chorus of women, of grandmothers, urging her to write. In a kind of magical synesthesia, orality and writing merge in the image of the "blunt" pencil that speaks. Her mother also describes the young Danticat silently writing in terms of sound: "But then she's not being quiet. You hear this scraping from her. Krik? Krak! Pencil, paper. It sounds like someone crying"(p. 220). These sounds, however – scraping, cracking and crying – evoke acts of violence more than they do a speaking human voice. We could read them as the traces of Danticat's conflict with her mother over becoming a writer and, indeed, all the difficult mother-daughter relationships of her fiction. Far from "speaking through her", her mother considers writing, like carnival, to be improper, "as forbidden as dark rouge on the cheeks or a first date before eighteen" (p. 219). Just as the mother's voice cannot be equated with the daughter's, these croaking sounds also bring our attention to the way in which the silence of writing cannot easily be equated with the voice, and the ways in which literature cannot simply replicate an oral culture, female or otherwise.

The fantasy of speaking in the voice of thousands of female forebears cancels out distances of time and place, as well as the differences between the internationally published text and the story told in a kitchen. The trope of the letter, however, foregrounds these very gaps. As Janet Gurkin Altman suggests: "Epistolary fiction tends to flourish at those moments when novelists most openly reflect upon the relation between storytelling and intersubjective communication and begin to question the way in which writing reflects, betrays or constitutes the relation between self, other, and experience."[15]

Danticat only occasionally writes in an epistolary form; she more often places letters within her fictions, as if to examine even more closely how writing functions between people. These letters encode the gulf between writing and speaking, but whether typed or handwritten, they also embody a textuality that seems less removed from the speaking voice than mass-produced forms of writing. Unlike novels or newspapers, letters can evoke the physical presence of their writer through the hand that writes and the tongue that seals the envelope; as Elizabeth Heckendorn Cook puts it in *Epistolary Bodies*, these texts can bear "traces of the body that produced them in inkblots, teardrops, erasures, revisions [and] a scriptive tremulousness that signifies iconographically instead of semantically".[16] Danticat's letters are above all treasured material objects, with specific histories inscribed upon their vulnerable surfaces. The singularity of these letters parallels, in a sense, the varied renditions of oral culture, in which each performance of a story or a saying makes it different. Both offer alternatives to the "mechanical" replications of mass society, or indeed contemporary global capitalism, which in Walter Benjamin's famous formulation "substitutes a plurality of copies for a unique existence".[17]

In *The Dew Breaker*, this sense of the unique materiality of the letter is particularly emphasized. In a letter to a nurse in America from her mother in Haiti, for example, the text becomes an iconographic palimpsest invoking a painful family history that the rather restrained words of the letter do not explicitly speak of: "The *a*s and *o*s, which had been struck over many times, created underlayers, shadows, and small holes within the vowels' perimeters" (p. 58). While letters can be a sign of absence and distance, because they stand in for someone who is not there, Danticat seems to be reaching here for a language of ghostly presences, an alphabet that signifies in multiple ways. This spectral language of shadows and holes is appropriate for *The Dew Breaker*, in which America is transformed into a landscape for refugees and fugitives, people hunted and haunted by the traumas and sins of the past. In these overlaps of orality and writing, Danticat is perhaps attempting to re-enchant the mechanized word, or as J. Michael Dash puts it in a brief discussion of her work, "English has become, for Danticat, the code of genuine feeling."[18]

The fragility of these letters begs the question, however, of whether this enchanted textuality is possible, or at least how far it can travel. Another much-examined letter in *The Dew Breaker* emphasizes emotional and geographical distance:

> It was written, as most of them were, in near-calligraphic style, in blue ink, on see-through airmail paper. . . . Every time she read the letter she tried to find something else between the lines, a note of sympathy, commiseration, condolence. But it simply wasn't there. The more time went by, the more brittle and fragile the letter became. Each time she held the paper between her fingers she wondered how her mother had not torn it with the pen she'd used to compose each carefully inscribed word. How had the postal workers in Port-au-Prince and Brookyn not lacerated the thin page and envelope? And how had the letter not turned to dust in her purse during the bus ride to and from work? (pp. 53–54)

This letter could be interpreted as a figuration of Danticat's anxieties about living and writing transnationally. The mother, left behind, writes with an anger that her daughter imagines as a pen tearing through paper, as the journey to America adds its own "lacerations", and the connections between the two worlds, perhaps even memories themselves, become more and more tattered. The letter is a sign here for the ways in which the ruptures of physical migration and political oppression prevent people from being able to speak directly to one another.

Krik? Krak! begins, significantly, with "Children of the Sea", Danticat's only epistolary short story in the collection, consisting of letters that will never reach the people they were written for. A young man flees Haiti by boat, made a fugitive because of his progressive political commentary on the radio – another form of democratic oral performance, perhaps – while his lover stays there with her parents. They both write clandestine letters to each other that are unsendable; the young man is finally forced to throw his notebook of letters overboard as the boat slowly fills with water, and we do not find out if he himself drowns. His lover is visited by a black butterfly that may signify his death. Just as his political speech is broken off, so too are their letters, and their society is also tragically rent apart by soldiers. The broken links of these unsent letters also parallel the broken sequence of Danticat's short story cycles, in which characters or their children sometimes appear in other people's stories, but sometimes do not. For example, we do not hear from the young letter-writing man in "Children of the Sea" again, but in "Caroline's Wedding", a story he tells in his letters about his boat-mates is told again in a church in America, which indicates that someone from the boat survived to tell their tale. People are lost through migration and political instability, but are also unpredictably re-encountered. The reader is also, of course, miraculously reading these letters lost at sea, in a kind of impossible eavesdropping. Like the thin blue letter in the passage above, these letters have somehow survived, and the stories they tell have come back into public circulation as spoken words in America.

The promiscuous, free-floating letter, written in intimacy and then sent into potential public view or hearing, is also a gendered object in a society so concerned with women's virginity and reputation. The first letter of "Children of the Sea" describes the sails of the boat the young man is fleeing on, which are made of "white sheets with bright red spots", inspiring him to think of his lover and imagine "the semen and the innocence lost to those sheets" (p. 3). She, meanwhile, is struggling with her father's anger over her decision to have a relationship with the young man against his wishes. Sheets of paper, sheets of a bed, sails of a boat; there is a connection between the unrestricted circulation of texts, migrant peoples and women's bodies. Danticat herself was accused of making the secrets of female sexuality and indeed the dirty laundry of Haitian culture too public with her first novel, *Breath, Eyes, Memory*, in which she negatively depicts the tradition of Haitian mothers "testing" their daughter's virginity.[19]

The loose letters of "Children of the Sea" contrast strongly with a letter of marriage proposal in *Krik? Krak!*'s "Caroline's Wedding", the story of a daughter marrying a non-Haitian man against her mother's wishes. This letter was originally the centre of a small public ritual in Haiti, and then becomes a much repeated family story in America, as when the mother tells it to her daughter here:

> Do you know how your father came to have me as his wife? His father wrote a letter to my father and came to my house on a Sunday afternoon and brought the letter in a pink and green handkerchief. Pink because it is the colour of romance and green for hope that it might work. Your grandfather on your papa's side had the handkerchief sewn especially in these two colours to wrap my proposal letter in. He brought this letter to my house and handed it to my father. My father didn't even read the letter himself. He called in a neighbor and asked the neighbor to read it out loud. (p. 162)

This is a beautiful ritual in which the oral and the written are combined. The letter is delivered by hand and read in person, and the bride thus safely delivered too. It is also, of course, a gendered circuit of exchange controlled by men. This bittersweet description perhaps shares the mother's nostalgia for a culture of presence, grace and wholeness, while gently pointing up the potential for oral traditions – and indeed "fatherlands" – to confine people within closed, conventional systems, which are paradoxically represented here through the carefully over-wrapped letter. This story thus casts oral culture in quite a different light from the tales of *lougarou* women and indeed the free play of the carnival at Jacmel.

Both the spoken word and the letter are thus written in a series of changing ways across Danticat's work. The unfettered, mobile sympathy of her writing refuses to insist on the primacy of either. We could interpret these constantly shifting figurations of the relationship between textuality and orality as contradictions, as signs of the insoluble incommensurability of folk culture and internationally published literature. The letter is an emblem of the distances – political, geographical and emotional – which prevent the potential communion of oral storytelling for the transnational writer. But the letter also suggests a possible space where the oral and the written can be put into conversation, and a new diasporan cultural politics can be brought into view.

Notes

1. See Edwidge Danticat, *After the Dance: A Walk Through Carnival in Jacmel, Haiti* (New York: Crown Publishers, 2004). Subsequent references to this work appear parenthetically in the text.
2. See Edwidge Danticat, *Brother, I'm Dying* (New York: Alfred A. Knopf, 2007).
3. See Edwidge Danticat, *Krik? Krak!* (New York: Vintage Books,1996). Subsequent references to this work appear parenthetically in the text.

4. See Edwidge Danticat, *The Dew Breaker* (New York: Alfred A. Knopf, 2004). Subsequent references to this work appear parenthetically in the text.

5. Keith Walker, "Mariama Bâ, Menopause, Epistolarity, and Postcolonialism", in *Emerging Perspectives on Mariama Bâ: Postcolonialism, Feminism, and Postmodernism*, ed. Ada Uzoamaka Azodo (Trenton, NJ: Africa World Press 2003), 247.

6. See Eileen Julien, *African Novels and the Question of Orality* (Bloomington and Indianapolis: Indiana University Press, 1992), 1–20.

7. Edwidge Danticat, *Breath, Eyes, Memory* (New York: Vintage Books, 1994), 138. Subsequent references to this work appear parenthetically in the text.

8. There is a great deal of debate about Vodou's intrinsic relationship to authoritarianism. Joan Dayan argues that the religion's preoccupation with the iconography of slavery and dictatorship – horses, whips, military titles – is a kind of radical history-telling, in which the terrors of the past and the present are ritually transformed and mastered. See *Haiti, History and the Gods* (Berkeley and Los Angeles: University of California Press, 1995). Richard D.E. Burton, on the other hand, sees Vodou's carnivalesque rituals of possession, in which the powerless temporarily get to be gods, as ultimately reconciling them to a hierarchical world view that is reproduced in the political arena. See *Afro-Creole: Power, Opposition and Play in the Caribbean* (Ithaca: Cornell University Press, 1997).

9. See Elizabeth McAlister, *Rara! Vodou, Power and Performance in Haiti and Its Diaspora* (Berkeley and Los Angeles: University of California Press, 2002). McAlister's ethnography-history draws a vivid picture of this emergent movement. One of the few female performers of the music associated with *rasin* is Emeline Michel, whose latest album, *Rasin Kreyol (Times Square)* includes a Danticat-esque song called "Zikap", which uses Haitian proverbs to talk about AIDS.

10. See, for example, Danticat's 2004 editorial about her uncle Joseph's death in US Customs detention, "A Very Haitian Story", *New York Times*, 24 November 2004, A23.

11. McAlister, *Rara*, 189.

12. The Dominican Republic (Spanish speaking) and Haiti (Creole and French speaking) share the island of Hispaniola, and are separated by the Massacre river – a border which has, tragically, earned its name more than once. Haitians known as "voyageurs" had been working mainly as sugar cane cutters and domestics in the Dominican Republic for generations when the then dictator Rafael Trujillo, influenced by the rise of fascism in Spain and Germany, ordered their massacre in the name of racial purity in October of 1937. Soldiers and citizens killed between twenty and forty thousand people, establishing their victim's supposed national origin through asking them to pronounce *perejil* – "parsley". Racialized division and hostility, not to mention mistreatment of Haitian immigrants in the Dominican Republic, is ongoing, as Danticat and Junot Diaz point out in a *New York Times* opinion piece. See "The Dominican Republic's War on Haitian Workers", *New York Times*, 20 November 1999, A13.

13. The Virgin Mary is a syncretic religious figure in Haiti, associated with the Vodou goddess Erzulie, whom Danticat also often invokes. She is also a potential political symbol: historian Michel S. Laguerre describes how "during the occupation of Haiti by United States marines (1915–1934), Haitian guerillas used the name of the Holy Virgin of Saut D'Eau to incite peasants to struggle against them" (p. 97). He also points out that the Duvalier regime banned students from taking part in the pilgrimage to the Saut D'Eau waterfall in 1964, when it appeared as though it might be a rallying point for resistance (p. 98). See *Voodoo and Politics in Haiti* (New York: St Martin's Press, 1989). Danticat thus seems to be deploying this Christian/Vodou female icon in order to summon up a more direct anti-authoritarian folk politics than even that of her stories. See Donette A. Francis, "Silences Too Horrific to Disturb: Writing Sexual Histories in Edwidge Danticat's *Breath, Eyes, Memory*", in *Research in African Literatures* (Summer 2004): 75–79, for an important account of the ways in which the Duvalier regime specifically targeted women.

14. In *Brother I'm Dying*, Danticat discusses how her uncle Joseph, who was a talented orator, lost his voice to throat cancer – and thus his ability to talk to her on the telephone – only a year after she left Haiti to join her parents in America.

15. See Janet Gurkin Altman, *Epistolarity: Approaches to a Form* (Columbus: Ohio State University Press, 1982), 212.

16. See Elizabeth Heckendorn Cook, *Epistolary Bodies: Gender and Genre in the Eighteenth-Century Republic of Letters* (Stanford: Stanford University Press, 1996), 2.

17. See Walter Benjamin, "The Work of Art in the Age of Mechanical Reproduction", in *Illuminations*, trans. Hannah Arendt (1955; repr. New York: Schocken Books, 1968), 221.

18. See J. Michael Dash, *Haiti and the United States: National Stereotypes and the Literary Imagination* (1988; repr., London: Macmillan Press, 1997), 161.

19. "Danticat's literary debut sparked controversy in the Haitian-American community. Some of the young novelist's fellow Haitians disapproved of her description of the traditional Haitian practice of 'testing'. . . . Most Haitian immigrants to the United States have abandoned this primarily rural practice, and many felt that by including this custom in the novel, Danticat would cause Haitian-American women to be viewed with continued suspicion, as primitive and abusive." See "Death is a Path" at http://www.haitiglobalvillage.com/sd-marassa1-cd/d-reviews.htm (17 August 2006). The paradox of this response is that Danticat, while critiquing certain aspects of tradition, is primarily engaged in transforming "rural" culture into a new diasporan writing that makes the notion of "primitive" and "civilized" cultures nonsensical.

CHAPTER 9

Being Haitian in New York
Migration and Transnationalism in Danticat's *Breath, Eyes, Memory*

Adlai Murdoch

The symbolic importance of Haiti's independence bicentennial year of 2004 reinforces the longstanding perception of Haiti's geopolitical punishment at the hands of myriad world powers, and illuminates the international impediments and obstacles consistently and diachronically directed against a black, revolutionary ex-colony laden with both material and symbolic importance. This process began with Napoleon's failed revisionist military attempts – backed by twenty-two thousand soldiers – to reintroduce slavery to the French Caribbean between 1802 and 1806. Recognition of Haiti's independence by France came only in 1825, and at the price of an imposing indemnity of 150 million francs, or about $18 billion in today's dollars, precipitating an endless round of international borrowing for the new nation. The subsequent repayment schedule amounted to 80 per cent of the country's GDP by the end of the nineteenth century, despite the debt's having been reduced to 90 million francs through a treaty signed with Louis-Philippe in 1838; the final instalment was paid to its French creditors in 1947. It also marks seventy years since US forces left Haiti in 1934 after a nineteen-year-long occupation beginning in 1915 – a period marked, *inter alia*, by the abolition of the constitutional clause banning foreign property ownership, the US takeover of the Haitian National Bank, and the arbitrary expropriation of land by both individual and corporate US concerns.

At the same time, Haitian society continues to be deeply riven by divisions of race, class and education, and beset by a series of socioeconomic travails that post-revolutionary regimes did little to alleviate. This is a country "brutalized by the dramatic polarization of wealth and power imposed by its tiny ruling elite", as Hallward puts it, perpetuating hierarchal extremes of income, education and language that trap both the peasantry and the urban poor in continuing cycles of oppression and deprivation.[1] Many of these patterns amount to nothing more than post-revolution redux, as Hallward claims, "Much of Haiti's subsequent history has been shaped by efforts, both internal and external, to stifle the consequences of this event and to preserve the essential legacy of slavery and colonialism – that spectacularly unjust distribution of labour, wealth and power which has characterized the whole of the island's post-Columbian history."[2] Despite these drawbacks, the momentous, pathbreaking creation of the Haitian nation continues to function as a paradigm of black identitarian consciousness for many nations and cultures into the present day, as Laurent Dubois points out, "The Haitian Revolution was a uniquely transcultural movement. The population of Saint-Domingue in the eighteenth century was not just majority slave; it was also majority African. These slaves had come from many different regions and political, social, and religious contexts, and they shaped the revolution with what they brought with them."[3] Here, then, is why Haiti's ongoing political and economic destabilization – including coups and countercoups, social violence and assassinations, joblessness and poverty, and the interminable, seemingly infinite postponement of election dates – continue to shape and feed its international diaspora and its patterns of exile. While its socio-economic stature may be delimited and diminished, its people's ethnic and cultural expressiveness most certainly is not.

It may be somewhat ironic, then, given the preceding panorama of US-driven privations, that the resulting phenomenon of large-scale migration has produced a Haitian diaspora in North America alone – the so-called tenth department located primarily in Miami, Boston, New York, Toronto and Montreal – that now numbers over 1 million people, a figure that includes second- and third-generation migrants who crucially – and similarly to their Caribbean counterparts in these and other North American and European locations – refer to themselves insistently as Haitian regardless of their place of birth. Indeed, the scale of flight from the *patrie* is somewhat staggering; given a demographic population of around 7 million,[4] fully 13 per cent of Haiti's population has chosen to abandon its shores for colder, northern climes. In addition, labour-driven Haitian communities numbering in the tens of thousands can be found within the Caribbean region from the Bahamas to the French Antilles and St Lucia, as well as in the neighbouring Dominican Republic. The predominant result of this drive for displacement, this insistent migratory movement, is that while the experience of Haitians in Haiti continues to be effectively and eloquently represented by authors like Frankétienne and Yanick Lahens, who remain resident there, a simultaneous expression of the ongoing vibrancy and continuity of Haitian national identity and culture is increasingly derived from beyond its borders, as its voices of exile are articulated through a series of migrant discourses.

Transnational movement on this scale has long been an integral part of the demographic makeup of the Caribbean region, and it is now critical to the ongoing reformulation of Haitian identity as an increasingly diasporic phenomenon. Stuart Hall effectively illuminates this plural context of cultural identity, "Cultural identity . . . is a matter of 'becoming' as well as of 'being'. . . . Cultural identities come from somewhere, have histories. But, like everything which is historical, they undergo constant transformation."[5] If demographic displacement engages a process of transformation, then recognizing its value also entails a concomitant acceptance of the erasure of homogeneity as the implicit basis for national identity, as Homi Bhabha points out, "The very concepts of homogeneous national cultures . . . are in a profound process of redefinition . . . there is overwhelming evidence of . . . the hybridity of imagined communities . . . the truest eye may now belong to the migrant's double vision."[6]

As these patterns of mixing and fusion began to replicate themselves in a number of North American metropoles, overlapping with pre-existing demographies and transforming and being transformed by them, hybrid Haitian migrant communities slowly began to take shape, driven by the ubiquitous presence of its diaspora. But given their emerging patterns of language and culture, these "new" Haitian communities soon come to embody diaspora identities, along the lines that Stuart Hall has posed for the comprehension of Caribbean population movement: "Diaspora identities are those which are constantly producing and reproducing themselves anew, through transformation and difference."[7] As the accepted criteria of what it means to be Haitian continue to evolve, the discursive patterns of diaspora identity establish themselves through the intersections of Haitianness with key attributes of its new host cultures, giving rise to new patterns of cultural expression and definition, which may or may not be encoded in French. Still, migrant Haitian communities from Miami to Montreal enthusiastically affirm their attachment both to their culture of origin and to that of their newfound, adoptive home, adopting a dual, double-voiced identitarian positionality that, in its simultaneous affirmation of both its Haitian and its American axes, makes the notion of a single definition of Haitian identity, or, for that matter, defining it through its traditional geopolitical boundaries increasingly implausible propositions.

It has long been clear that culture represents an ongoing outlet of social vibrancy and national pride for the Haitian people. Indeed, as Nick Nesbitt points out, the depth and complexity of this phenomenon is nothing short of remarkable, "Haitian society is one of the most vibrant and dynamic in the world. Its people are extraordinary, having produced one of the most original and vital cultural traditions of the twentieth century including music, religion, literature, and visual art." This penchant for cultural and artistic expression is arguably intensified in the diasporic communities, since a primary facet of their continuity is the reinscription and expansion of cultural and communal ties with the homeland they have left behind, to recreate, as it were, a simulacrum of "home" that can contest the disconnection of being "away".[8] As a result, much Haitian literature, music and painting pervades, is produced in and exported from these metropolitan locations whose ever-expanding communities of migrants make them an integral part of the transnational, migrant-inflected landscape of late modernity. For example, as Haitian literature seeks to incorporate the composite characteristics of mutability, malleability and doubleness generated by the migrant experience of transplantation and transformation into the identitarian framework of the nation, exile itself is increasingly inscribed as an enabling construct. As Yanick Lahens points out, "exile is certainly one of the dimensions which, along with resistance and syncretism, give Haitian culture its coherence".[9] Given this paradoxical framework, the transnational transformation and reinscription of Haitianness reinvents and redefines identity as a protean discourse of self-expression and self-assertion whose concerns and subjects escape traditional boundaries of location, geography or history; rather, the terms and conditions that have historically positioned this literature within clearly visible geographic boundaries now give way to a fluid construct born of both displacement and difference. To take another example, the compound, even contradictory paths traced by Haitian author Dany Laferrière's trajectory from Haiti through North America are an apposite example of this double inscription. Jana Evans Braziel points out that "as a migrant writer, Laferrière's feelings for both, country of adoption and homeland are deeply ambivalent. . . . Laferrière resists both nostalgia and migration, nomadically traversing and deterritorializing the territories of each."[10] This ambivalence is often the price paid by elements of the modern diaspora, and as Haitian literary identity is increasingly perceived through its diasporic component, the production of new and extended definitions of Haitianness becomes more and more bound up with techniques for its inscription that incorporate complex issues of language, place, race and world view.

In a key article, Léon-François Hoffman insists on this increasing visibility of the representation of the migrant experience by the Haitian diaspora over time: "The diaspora could not fail to broaden considerably the sphere of experience and observation of the novelists. . . . As a result of the diaspora, novelists are, with increasing frequency, choosing Haitian life abroad as a theme."[11] Indeed, as the patterns and paradoxes of exile begin to predominate in the literature, the work of such expatriate authors as Laferrière and Danticat has veered away from politics and autobiography and begun instead to look squarely at the tensions and contradictions of exile and migrancy and their implications for Haitian and hemispheric self-definition. In Laferrière's case, for example, his writing increasingly shifts critical focus onto intersecting Antillean and Canadian patterns of transnationalism, challenging his readers to rethink supposedly settled North American histories and identities as complex sites of cultural exchange. As Laferrière himself has pointed out, "I was not interested in imitating other Caribbean writers I knew who kept writing about the country they came from after living thirty years in New York, Paris, Berlin or Montréal. I wanted to give an account of the life I was leading at the moment, not of the past."[12] In tandem with the steady growth of the migrant community, integral, long-held concepts of national boundaries, cultural authenticity and belonging began to be discarded in favour of wider-ranging notions of self and place articulated by authors of Haitian descent or origin, living and writing about the challenge of confronting the continuity or transformation of Haitian identity and culture in Montreal, Havana, Paris and New York, and of doing so in French, English or Spanish. As these new spatial and linguistic patterns are inscribed as key components of a hybrid, extended Haitian discourse, its patterns and principles are perhaps best embodied in the work and persona of Edwidge Danticat. Born in Haiti in 1969, Danticat came to the United States at the age of twelve and attended Barnard College and Brown University. She is the recipient of numerous nominations and awards for her published work, the first of which, *Breath, Eyes, Memory*, appeared when she was twenty-five; more importantly, English is Danticat's chosen language of creative expression and national identity. In breaching the boundaries of the traditional treatment of identity and nation, Danticat and others work to liberate their literature from the constraints of autobiography, linearity and the intersection of language and history. Such subversive strategies are particularly apparent in the work of Dany Laferrière, whose work develops multiple, intersecting narrative discourses and subjective perspectives through which the traditional ties linking identity to ethnicity, language and place are effectively undermined. Thus, longstanding and largely restrictive discursive patterns have now been superseded by the explosive growth and influence of continental expatriate communities and their ongoing redefinition of Haitian writing, Haitian culture and Haitian belonging.

II

Before turning to close consideration of the representation of migrant Haitian identity as inscribed in Edwidge Danticat's work, it should be noted that the demographic and discursive developments outlined above speak directly to the radical transformation of the terms in which the Haitian diaspora articulates its experiences, where the concatenation of communities, generations, visibility, and artistic and cultural articulation have resulted in the emergence of pluralized discourses of identitarian expression. Clearly, as Hoffman suggests, the literary axes of writing and publication are increasingly being shaped by this diasporic growth and visibility; as he puts it, "Because of the diaspora, the most significant events for Haitian literary life have occurred outside the country."[13] And indeed the extreme scope of such events is ironically underlined by the recent tragic and unnecessary death of Edwidge Danticat's uncle, the Reverend Joseph N. Dantica, whose medical condition during his refugee incarceration was ignored by the US Department of Homeland Security.[14] From a more literary standpoint, however, the dualities and alternating axes of identity embodied by Danticat's protagonists, Sophie and her mother, Martine, figures their inscription as subjects doubly and simultaneously rooted in both New York and Haiti. They carry with them the indelible traces of this cultural hybridity, traces that are increasingly a hallmark both of the specific discourses of Haitian identity and a more generalized articulation of identity in a migrant postcolonial context. As Stuart Hall explains,

> Such people retain strong links with their places of origin and their traditions, but . . . are obliged to come to terms with the new cultures they inhabit, without simply assimilating to them and losing their identities completely. They bear upon them the traces of the particular cultures, traditions, languages and histories by which they were shaped . . . they are irrevocably the product of several interlocking histories and cultures, belong at one and the same time to several "homes". . . . They must learn to inhabit at least two identities, to speak two cultural languages, to translate and negotiate between them.[15]

Being Haitian in New York

The patterns of these doubled identities and their hybridized cultural affiliations come increasingly to characterize the modern Haitian migrant condition, portraying a subjectivity that effectively derives its validity both from the host nation and from the patterns of nation and culture of the country of origin. When Édouard Glissant speaks of "identification . . . with a culture, not yet with a nation", it is the articulation of cultural affiliation and its varied modes of expression that is of paramount importance.[16] Ultimately, Danticat probes the parameters of what it means to be Haitian and affirms the valency of the hybridized, exilic Haitian subject who asserts her attachment to her homeland even as she interrogates the pros and cons of her own experience of migrancy.

Breath, Eyes, Memory[17] is Edwidge Danticat's semi-autobiographical, English-inscribed evocation of the dualities and tensions produced by this enforced separation from the Haitian homeland, and in it she addresses many of the positionalities and paradoxes of exile that we have discussed thus far, making it in many respects a paradigmatic example of contemporary Haitian novelistic discourse. Having spent the first years of her life with her surrogate mother, Tante Atie, Sophie Caco's story begins when a letter arrives, summoning her to a new life in New York with the mother she has never known; symbolically then, her mother, Martine, comes to represent the unknowns of the migrant life, while Sophie's intimate relationship with Tante Atie can be read as her inscription in a homeland that somehow still manages to keep its distance. Once in New York, Haiti's looming presence in their migrant lives – and its concomitant production of a set of hybrid cultural practices – is evoked in myriad ways; from language (creole) to food (*boudin*), to the pressing presence of Haitian convenience stores and restaurants that punctuate the community and alleviate their sense of exile. Indeed, a major and overarching theme of the novel is a paramount and penetrating trauma and conviction of guilt at having "escaped" that characterizes the New York lives of both Sophie and Martine. In addition, there is the communication with and transfers of money to those still at home, and the ever-present primacy of Haitian beliefs, customs and social stratification in their lives. At the same time, the downside of this exile is also clearly proclaimed; the social segregation, stigmatization and difference that afflict the day-to-day condition of the Haitian migrant in America, inherent in such appalling characterizations as HBO – an American acronym for Haitian body odour – or the widespread association of Haitians with AIDS, is a clear sense of the range of intractable differences that continue to separate the Haitian migrant community both from the black American community and from American culture at large.

The pressing paradoxes of Haitian migrant life delineated above – as well as the further specificity of their non-French inscription – illustrate the extent to which the varied, and even contradictory, character and experiences of the Haitian diaspora cannot be simply or neatly categorized. Indeed, the complexities lived by Haitian communities both on and off the island are powerfully indicative of what the Haitian critic Marie-Denise Shelton calls "the contradictions of the modern Haitian diaspora . . . . What emerges . . . are images, of fragmentation, separation, moral and economic distress, human loss, but also of faint hope."[18] Now, if the "separation" and "distress" to which Shelton refers are themselves ultimately juxtaposed to the possibility of "faint hope", then the mother's ongoing alienation and searing nightmares, from which she is awakened screaming by Sophie almost every night, bespeak both a fundamental lack of coherence with her adopted culture and a symbolic, ongoing homeland-driven trauma resulting from her rape in Haiti by an anonymous *Tonton Macoute*. In a larger sense, this violent encounter makes of Martine the novel's chief symbol of the suffering of the Haitian nation itself, one carried out at the hands of Martine's national counterparts. This symbolic inscription of Haitian life as implying the ongoing and overwhelming risk of victimhood is later echoed, retrospectively, by the scene of sadistic violence at the airport – again involving a *Tonton Macoute* – that marks the moment of Sophie's departure from Haiti, and its ineradicable resonances generate a basic dis-ease in Martine that ultimately also marks her complex, contradictory relationship to a country and culture that – simultaneously familiar yet estranged – once oppressed and yet still beckon to her. While she praises the less restrained cultural mores of her new American home, which sets no constraints on her relationship with her boyfriend, Marc – "In Haiti, it would not be possible for someone like Marc to love someone like me. He is from a very upstanding family" (p. 59) – she also pursues specific traditions from the old country, like "testing" Sophie to see if she is still a virgin. This tradition represents nothing but a perpetuation of mores of maternal power that are at odds with her own personal history even as they turn her into her own daughter's primary oppressor. Indeed, this odious and repeated practice of "testing", particularly read in conjunction with the prevalence of rape in the novel, provides a symbolic means of examining Haiti's longstanding political instability. The overt intimacy and sexualization – and their attendant suffering and humiliation – implied in this act opens up a number of possible referents, among which are Haiti's bloody succession of political rulers and the generations of abuse that is their heritage. In her turn, as she is increasingly made subject to the "racial" perceptions of otherness that are the seamy underbelly of American life, Sophie conveys the searing combination of stereotyping and denigration that is still the untold lot of Haitian migrants to the land of the free, "It was as if I had never left Haiti.... Outside the school, we were 'the Frenchies', cringing in our mock-Catholic school uniforms as the students from the public school across the street called us 'boat people' and 'stinking Haitians' " (p. 66). Ultimately, then, Sophie has simply exchanged one form and place of alienation and oppression for another, begging the question of whether this is an adequate price to pay for the separation and the prejudices that are part and parcel of exile.

When Sophie meets the older, American-born Joseph, it might be said that her interest is piqued by his interest in her; in a very important way, it seems that she comes to desire his desire, rather than Joseph himself, and her problematic, indeed conflicted, association with him marks her incomplete inscription in both the racial and the cultural frameworks of her exilic home: ultimately, she rationalizes to herself his symbolic representation of a certain protectiveness and familiarity. Importantly, however, this relationship itself is also drawn into, and is driven by, Sophie's ongoing battle of wills with her mother; finally, this conflict engenders physical suffering bordering on masochism, as Sophie deliberately violates herself with a pestle so that she can fail her mother's continuing practice of "testing" by implying sexual activity with Joseph, her American boyfriend whom she has represented to her mother as Haitian, as a way of pre-empting disapproval and anger on the part of Martine. Since any sexual activity is in reality unconsummated, Sophie uses this relationship to escape her mother's domineering intrusiveness on the one hand, materially and symbolically exacerbating her own subjugation in the process, while she eventually finds that she experiences limited pleasure – rather, indeed, real discomfort – in her ultimate conjugal relationship with Joseph on the other. This double disjuncture from both sex and masculinity in the novel sets up the identitarian alienation of Sophie herself, since she now undergoes both physical and mental suffering symbolic of her material and affective displacement from her family and from her place of origin. When it is ultimately revealed that she is the biological result of her mother's rape, this chilling fact analeptically provides the overarching context for the multiple facets of Sophie's social and cultural disease and, through her, for the diachronic victimization of the Haitian people by disparate forces in various places, a fact also signified through Martine's continued suffering following her encounter with the *Tonton Macoute* rapist. Even as this relationship with Joseph develops, and Sophie spins a web of lies to explain Joseph away to her mother, these double axes of female suffering symbolically represent the broadbased trauma of the Haitian body politic, represented through the double disjunctures of both Sophie's and Martine's tentative inscriptions in their new migrant culture and Martine's conflicted attitude to the one she left behind. Accepting Sophie's reconstruction of Joseph as the scion of a Haitian immigrant family – a lie Sophie knows her mother wants to hear – Martine proceeds to warn Sophie – herself transplanted, if not exactly "new-generation" – of the pitfalls of migrant patterns of belonging, particularly with regard to "metropolitan" Haitians, " 'It is really hard for the new-generation girls,' she began. 'You will have to choose between the really old-fashioned Haitians and the new-generation Haitians. The old-fashioned ones are not exactly prize fruits. They make you cook plantains and rice and beans and never let you feed them lasagna. The problem with the new generation is that a lot of them have lost their sense of obligation to the family's honor' " (p. 80). This exchange illuminates a plurality of perspectives on the migrant condition, not least the ways in which its paradoxical patterns of migrancy and belonging can change from generation to generation. Further, Stuart Hall's critical articulation of the Caribbean as having been engendered in diaspora, one whose patterns and boundaries continue to extend and transform themselves across both time and space, receives implicit approbation through this categorical juxtaposition. For Martine, transplanted Haitians constitute an identitarian dilemma, caught between rice and beans, and lasagna. They are caught between home and away, with those born in Haiti showing a blind adherence to past practice and a negation of modernity, while those of the new hybrid communities lack a sense of history and cultural continuity, as they seek to conform to the patterns and practices of the only home they have really known. Ultimately, this dichotomy threatens to place the concept and continuity of Haitianness itself into question. In this sense, then, the various filaments of this symbolic, attitudinal triangle of Marc, Martine and Joseph foregrounds the myriad undecidabilities that paradoxically underscore for Martine what it means to be Haitian.

Eventually, confronting these tensions becomes too much for Sophie, and with their daughter, Brigitte, she summarily abandons Joseph to return to the *patrie* and, more particularly, to her surrogate mother Tante Atie. Following this voyage of rediscovery and a reinscription into her half-forgotten, half-unknown culture that becomes a sort of pilgrimage, she visits the cemetery with her aunt, becomes reacquainted with the branches of her family tree, the Cacos, and, in a sense, relearns what it means to be a Haitian woman, integrating bits of folklore that have long determined local feminine identity, "According to Tante Atie, each finger had a purpose. It was the way she had been taught to prepare herself to become a woman. Mothering. Boiling. Loving. Baking. Nursing. Frying. Healing. Washing. Ironing. Scrubbing. It wasn't her fault, she said. Her ten fingers had been named for her even before she was born" (p. 151). Faced with this literal and figurative synecdoche of the domesticated role expected of women in Haitian society, Atie does express a recognition of the social and sexual subjection of women that such a role represents and a certain wistfulness that things could be otherwise: "Sometimes, she even wished she had six fingers on each hand so she could have two left for herself" (p. 151). Sophie, however, appears to have no opinion on the matter, still unable herself to come to terms with the implications of this (re)discovery of her hybrid cultural identity.

Joseph, in his turn, is surprised when, near the end of the novel, Sophie refers to Haiti for the first time as "home" following her return from this voyage, one that functions as rediscovery, reassessment and redemption, as well as a voyage of baptism for Brigitte. While her response, "What else would I call it?" seems to point towards a final recognition and inscription of origins and belonging, Joseph's rejoinder, "Home has always been your mother's house, that you could never go back to" (p. 195), suggests that he has always seen her as a (transplanted) American, without a past, rooted only in that soil, tracing a life begun only at the moment of her arrival in New York, and primarily marked by her rebellion against the maternal authority figure. Joseph thus simultaneously recognizes and denies the value of the Haitian axis in Sophie's life. But when, ironically, her mother then voices similar sentiments, telling her, "You have become very American. . . . You are different, but that's okay. I am different too" (pp. 179–80), it becomes clear that the mother's implicit claim of shared experience is substantially different from Sophie's doubled sense of difference and otherness. It is also a tacit acknowledgement of the primal psychoses of rape and its corollary of trauma that are irrevocably associated with the homeland. Martine's suicide upon becoming pregnant again ultimately provides proof positive of the ineradicable trace of this event. Sophie accompanies the body back to Haiti for burial, and the symbolic resolution engendered by this moment finally permits her a moment of extraordinary subjective and cultural insight, "I come from a place where breath, eyes, and memory are one, a place from which you carry your past like the hair on your head" (p. 234). In this ultimate acknowledgement of the ineluctable continuity of roots and origins,

Sophie, critically, does not overtly choose a single cultural path, does not deny either her Haitianness or her Americanness. Thus it is that when, at the novel's end, Tante Atie again asks her the critical question, strategically and uncoincidentally voiced in the cadences of Creole, "*Ou libéré?* Are you free my daughter?" Atie is able to see the response to her own question, "Now . . . you will know how to answer" (p. 234). Sophie's liberation, here, is both subjective and cultural; what Tante Atie perceives, and elliptically articulates, is Sophie's relocation beyond national boundaries of identity and belonging; that while she may not still live in Haiti, Haiti will always live within her, and she is both product and symbol of this critical encounter between positionality and place, tradition and modernity. In the end, Sophie may be *in* New York, but is not *of* it; likewise, she is simultaneously *of* Haiti but not *in* it, and it is in this doubled positionality, representing a range of affective attachments, whose importance supersedes physical location that determines who she is and where, ultimately, her allegiances lie.

Language plays a key role in this migrant reordering of identity, and the myriad moments when Haitian Creole intersects with the English narrative structure of *Breath, Eyes, Memory* serve to remind us both of the impenetrability of Creole – the impossibility of a complete rendition of its myriad communicative nuances into English, French or any other metropolitan language – and of its critical mediation of cultural difference and cultural continuity, particularly as regards the separation suffered by migrant communities. The inscription of Creole in this text, then, sporadic as it may be, is meant both to mark the continuity of Haitian culture beyond national borders and to illuminate the psychic and positional duality that marks the migrant subject. Indeed, as Frantz Fanon reminds us, speaking a language "means above all to assume a culture, to support the weight of a civilization".[19] The linguistic pattern that Fanon points to here, mirrored in the continuing demographic movements toward the modern metropolis, emphasizes the problematic nexus between language, place and identity, a complex conundrum which was once a function of the colonial encounter, but now increasingly marks the migrant moment. In this insistently anglophone culture, the suturing role played by Haitian creole in engendering and maintaining Haitian cultural identity beyond Haitian shores appears to be an ineluctable one, a transcendence of geographic boundaries and a contestation of exile through a sort of umbilical psycholinguistic connection that we see inscribed into texts not only from Haitian authors, but from the wider French Caribbean as well.

Danticat's *Breath, Eyes, Memory* is thus a paradigmatic example of the intersecting themes and tensions that converge in the writing and representation of the Haitian experience today. Her insistence on figuring this experience through the mother-daughter dyad, for example, draws on a long-familiar trope for reading the politics of colonialism and independence in the Caribbean, and their larger political implications; indeed, it allows her to critique both the condition of contemporary Haiti and the complex corollaries that frame its ever-growing diaspora. Danticat accomplishes this largely by displacing traditional female generational tensions into complex sociopolitical contexts, such that, as Marianne Hirsch argues, the polyvalent layers and complexities of the mother/daughter plot ultimately create a situation in which "Oedipal frameworks are modified by other psychological and narrative economies".[20] As a result, the deliberate conjunction of the contradictions of migrant life with the trauma of the politicized Haitian body engenders a reconfiguration of the concepts of Haitian subjectivity and belonging and the terms of their representation as they occur both inside and outside Haitian borders.

Gender and culture are thus critical tools that are incontrovertibly intertwined for Danticat's exploration of contemporary Haitianness. In both theme and form, her work is at the representative cusp of today's multinational, multilingual and multicultural Haitian experience. These twin analytical axes displace discourse and identity into a new framework, as together they illuminate key aspects of the pride in and paradoxes of Haitian identity. Danticat's specific shaping of the cultural identity through which the Haitian people seek to represent themselves is especially cognizant of the material and symbolic tensions of this maternal axis; "the result", as Carole Boyce Davies writes, "is that a shared exploration of gender and heritage is an inseparable aspect of a singular articulation of cultural identity".[21] As the multiple sites and resonances of the Haitian experience, in the Caribbean and beyond, are translated into international patterns of language and subjectivity, the traumas that are the product of history and politics ultimately cannot impede a prideful Haitian identity from assuming its rightful place and articulating its right to be heard.

In conclusion, I would like to suggest further that the complex case of contemporary Haitian writing embodies in fine the creative, polymorphous paradoxes posed by the larger case of migrant writing, in all its many guises; indeed, it is not simply borders, but our traditional perspectives on and definitions of nationalism and cultural identity and their implicit limits that must undergo revision and amplification. Writing the compound Haitian migrant experience from beyond Haiti's geopolitical borders, while marking a bold new axis of Haitian creative expression on the one hand, also risks fragmenting the broader Haitian community into an artificially constructed series of oppositional fragments. In this regard, Yanick Lahens aptly warns against an implicit and incipient binarism, as well as its attendant essentialist corollaries, of "paradigms of outside/inside referring once more to an essentialism whether territorial or national", and encourages us to "rethink the question of identity, of nationality, and of origin in order to get out of the inside/outside alternative".[22] Implicit in Lahens's critique is the all-too-common notion of a singular and integral Haitian identity, one that excludes specific groups and practices based on particular patterns and strictures of origin, language or location, and takes a geographically grounded positionality as its enabling construct. But the representations and redefinitions of Haitianness, essayed by writers like Danticat, encourage us to broaden both our perspective and our principle of inclusiveness by suggesting that any act of cultural affiliation is a moveable feast, one that is both independent of any fixed location and the product of subjective strategies of self-representation. Through this conjunction of culture, discourse and geopolitics, new boundaries, spaces and frameworks for identity and nationality are engendered; if we accept that, as Stuart Hall puts it, "a nation is not only a political entity but something which produces meanings – *a system of representation*",[23] then it will be those transnational strands of identifiably Haitian discourses and cultural practice that together will fashion a certain commonality of vision for the island's people through their scattered yet ineluctably conjoined voices.

Notes

1. Peter Hallward, "Option Zero in Haiti", *New Left Review* 27 (May–June 2004): 47.
2. Ibid., 26.
3. Laurent Dubois, *Avengers of the New World: The Story of the Haitian Revolution* (Cambridge, Mass.: Harvard University Press, 2004), 5.
4. See Jan Rogozinski, *A Brief History of the Caribbean* (New York: Plume, 1999), 267.
5. Stuart Hall, "Cultural Identity and Diaspora", in *Identity: Community, Culture, Difference*, ed. Jonathan Rutherford (London: Lawrence and Wishart, 1990), 225.
6. Homi Bhabha, *The Location of Culture* (New York: Routledge, 1994), 5.
7. Hall, "Cultural Identity and Diaspora", 235; emphasis in the original.
8. Nick Nesbitt, "Troping Toussaint, Reading Revolution", *Research in African Literatures*, special issue, Haiti 1804–2004: Literature, Culture, and Art, 35, no. 2 (2004): 19.

9. Yanick Lahens, "Exile: Between Writing and Place", *Callaloo* 15, no. 3 (1992): 736.

10. Jana Evans Braziel, "From Port-au-Prince to Montréal to Miami: Trans-American Nomads in Dany Laferrière's Migratory Texts", *Callaloo* 26, no. 1 (2003): 236.

11. Léon-François Hoffman, "The Haitian Novel during the Last Ten Years", *Callaloo* 15, no. 3 (1992): 761–62.

12. "Dany Laferrière: An Interview", Carroll F. Coates, *Callaloo* 22, no. 4 (1999): 911.

13. Hoffman, "The Haitian Novel", 765.

14. See Danticat's account of this series of events, "A Very Haitian Story", *New York Times*, op-ed page, 24 November 2004.

15. "The Question of Cultural Identity", in *Modernity and Its Futures*, ed. Stuart Hall, David Held and Tony McGrew (London: Polity Press, 1992), 310; emphasis in the original.

16. See Édouard Glissant, *Poetics of Relation*, trans. Betsy Wing. (Ann Arbor: University of Michigan Press, 1997), 13.

17. Edwidge Danticat, *Breath, Eyes, Memory* (New York: Vintage, 1994). Subsequent references to this work appear parenthetically in the text.

18. Marie-Denise Shelton, "Haitian Women's Fiction", *Callaloo* 15, no. 3 (1992): 776.

19. Frantz Fanon, *Black Skin, White Masks*, trans. Charles Lam Markmann (London: MacGibbon and Kee, 1968), 17–18.

20. Marianne Hirsch, *The Mother/Daughter Plot: Narrative, Psychoanalysis, Feminism* (Bloomington and Indianapolis: Indiana University Press, 1989), 8.

21. Carole Boyce Davies, "Writing Home: Gender and Heritage in the Works of Afro-Caribbean/American Women Writers", in *Out of the Kumbla: Caribbean Women and Literature*, ed. Carole Boyce Davies and Elaine Savory Fido (Trenton, NJ: Africa World Press, 1990), 59.

22. Lahens, "Exile: Between Writing and Place", 745.

23. Hall, *Modernity and Its Futures*, 292; emphasis in the original.

Chapter 10

Dancing at the Border
Cultural Translations and the Writer's Return

Elizabeth Walcott-Hackshaw

There are two important moments for a traveller . . . the moment of departure and of return.

– Dany Laferrière

Embrace me without fear . . . then I will speak for you.

– Aimé Césaire

When we think of the diaspora and literature of the diaspora, we should recall Stuart Hall's idea that the Caribbean itself has always been a diaspora[1] and as such has always had diasporic writers. Emphasizing the dynamic process of constant transformation, cultures, as Hall states, are always in translation: "Jamaican culture is a translation of European and African and Indian cultures. And Jamaican culture in England is a translation of that translation, composed out of African, European, and Indian cultures in the Caribbean, now further translated in relation to twenty-first-century Britain and Europe. That is what culture is: it's not something which stands still, which never moves."[2]

This notion of translation destabilizes the concepts of fixed locations of "here" and "there", since one of the two locations, depending on where you are, is supposed to have the "pure" culture and the other is a modification or translation of that culture. But for Hall, both "here" and "there" exist in perpetual translation; each generation modifying and generating its culture. Locating Caribbean culture has always been about crossing borders, borders that have been both physical and imaginary, borders that also exist within the islands themselves.

But how do we locate Caribbean diasporas when we are still grappling with basic questions that become even more complicated when polemic constructs are removed and when fusion (or perhaps confusion) is taking place between "here" and "there"? How do we define or locate Literatures of the Caribbean in this era of *errance* and migration? What does it mean to be a Caribbean writer? A Haitian writer? How do the writers of the diaspora define themselves and their literature? And, more importantly, do they even need to?

With the echo of these haunting questions still hovering, I would like to formulate and interrogate other questions by focusing on an old, reoccurring theme in Caribbean literature, that of the writer's return to his "native land" and the treatment of this theme by two authors of Haitian origin, Edwidge Danticat and Dany Laferrière. Both writers, now based in North America, navigate returns to Haiti with the gaze of both observer and participant. In his work *Pays sans chapeau*[3] (1997), Laferrière relates the account of his writer-personage Vieux Os's[4] return to Port-au-Prince after twenty years in Montreal and Miami. In *After the Dance*[5] (2002), a work that can be characterized as part travelogue, part memoir, Danticat returns to Haiti to experience Carnival in Jacmel for the first time. My interest in these texts stems from the manner in which these two writers translate and represent their experience of a return "home" in two distinct manners. Although they both engage in a discourse of return and share similar preoccupations, their experiences and treatment of return are unique. In order to expose the individual nature of each text I would like to investigate the following questions: What is the role of location in the writers return? How do these diasporic writers reconstruct the island space? How do they negotiate feelings of liminality, cultural indeterminacy and dislocation? And, finally, how do we compare the returns of Danticat and Laferrière to that of Césaire's? The choices made by these writers in their selection of spaces, and the (non)-identification between self and landscape, help shape the argument. These interrogations, informed by Stuart Hall's notion of culture as translation, are the preoccupations of this paper.

Lived Borders of Dream and Reality or Location Ambiguities

In exploring the notion of a writer's return, Aimé Césaire's seminal work, *Cahier d'un Retour au pays natal*, provides an important if obvious *point de départ*. In the *Cahier* there is seemingly the total integration between self and territory; we see this particularly at the end where the poem reunites, in a celebratory note, self and native land with the famous lines, "Et nous sommes debout maintenant, mon pays et moi"[6] (And we are standing now, my country and I). There is a complete identification between poet and homeland. The island space is inhabited in an unambiguous manner; there is no ambiguity of location, no uncertainty at the border. But the *Cahier* does not begin on this secure footing with a rooted identification between self and native land, instead, the text situates the homecoming in a liminal space. Gregson Davis, in *Aimé Césaire*,[7] argues that at the beginning of the poem both speaker and audience are located on an indeterminate time threshold that is neither day nor night. According to Davis, "This liminal space occupied by the poetic creator is precisely what Césaire emphasizes in his own aesthetic manifesto, 'Poetry and Knowledge' ('Poésie et Connaissance'),[8] which locates the poet 'at the lived borders of dream and reality, of day and night, between absence and presence' ('aux confins vécus du rêve et du réel, du jour et de la nuit, entre absence et présence')."[9]

This in-between state is created by the poet's ambiguous location in the poem's first lines. The refrain, "Au bout du petit matin" (At the end of early dawn), Davis contends, positions the poet between two worlds, at the margins where cultures intersect, and above all where lines of identity become blurred.[10] The trajectory in the *Cahier* moves from the liminal, an in-between state, to one of complete identification with the landscape and the people. These ambiguities in location are the result of the fusion/confusion that is created as the writer moves between two states of territorial identification between *moi* and *territoire* or the inverse, non-identification between the writer's "I" and the territory. Both, Danticat and Laferrière occupy liminal spaces between the *Pays Rêvé* and the *Pays Réel* at different times during their return to Haiti; it is at these times that they inhabit Césaire's borderland of dream and reality.

The notion of liminality and of alternating between states of dream and reality is apparent in Laferrière's construction of *Pays sans chapeau*; the first and last chapters of the novel are entitled "Un Écrivain Primitif". In fact, Laferrière claims that when he writes, he tries to create a similar effect as the primitive Haitian artists, "when I write, I try to do as they do. . . . I try to mesmerize the reader so that he can only imagine the universe that I have created".[11] However, the rest of the work alternates for the most part between the headings "Pays Rêvé" and the "Pays Réel" with the exception of his voyage to the "Pays sans chapeau" and the final chapter which is entitled "Pays Rêvé/Pays Réel". This division and structural pattern play an important role in the writer-personage's negotiation of his return. Not only do the alternating chapter titles differ in their structure but also in treatment and content. In the "Pays Réel" chapters, Laferrière uses the technique of short subheadings that focus on a particular object, idea or incident. In the first "Pay Réel" chapter alone, we have a wide range of subheadings including: *The Suitcase, Time, The Hill, The New House, Coffee, The Gray Dress, The Objects, Spaghetti* and *The Prayer*. Laferrière, a master of dialogue, often uses these short studies as a way to insist on the ordinary or the real and at the same time expose the sometimes extra-ordinary quality of the everyday. In the conversations with his mother, or Tante Renée, and later with other Haitians on the streets of Port-au-Prince, we see this ability in Laferrière to combat misery with every day humour, to inject the tragic with the comic in the tone of the quotidian. This is very much in keeping with Laferrière's ideas of the fusion between literature and life: "Literature and life have always merged for me. . . . This is not a concept, an ideology or some marketing strategy. It's life and in life you bump into objects. These signs of daily life. The telephone, car, bicycle, a watch. . . . And these objects tell the story of our lives. . . . For me the quotidian is fundamental, it prevents us from dreaming beyond our means."[12]

In the "Pays Rêvé" chapters, although Laferrière's maintains a clearly conversational tone, the structural treatment differs. The writer himself states: "For me the reader is someone that I am having a conversation with."[13] These chapters are no longer divided into short studies or short exchanges; here the focus is on his work as writer, and as we will see later on, a central concern is the world of the dead. In Laferrière's novel, a sense of in-betweeness, of alternating states, is created by the movement between "Pays Réel" and "Pays Rêvé".

With Danticat, a similar feeling of liminality occurs as the writer describes the experience of Jacmel before and after Carnival. In the travelogue/memoir, Danticat, combines personal history, Haitian history and the island's present political situation with a plethora of allusions to other voices that inform the writer's own interrogation of return. The temporal shifts from past to present in the text help perpetuate the feeling of errancy.

These questions of liminality and ambiguities of location are central to our understanding of the writer's return. In fact, the title of Laferrière's text immediately engages the reader into an interrogation of location. *Pays sans chapeau* is the world of the dead, so named, Laferrière tells us, because the dead are not buried with their hats. Laferrière's journey to Haiti is also a journey to a *Pays sans chapeau*. Early in the novel we learn from Laferrière's mother that Haiti has become a land of zombies, of the walking dead. Haiti in fact epitomizes an ambiguous, liminal location where living and living-dead coexist.

> – You know, Old Bones, this country has changed
> – I've definitely seen that mama.
> – No, not how you think. This country has really changed. We've hit rock-bottom. They are no longer human.[14]

His mother goes on to describe a growing army of zombies and a cemetery emptied of its dead. Typical of Laferrière's provocative style, seemingly extraordinary, fantastic ideas are examined in the most logical, scholarly manner. Vieux Os decides to investigate what his mother has told him about the zombies by talking to authorities on the subject. He visits Professor J.B. Romain and learns that an army of zombies does exist, probably created by "le vieux Président" to fight against the American army.[15] This is confirmed in another discussion with yet another authority on the subject, professor and psychiatrist Legrand Bijou: "Laferriere, we are different. The Americans take away their dead, we Blacks continue to add to ours."[16]

According to Legrand, the CIA has often toppled Third World leaders by starving their peoples. But with an army of zombies who do not need food, this weapon is ineffective. The Americans, he claims, are secretly studying the phenomena of Haitian zombification; they have also set up a Space Station and, according to a friend of Laferrière's mother, a Haitian, not an American, was the first person to land on the moon: "It seems that Kennedy got into a mad rage when he found out about the Haitian on the moon who had obviously gotten there before Armstrong."[17] All of these discussions about the army of zombies, the Haitian on the moon and empty cemeteries take place in the "Pays Rêvé" chapters as if to reinforce the context of the unreal or even the surreal. But Laferière also paints a hyper-reality which forces us to see that many Haitians are in fact zombified beyond hunger, or even starvation. Laferrière wants to understand how "the Haitian mind works",[18] particularly within the context of their tragic circumstance.

Danticat shares Laferrière's preoccupation with the dead and the possibilities of understanding a culture through that culture's treatment of death and the dead. In *After the Dance* Danticat talks of her interest in cemeteries: "I have always enjoyed cemeteries. Altars for the living as well as resting places for the dead, they are entryways, and I think, to any town or city, the best places to become acquainted with the tastes of the inhabitants, both present and gone."[19] According to her cemetery guide, the poet Rodney Saint-Eloi, the best way to enter a cemetery is from the back since it alerts the dead that they are not here to stay.[20] For Danticat, cemeteries are historic, cultural, artistic spaces. But in Haiti they are places that hold the memories of tragedy and tyranny. She reminds the reader of François Duvalier's ("Papa Doc's") legacy; the dictator would dress like the figure, Baron Samedi, the keeper of the cemeteries, to remind all Haitians that he "literally held the key and could decide at will who the next inhabitants would be".[21] Danticat also identifies the phenomenon of zombification that exists during and after the carnival in Jacmel. She describes the carnival zombies on the Sunday before carnival and remembers that, in an interview with a reporter, Haitian writer René Depestre referred to Jacmel itself as a zombie affirming that "Jacmel is no longer Jacmel".[22]

Both writers' preoccupation with death and zombification is also framed by their notion of return, for within the celebration of prodigal returns, these two writers are forced to confront and translate onto the page the purgatorial existence of Haiti as a *Pays sans chapeau*. Each writer has a different landscape of return. The primary location of Vieux Os's return is to his mother's home, a return to the interior. There is in fact a direct link between Laferrière's return to Haiti and the return to his mother's home; she is Haiti to him: "My mother will never leave her country. But if ever she does, I will feel that there is no longer a country. I completely identify my mother with this country."[23] Only after we get a clear sense of that home does Vieux Os move outside, into the streets of Port-au-Prince.

The contrast here with Danticat is quite stark. Although her interior dialogue is what paints her image of Haiti, Danticat's descriptions focus on the physical landscape of Jacmel, both human and natural. She takes us through the countryside, the towns, and we meet different people along the way that enrich the experience of her return. This is in keeping with her desire to become a participant in Jacmel Carnival; the landscape of Danticat's return is exterior in this regard.

As a child growing up in Haiti, raised by her uncle, who was a Baptist minister, Danticat was forbidden to "join the Carnival". This return is part of a pilgrimage to exorcise her carnival demons; she is "aching for a baptism by crowd here, among my own people".[24] And at the end of the work she describes how this baptism has been attained, revealing the cathartic effect of the carnival, allowing her to experience seemingly contradictory states of anonymity and belonging: "At last, my body is a tiny fragment of a much larger being. I am part of a group possession, a massive stream of joy. . . . There is nothing that seems to matter as much as following the curve of the other bodies pressed against mine. In that brief space and time, the carnival offers all the paradoxical elements I am craving: anonymity, jubilant community, and belonging."[25]

The real and imaginary landscapes of the two writers alternate between interior and exterior locations, between feelings of individuality and belonging. In *Pays sans chapeau*, the feeling of movement between mental and physical landscapes is constant. In both worlds, the "Pays Réel" and the "Pays Rêvé", the writer-personage is either walking through the streets of Port-au-Prince, in a taxi with his mother, in the market with his mother, visiting a professor, visiting old friends or travelling through yet another world, even of the dead. In this respect it is as much a log of Laferrière's return as it is of Danticat's.

The title of Danticat's text proves useful when considering this sense of travel and movement; in the text we experience more of "after" and "before" the dance than the dance itself. Much of the discussion on carnival remains descriptive and seldom evokes the movement, music or rhythm of carnival, until the end when Danticat takes part in the dance herself. Before then it is the gaze of the observer who is trying hard to become less distant and whose dream it is to become one with the other revellers. With Laferrière we are seldom still. Even the conversations in *Pays sans chapeau* demand a mental journey to another place. This movement of the imagination on the page is typical of Laferrière's style: "I make the words dance on the floor of a white page."[26]

There is then a paradoxical movement in both texts. In *After the Dance* we see Danticat's desire to be a part of the dance, but she remains at the border until the very end of her journey; in Laferrière's case, the writer-personage is engaged in movement or dance with his *pays* from the beginning, but unlike Danticat, he never feels the need to express this desire to be part of it. How then do we read this complex play on movement between individual and community, or interior and exterior within the context of identification and non-identification? What does it say about the writer's relationship with his native land?

Passport Please: Masks, Mirrors and IDs

Navigating the writer's "I" in both Laferrière and Danticat leads to a greater understanding of how each writer negotiates the question of (self)-identification. Both

Laferrière and Danticat use the writer's "I" to engage the reader in a game of masking and unmasking, of identification and non-identification. The question of the writer's identity and the writer as personage is particularly relevant in the case of Laferrière, who uses the personage of Vieux Os as a protagonist in his works. However, in *Pays sans chapeau*, the last novel of his "Autobiographie américaine",[27] Laferrière refers to himself, for the first time as Laferrière. Bernard Magnier, in his interview with the writer, asks whether the reference to himself as himself in *Pays sans chapeau* marks an end to his creative journey. Laferrière's reply is instructive:

> In Haitian mythology, once someone says his real name it's over, he's lifted the mask. He's shown his real face. . . . Vieux Os is a childhood character, one of intimacy. My grandmother called me by that name and my mother kept it all through my adolescence. Old Bones is the character that the author created in order to be able to survive the North American Jungle. . . . In *L'odeur du café*, the first of this "American Autobiography", the narrator says that if someone knows your real name that person can make you his slave. In the last novel *Pays sans chapeau*, Old Bones reveals his real name.[28]

But if Laferrière has called his opus "Une Autobiographie américaine" are we thus supposed to see the "I" as autobiographical? Philippe Lejeune contends that in autobiographical works there is a "pacte autobiographique"[29] (an autobiographical pact) in which author, narrator and character are identical. However, the "I" in Lafèrriere is situated in a unique, liminal location; it is neither "autobiographie" nor "autofiction"[30] but located somewhere in between.

Laferrière has spoken on numerous occasions about the use of his writer's "I". In *J'écris comme je vis*, he clearly states that he writes about his life using characters, events and adventures from his own life; he combines his *vie réelle* with his fictional life, his *vie écrite*. Laferrière insists on the unity of the two: "I do not see any distance between my life and my books."[31] It is the personage of the writer in Laferrière that helps him to travel and to exist without borders: "The real creation is the writer's character. This writer-personage allows me to infiltrate any place, into the most private lives, into the most exclusive clubs; it allows me to cross classes, races, and countries. This character is not married and has no children while I am married and have three children. This writer-personage allows me to travel. . . . It's a character without roots."[32]

This notion of creation, combined with the use of autobiography and autofiction, makes it difficult to make clear distinctions between the "I" of the *vie réelle* or the "I" of the *vie écrite*. A hybrid action takes place between the truth of real life and the truth of the text. But it is the use of Laferrière as the "I/protagonist" or "I/narrator" that is unique, especially since we are unable to make clear distinctions between the voice of Laferrière and the voice of the character:

> Certain uses of "I" are simply a narrative strategy to make the work easier to read: the reader is used to "I" so give him "I". On the other hand, there is another "I" more commonly used, in manner that is truly appropriate, very discreet, and very natural: that is the "I" in *L'odeur du café*, in *Charme des après-midi sans fin*, *Chronique de la dérive douce*, and *Pays sans chapeau* . . . my novels are an autobiography of my emotions, my reality, my fantasies. None of these aspects of my personality is more authentic than the other.[33]

This unfixed, liminal, rootless, multiple, plural "I"[34] is in keeping with the manner in which Laferrière defines himself; there is first the insistence on non-identification with the range of possible identifications: "Immigrant writer, Ethnic writer, Caribbean writer, cross-cultural writer, Post-Colonial writer, or Black writer . . . . I am condemned to having a label stuck to my back no matter what stance I take."[35] He states emphatically, "I am a Haitian, I am a writer, but I am not a Haitian writer."[36]

Laferrière would no doubt resist the classification of a Disaporic writer. For he is "too ambitious to belong to any one country. I am universal."[37] Identification with a place or an identity in Laferrière's work is as much a question of location, both physical and psychological, as it is one of national, ethnic, cultural or any other identity. Just as his writer's "I" has no fixed or rooted nationality, so too does Laferrière inhabit a liminal identity, dancing at the borders, forever in motion. *Pays sans chapeau* translates this movement, this lack of rootedness. He has not returned in *Pays sans chapeau* to proclaim his Haitianness, nor has he a desire, like Danticat, to be identified as part of a collective. He has not returned to be the voice of his people adopting a Césarian stance. He has not returned to proclaim his Négritude or his Créolité. For Laferrière, the return is the end of a cycle of the "Pays Réel" and the "Pays Rêvé" ending a cycle of this writer's plural I-dentities.

In *After the Dance*, Danticat uses the trope of masking throughout her travel-memoir. In the opening pages she admits to "wearing my own mask of distant observer",[38] of her desire to "throw away the mas"[39] and show her true colours, to reveal herself. For Danticat, carnival becomes a metaphor of identification with the collective and a means of liberation, allowing her to temporarily let go of her distant observer-writer personage. Danticat's plural "I", like Laferrière's, is linked to her negotiation of the many representations of the "I" as writer-observer or reveller-participant. Removing and replacing these masks is the manner in which Danticat is able to understand her experience of return.

After the Dance traces a return that resembles a Césairian trajectory in which identification with the community is essential. In the opening pages of Danticat's work, there is the confusion created by the writer's liminality expressed by her desire to be part of the collective and her psychological position as distant observer. But by the end of the work the hope of identification with the carnival revellers is finally realized.

Danticat's return also contains many elements of a spiritual quest, something that is not at all evident in Laferrière. Danticat alludes to a pilgrimage as a way to exorcise and confront her carnival demons. She is "aching for a baptism by crowd, among my own people".[40] Later in the work she goes on to say: "I am one of those marchers and migrants, back from the *purgatory* of *exile, expatiating sins* of coldness and distance."[41] The trajectory is one of a confession of distance that allows a movement from the purgatory of exile to baptism and renewal. The feelings of exteriority that she hides in the beginning are no longer apparent:

> I do not mention it to Divers, but this is the first time that I will be an active reveler at carnival in Haiti. I am worried that such an admission would appear strange to someone for whom carnival is one of life's passions. A Haitian writer (me) – even one who'd left the country twenty years before, at age twelve – who has never been to carnival in her own country? I imagine him asking. What was that about?[42]

Carnival becomes a transformative experience for Danticat, allowing her to free herself from the troubling echoes of her childhood; it is no longer "sinful" but signals a renewal. It has been translated into a celebration of community and freedom: "My head is spinning, but I don't care. There is nothing that seems to matter as much as following the curve of the other bodies pressed against mine."[43]

If Danticat is seeking redemption, Laferrière's return shows no evidence of this. The writer-personage, Vieux Os, does not carry a burden of guilt, of exile, of abandonment, of distance or forgetting. He does not carry the burden of the "dyaspora".[44] But in Danticat's return visit there are echoes of all of these: the word "dyaspora" does not appear in *Pays sans chapeau*, there are allusions to *là-bas*, there are allusions to the twenty years spent abroad, but no identification with the dyaspora. Danticat draws the reader's attention to one of the theatrical pieces in the carnival that mocks the fake, newly adopted mannerisms of a dysapora, or as Danticat says, "a Haitian living in the United States".[45] Danticat also introduces the notion of forgetting, linked to the dyaspora's experience with the sabliye tree: "People who leave Haiti and don't call, write, or return are said to have gone under the sabliye tree . . . the last two syllables placed before the first is bliye sa, or forget it."[46] But in *Pays sans chapeau* Vieux Os insists from the beginning of being "chez moi". He describes this ability to clearly locate himself in his home and of being able to see it clearly in its misery and beauty:

> I feel this country physically. From head to toe. Here, I recognize each sound, each shout, each laugh, and each silence. I feel at home here, on this pebble in the sun, not far from the equator where seven million men, women and starving children, hold on. . . . I am at home here with the music of flies over a dog's body. I am at home with this rabble that tears each other to pieces like mad dogs.[47]

Structurally and stylistically, both texts have a liminal quality that characterizes a transient rather than rooted return. These writers are not here to stay, they have not returned to set up roots, they are in transit. This is a return visit. With the passing of time, a natural distance has been created between the writer and the human and natural landscapes. Both writers use guides in their travels: Danticat's primary guide is Michelet Divers, Jacmel's best-known carnival expert, but she has others throughout her visit. Laferrière is guided by Lucrèce to the *Pays sans chapeau*, and his mother guides him through the market jungle of Port-au-Prince.

With both writers there is also the sense of liminality in location and identity. But identification between *moi* and *territoire* is where the greatest distinction lies. Danticat expresses this desire for community and belonging in no uncertain terms. She wishes to identify with "my own people".[48] In Danticat's "I" there is also the need to be a part of the communal "we". But this is not the case for Laferrière; his "I" does not seek this reassurance. Laferrière's "I" is liminal as a result of its fictional plurality, and his desire for (non)-identification with any particular location.

Danticat and Laferrière reconstruct an island space that must negotiate time and distance as well as the real country (the *Pays Réel*) with the imagined one (*Pays Rêvé*). At the end of the novel, as Danticat puts back on her mask of the writer-observer, she talks of such negotiations between the *Pays Réel* and the *Pays Rêvé* having experienced two carnivals, the carnival of her imagination and "the one I'd been part of today".[49] If we return to Stuart Hall's view of culture as continually in translation, which corresponds with Édouard Glissant's idea of culture as a dynamic process,[50] then identification with an ever-changing culture is informed by personal locations in time. The writer tries to frame images of a real and imagined culture in time. Nostalgia is framed by time, as is memory or sensations from the past. The concept is of course Proustian, where sensations, tastes, smell, even locations trigger identifications with a past, with another time. A return home becomes a journey in time of the past and the present. Laferrière describes this when he says that we can never return to the same place that we have left, and even though we may act as though the country is the same, we know very well that it is not the country that we once knew.[51] And so twenty years away from a home must pass through the translation of time. And that time can never be recaptured, only described on the page. In fact, the primary location of return for these writers *is* the page. And what is created on those pages is neither *Pays Réel* nor *Pays Rêvé* but another country.

Notes

1. See Stuart Hall, *Myths of Caribbean Identity*, Walter Rodney Memorial Lecture (Coventry, UK: Centre for Caribbean Studies, University of Warwick, 1991), 4. Hall argues that "the Caribbean is the first, the original and the purest diaspora".

2. Stuart Hall, "Culture Is Always a Translation", *Caribbean Beat*, no. 71 (January/February 2005): 37.

3. Dany Laferrière, *Pays sans chapeau* (Paris: Le Serpent à Plumes, 1999).

4. Vieux Os is the writer-personage in Laferrière's novels. Laferrière was given the name Vieux Os by his grandmother when he was a young boy. See Dany Laferrière, *J'écris comme je vis*, interview with Bernard Magnier (Outremont: Lanctôt, 2000), 184; all translations are my own unless otherwise indicated.

This chapter will also look at the manner in which Laferrière manipulates the use of the writer's "I"; it will also use both names, Vieux Os and Laferrière, to refer to the writer-protagonist.

5. Edwidge Danticat, *After the Dance* (New York: Crown Journeys, 2002).

6. Aimé Césaire, *Cahier d'un retour au pays natal* (Paris: Présence Africaine, 1956), 125.

7. Gregson Davis, *Aimé Césaire* (Cambridge: Cambridge University Press, 1997).

8. See Lilyan Kesteloot and Bartelemy Kotchy, *Aimé Césaire, L'homme et l'oeuvre* (Paris: Présence Africaine, 1973), 112–26.

9. Ibid., 24.

10. Ibid.

11. Laferrière, *J'écris comme je vis*, 104.

12. Ibid., 183–84.

13. Ibid., 97.

14. Laferrière, *Pays sans chapeau*, 47.

15. Ibid., 75.
16. Ibid., 94.
17. Ibid., 113.
18. Ibid.
19. Danticat, *After the Dance*, 25.
20. Ibid., 27.
21. Ibid., 30.
22. Ibid., 69.
23. Laferrière, *Pays sans chapeau*, 150.
24. Danticat, *After the Dance*, 15.
25. Ibid., 147.
26. Laferrière, *J'écris comme je vis*, 99.
27. Laferrière has called his collection of novels his "Une autobiographie américaine". See *J'écris comme je vis*, 107, where the writer discusses this: "le titre que j'ai donné à l'ensemble de mes livres: 'Une autobiographie américaine'."
28. Laferrière, *J'écris comme je vis*, 184–85.
29. See Lejeune as quoted in Ursula Mathis-Moser, *Dany Laferrière: La dérive américaine* (Montréal: VLB Éditeur, 2003), 253. Lejeune goes on to define autobiographical fiction as a "récit rétrospectif en prose qu'une personne réelle fait de sa propre existence, lorsqu'elle met l'accent sur sa vie individuelle, en particulier, sur l'histoire de sa personnalité".
30. For my definition of autofiction I rely on Serge Doubrovsky: "Fiction, d'événements et de faits strictement réels; si l'on veut, *autofiction*, d'avoir confié le language d'une aventure à l'aventure du langage, hors sagesse et hors syntaxe du roman, traditionnel et nouveau." See Mathis-Moser, *Dany Laferrière,* 255.
31. Laferrière, *J'écris comme je vis*, 73.
32. Ibid., 45–46.
33. Dany Laferrière as cited in Mathis-Moser, *Dany Laferrière*, 259.
34. Ursula Mathis-Moser characterizes Laferriere's "Autobiographie americaine" as typically postmodern: "Nous avons mentionné à maintes reprises le caractère postmodern de l'oeuvre, subsumant sous ce titre la fragmentation du récit, le mélange des genres, intertextualité et intermédialité, le moi pluriel et instable, la juxtaposition du divers, l'accumulation du même, le refus de linéarité, le refus d'une prise de position, le caratère ludique. Tous ces traits concourent à créer un effet d'hybridité esthetique qui stimule et deconcerte à la fois." Mathis-Moser, *Dany Laferrière,* 274.

Laferriere himself resists classifications or "etiquettes" at all costs and yet the world he creates which celebrates the ordinariness of daily life lends itself to Moser's complex classification of esthetic hybridity. There is perhaps no greater example of the destabilizing and at the same reassuring effect that Laferriere creates in his work than the use of the writer's "I". The plural I or "le moi pluriel" is unique, playful, transient and as such somewhat disconcerting. Locating Laferrière's "I" draws the reader into a fictional world that presents what is seemingly real and obvious; the tone is sincere, the description seemingly non-judgmental, the narrator's perspective adopting a stance of presenting things as they are.

35. Laferrière: "J'ai l'habitude de dire que je suis un homme en trois morceaux: mon coeur est à Port-au-Prince, mon esprit à Montreal, et mon corps et à Miami" (*J'écris comme je vis*, 49) ". . . je ne veux plus de frontière" (ibid., 72).

36. Ibid., 85.

37. Ibid., 107. Laferrière also says: "Je suis du pays de mes lecteurs. Quand un Japonais me lit, je deviens un écrivain japonais" (ibid., 9).

38. Danticat, *After the Dance*, 16.

39. Ibid.

40. Ibid., 15.

41. Ibid., 147; my emphasis.

42. Ibid., 12.

43. Ibid., 147. Danticat also quotes Bakhtin and his idea of the carnivalesque disaster which turns into a "sequence of gay transformations and renewals" (ibid., 146).

44. The terms "dyaspora" as well as "Haitian diaspora" are used by Danticat in the novel. Ibid., 11, 142.

45. Ibid., 12.

46. Ibid., 19.

47. Laferrière, *Pays sans chapeau*, 11.

48. Danticat, *After the Dance*, 15.

49. Ibid., 152.

50. Glissant's concept of *Antillanité* stresses the notion of cultures that are not static; they are instead engaged in a permanent revolution. They are in constant translation and transformation.

51. Laferrière, *J'écris comme je vis*, 150.

Chapter 11

Hatred Chérie
History, Silence and Animosity in Three Haitian Novels

Martin Munro

> *Silences are inherent in history because any single event enters history with some of its constituting parts missing. Something is always left out while something else is recorded.*
> – Michel-Rolph Trouillot
>
> *This hatred you have for each other, where does it come from?*
> – Marie Chauvet

Contrary to what discourses of nationalist or racial brotherhood and solidarity might claim, we hold a special contempt for those who most resemble us in terms of class and colour, and for those with whom we share space most intimately. In colonial and postcolonial situations, this peculiarly virulent neighbourly hatred is magnified. Stunted and deformed by colonialism's methodical imposition of a deep inferiority complex, colonized peoples at once tentatively reject and unconsciously internalize what they have been told about themselves and their innate moral, physical and intellectual failings so that even if they manifest an outward contempt for the oppressor, they nurture at the same time an impregnable core of antipathy towards themselves and "their people". There is, in postcolonial societies, a residue of guilt and shame, and a nagging doubt that maybe the colonizers were right after all; maybe we are inherently incapable. As an unconscious way of attacking one's own assumed feelings of inferiority, violence against those closest to us in society feels justified, almost a right. It is this toxic blend of unfinished psychological colonialism, powerlessness and self-hatred that underlies the epidemic of violence, drug addiction and murder inside Caribbean ghettos from Kingston to Port of Spain.

Perhaps nowhere in the postcolonial world is the disjuncture between the nationalist rhetoric of racial solidarity and lived, everyday hatred starker than it is in Haiti. Their new nation under siege politically and economically, Haitian intellectuals in the nineteenth century often charged themselves with the task of promoting Haiti in the eyes of the world. In his monumental *The Equality of the Human Races* (1885), Anténor Firmin promotes Haiti as the foremost example of what the "black race" could achieve, and sees Haiti's primary role in its standing as an "edifying" symbol of black achievement that could generate "the rehabilitation of Africa".[1] A common understanding and acceptance of race is therefore, to Firmin, what binds Haitians together and what ties them to Africa and others of the same race.

Modern Haitian nationalism was revitalized during the American occupation of 1915–34, even if, apart from Charlemagne Péralte's *caco* revolt of 1918–20, and despite the troubled relationship between the Haitians and the Americans, there was little sustained, overt resistance to the occupation until 1929, when a student strike at the School of Agriculture at Damiens sparked a series of sympathy strikes in Port-au-Prince. The previous year, in a short article in the newspaper *Le Petit Impartial*, Georges J. Petit and Jacques Roumain had demanded, "Youth, where are you? For twelve years the white man has trampled like a master over the sacred soil that our phalanx of heroes watered with their blood."[2] Born out of the need to resist the easily identifiable white, foreign enemy, early Haitian indigenism (in which Roumain was to play a major role) was, like Firmin's earlier thought, founded on an all-subsuming notion of Haitian togetherness, beyond race, colour and class, which is demonstrated in Petit and Roumain's call in April 1928 for a "union of all factions, all classes". For, faced with the American oppressor, "there were no blacks, no mulattos, no rich, no poor", only a "mass united by the same aspirations, the same suffering".[3]

The fundamental problem of a movement such as Haitian indigenism that is born from and evolves around a poetics of resistance arises when the focus of resistance shifts, changes or disappears. Indigenism was held together by the shared desire to resist the white menace of the United States, but when the Americans withdrew in 1934 and the question of national reconstitution became all the more pressing, the differences between Haiti's various internal factions became more polarized. Whereas Haitian Marxists, such as Roumain, retained the loosely defined notions of race and cultural authenticity of indigenism, Africanists such as Denis Lorimer and François Duvalier tended to solidify and fix racial identity into a rigid, essentialized ideology. In the thirties, as Africanism slowly mutated into the Griot movement, a distorted racial ideology became the vehicle for a black, racially motivated politics looking to redress its sense of historical injustice and political isolation, which it blamed on the mulatto elite. The Griots' racial ideology implied a sliding scale of authenticity: the true Haitian soul was black, and the fairer the skin, the less Haitian one was. In contrast to the indigenists, for whom the rediscovery of Africanity and popular culture had been a creative and open-ended act, the Griots were strategically reductive, and systematically closed down the meanings associated with blackness and Haitian authenticity. Africanity and racial authenticity became the tenets of the political ideology of the rising black middle class, who saw in this ideology "the rationale for a black cultural dictatorship".[4]

In effect, the Griots laid bare the historical colour and class conflicts that anti-American nationalist rhetoric had strategically ignored but that had far from disappeared from Haitian society. The disavowed prejudices and hatreds that are the legacy of colonialism and Haiti's postcolonial perpetuation of colour division resurfaced, literally with a vengeance. In this chapter, my broadest interest lies in trying to understand the causes and manifestations of hatred and violence in Haiti: how and why does this intimate antipathy manifest itself? My primary sources are three novels – Marie Chauvet's *Amour* (1968), Yanick Lahens's *Dans la maison du père* (2000) and Lyonel Trouillot's *Bicentenaire* (2004) – which, far from reiterating nationalist ideals of solidarity, deal with Haiti's internal animosities, violence and the realities of a silenced people, alienated and exiled in their own nation.[5] As I will show, at the heart of each of the works are the questions of inter-class and colour mistrust and contempt that manifest themselves in cycles of violence, and in the deep, unrelenting though often disavowed self-hatred of Haiti's people.

Set in 1939, during the presidency of Sténio Vincent, who punished those "'light-skinned' aristocrats who had never fully accepted him", Chauvet's *Amour* indirectly charts the rise of black nationalism in everyday Haitian life.[6] The central character Claire's alienation and self-hatred are determined largely by the dark shade of her skin; her two sisters, Félicité and Annette, are light-skinned, but Claire is "stained" by darkness, "the surprise that mixed blood held for our parents" (p. 12). In her insular middle-class milieu, Claire's dark skin is a source of unacknowledged shame for her family, and her life is lived almost exclusively within the walls of the family home. Claire is doubly alienated in that her dark skin sets her apart from the light-skinned bourgeoisie and, conversely, her middle-class background differentiates her from the dark-skinned lower classes.

Locking herself in her room, she is excluded from the "drama" of her sisters' lives, "erased", as she says, "like a shadow" (p. 9). The romantic novels and pornographic postcards that she secretly "devours" (p. 17) are dual figurations of her emotional and sexual deprivation. Even if she is excluded, however, she manipulates the drama that takes place in the closed household, willing Félicité's white French fiancé Jean Luze to give in to his desire for Annette. "When is it all going to untangle?" she asks, "I am in the wings and they think I don't exist. It is me who is the director of the scene" (p. 12).

The novel's critique of black nationalism is effected largely through the presentation of the commander Calédu, a "black imbecile" (p. 26) who avenges his own past of colour discrimination by raping lighter-skinned, middle-class women, and who at once repels and fascinates Claire. Distorted by the strictures that have created her own internal exile, she gives up on her idealized dreams of love, previously figured by her secretly reading romantic novels, and adopts a "realist definition" of love as the "rubbing together of two pieces of flesh" (p. 83). Unconsciously, she is attracted to Calédu's "big, black, muscled body" (p. 83), dreams of his "enormous phallus", and of herself at his feet, "at once submissive and rebellious" (p. 145). Therefore, as in many Haitian fictions, the desire for revenge is what compels characters' actions, and it is what assures the perpetuation of the cycle of violence and retribution. If Claire's initial solution to her alienation and self-hatred is to seek love, she comes to realize that in her society such a solution is impossible, and that "one can only respond to hatred with more hatred" (p. 144). What is at once terrible and fascinating in this work of internal exile and intimate hatred is the breakdown of conventional binaries of meaning: Claire, the dark-skinned, "old little girl" with a name that means "light" is rebellious and submissive at once; her "joy" is "nasty" (p. 81). The internal, private space is invaded by the exterior and the public; love and hatred become enmeshed, inseparable, and a book entitled *Amour* presents some of the most appalling acts of hatred imaginable. Chauvet's fundamental question, indeed the fundamental question of so many Haitian novels, is put by the outsider Jean Luze, who asks: "This hatred you have for each other, where does it come from?" (p. 56). Haitian novels, such as Chauvet's, that present internal antipathy and alienation in this way often counteract the nationalist rhetoric of racial and national plenitude; if indigenism had sought to valorize the "Haitian soul", Chauvet suggests the radical alienation and emptiness ultimately created by racial rhetoric in her character Claire who is a "body without soul" (pp. 82–83).

One of the binary oppositions that dissolve in this novel of internal exile is that between silence and utterance. Claire's voice, one of the most directly eloquent in Haitian writing, is largely an interior monologue; her silence, she says, is her "revenge" (p. 9). Similarly, in Yanick Lahens's *Dans la maison du père*, silence connotes not just alienation, but internal, inviolable resistance. Lahens's novel is a worthy successor to Chauvet's fictions, a work that presents its alienated female protagonist Alice Bienaimé in similar situations: a repressed, silenced existence in a middle-class household. Like in *Amour*, the house is a kind of stage upon which different actors play out their personal dramas, and for which Haitian history provides the backdrop. The novel's historical scope ranges from the departure of the Americans in August 1934, through the 1937 massacre of Haitians in the Dominican Republic, the Second World War, the anti-superstitious campaign, the turbulent promise of the 1945–46 revolution, the presence of André Breton and Wifredo Lam in Haiti, the rise and violent reign of Duvalier, the exiles of the sixties and, finally, the protagonist's post-Duvalier return to Haiti. The private space of the house is not therefore a haven from history. Nor, however, does history determine absolutely the course of the characters' lives; the women in particular, like Chauvet's Claire, in their silent submissiveness, articulate a muted rebelliousness.

To use one of the central symbols of resistance in the novel, Lahens's work *dances* with history; dance offers movement, freedom and, ultimately, escape, as the narrator Alice leaves for New York in 1946, where she says she is "free to dance my life, to love and to say no as I please, all the knots of my heart undone" (p. 149). Dance to Alice is her "own way of teasing life, of throwing light into its darkest corners" (p. 85). It is moreover a means of attaining the desired state of silence, for as she says, "to dance is to be silent" (p. 138). If in *Amour*, Claire's act of writing her journal only reflects and records her imprisonment, Alice's dance permits her to escape both emotionally and physically the prison of history, and her incarceration in the house. Also, whereas in *Amour* Claire tends to view the outside from behind closed windows, in *Dans la maison du père*, political discussions between the father and Uncle Héraclès take place on balconies, their words apparently passing with the breeze through the house and out of the open windows. Music also interrupts the political discourse; in the opening scene, for instance, Alice describes the house, with "all its doors and windows open. A popular ragtime tune was playing on a gramophone." From the first notes, she says, "I turned in my blue dress. I moved my feet, laughing. Clapped my hands" (p. 11). Even if Lahens's house is in many ways as morally and emotionally stifling as Chauvet's, Lahens is careful to suggest the child's resistance to the authority of the father and mother through movement, dance and music, as well as their subtle interplay with politics and history.

This greater sense of freedom in Lahens's novel is illustrated in Alice's relationship to language. For Claire in *Amour*, French language is one element of the prison of history, a leftover from colonialism that Haitians cling to, just as they do to self-hatred and torture: "We have practiced slitting each other's throats since Independence. Hatred between us was born. From this hatred came the torturers. They torture before slitting throats. It is a colonial heritage we cling to, just as we cling to French language" (p. 14). Claire's silence is therefore, to some extent, a retreat from colonially imposed language. Alice's silence, by contrast, is never presented in terms of anti-colonial resistance. On her first day at school, silence is her reaction to feeling "abandoned", it is her "first refuge", her "first retreat" and her "only standard", where she liked to "set up camp as in a fortress, certain of being protected by this absence, this momentary death of words" (p. 40). Alice uses the word "standard" here in the sense of a banner or flag, a marker of identity, and unlike Claire, whose silence is her revenge, Alice sees her wordlessness as a liberation, a different standard. Words for her were "without a homeland, without a flag" (p. 41). Silence is therefore, to Alice, a means of bypassing the dominant male discourses of belonging, while retaining the right to belong, but in a different way.

This reworked, reduced notion of belonging is further suggested in a scene where the young Alice ventures into the back yard, which, with its thick vegetation and "murmuring odours", is to Alice as "wild as the Amazon" and the affective and symbolic counterpoint to the ordered, respectable front garden (p. 32). The back yard was, she says, the "reverse of her world at seven years old"; it is moreover where Alice is initiated into the folkloric world of Man Bo, who is the archetype of the stoic, suffering yet resilient black maid (p. 32). Playing on and subverting the traditional male nationalist preoccupation with possessing land, Lahens's Alice treats the land with reverence; her first act, she says, on treading upon this "reserved territory" was to remove her shoes. Here and there, she says, the soil was wet and muddy, and this gave her the feeling of "taking root there and existing like a tree". Nothing could ever take from her the "taste" of this land, even if she stood by mistake on hot charcoal, splinters or pine needles. Her enduring attachment to the land of the back yard is therefore something of a metaphor for her continued bond with Haiti itself, no matter what injuries it may inflict upon her. It is in that piece of muddy land, she says, that her "silent fidelity" to Haiti still exists. And to underscore the difference between traditional expressions of nationalist belonging and her own silent bond, she says that her attachment is "without cockade, with neither discourse nor flag" (p. 33). Like *Amour*, therefore, *Dans la maison du père* deflates the pomp and circumstance of nationalist manifestations of Haitian identity, and insists on a more intimate, wordless bond with the land.

One of Lahens's most convincing and important contributions in this novel is her implicit response to Jean-Luze's question in *Amour* on the source of Haitians' self-hatred (p. 56). Through Alice's experiences in the school run by the Védin sisters, Lahens suggests that education upholds and perpetuates the prejudices and inferiority complexes that in turn create class and colour conflicts in Haitian society. School is to Alice like a foreign country; she and her friend Thérèse passed their schooldays, she says, as if they were "a settlement of exiles" (p. 79). The Védin sisters' project is classically colonial and is apparent from the first day of school: "to turn the young negresses that we were into coloured daughters of France". Alice sees in this project a pathological mistrust of and disdain for all that is not European and "civilized" and asks: "Why did they go to so much trouble to force me to construct an amputated life? A clumsily-copied life?" (p. 41). The Védin sisters, like their students, were descended from Africans but, Alice says, "found in this condition a source of self-hatred and scorn that they thought they should pass on to us so that we could all carry this burden". Simply put, the Védin sisters "did not like themselves. They lacked this support, which was indispensable for existence" (p. 41). This, suggests Lahens, is the root of Haiti's problems: the bourgeois denial of anything other than French culture and manners implies a deep self-hatred, which is transmitted through institutions such as education with the result that mutual empathy and respect between different colours and classes are virtually non-existent. Few students, Alice says, "truly liked each other", but given their inherited self-hatred, how, she asks, "could we have liked each other?" (p. 42).

The silence motif reappears in another work of Haitian antipathy and internal exile, Lyonel Trouillot's *Bicentenaire*, a short, powerful novel that relates the intersecting lives of a diverse cast of Port-au-Prince characters during the political unrest that marked the end of 2003 and the beginning of the bicentenary year, 2004. In the novel's preface, an author figure asserts that "Everything here refers only to the incommunicable, to the silence hidden by the sound and the fury" (p. 9). The student protagonist Lucien Saint-Hilaire says (to himself) that if ever he were to write a novel, the "hero would be silence" (p. 12). In Trouillot's novel, the hero is indeed silence, a kind of urbanized wordlessness, far removed from the earthy loquaciousness of Lucien's mother, a peasant woman who "has never been able to make peace with silence, who has always used words as the only exorcism" (p. 14). The internal exile, and the colour and class animosity in this novel are thus figured around language and communication; the hinterland is a repository of folk proverbs, a place where "there are rules and the rules are clear" (p. 15), but these rules, these words, do not translate easily into the shifting, chaotic world of the city where, the mother says, "there are too many ideas" (p. 14). The novel's intention is not to enrich the city with the lost folk knowledge, with the lost language of the hinterland, but to listen to, register, and "let silence be" (p. 14).

It is not that Lucien is uncommunicative – he "really liked to speak to people" (p. 39) – but that, in the city, communication is distorted by fear, mistrust, insecurity and class prejudice. The role of class divisions in impeding communication is underscored in Lucien's exchanges with the unnamed doctor, whose video-game-obsessed son is tutored in French language by Lucien. During their meetings, there are two conversations occurring simultaneously between Lucien and the doctor: "the audible and the inaudible" (p. 25). In the audible conversation, the doctor inquires about the student political movement, and Lucien responds politely. The inaudible dialogue, on the other hand, enounces their mutual, class-based antipathy: the doctor says "But I know in truth that you detest me and say to yourself that it is not fair that I live in this house, which my imbecile son will inherit while you, who go to the theatre in your books, probably live nowhere", while Lucien silently responds "you are nothing but a brute who is good with his hands and has money to burn. Even if you multiply by four the pittance that you pay me, your son will never learn a thing" (p. 25).

Lucien can be read as a tattered revenant of previous student militants, a muted reincarnation of the 1946 generation, only now the strident volubility of Alexis, Depestre et al. has been reduced to the silent protest of Lucien and his hesitant group of students. In one of the novel's most revealing and poignant scenes, Lucien and some fellow marchers flee the police, seek refuge in a house, and in the general panic, an unnamed older man assures a woman that the gas fired by the police will kill nobody, "that their cause is just", and that they must regroup and continue the march (p. 99). The man is "almost old" and "takes in hand hope, willpower, courage". Thinking themselves to be the first to "say no", the students are impressed by the man's calm determination, and Lucien wonders "What acts have preceded mine?" The older man is himself a reminder of Haiti's militant past, brought out of his own long silence by the march and the impending bicentenary. The realization that he is not the first to rise up in Haiti causes Lucien to reflect on his own narcissism as well as that of the Haitian people in general: "What kind of country is it where each individual thinks himself to be the centre of the world, the only supreme being, the beginning and the end?" In a nation where history weighs heavily on the collective memory, the amnesia that has erased the older militant from the minds of the young students causes Lucien to reflect pointedly that "One always has either too much memory or not enough" (p. 100).

Lucien is connected to previous generations of militants through his continued, if commuted and compromised, attachment to language and reading. His only "weapon" is the old grammar book that he carries around, giving classes to the uninterested children of rich families (p. 23). And yet, as he realizes, he is "losing the war" (p. 23); words may refuse to be quiet but they say little, mean little: "Words are empty. Words no longer say anything. Words have no presence and expect no reply. . . . Words are dead" (pp. 68–69). If language and reading are Lucien's only weapons, they are ill-suited to the realities of a city that renders communication impossible. What thrives and what makes sense in the city is the stilted yet eloquent language of violence. Lucien's younger brother, the self-styled gangster "Little Joe", adapts to the city and its violence in ways that Lucien is unable to, becoming part of its chaotic, amoral discourse. Little Joe has made for himself, "with the little he had, violently", an existence based around drugs, rape and other violent crimes that somehow make sense in Port-au-Prince (p. 17). In contrast to Lucien, Little Joe "has never been a great reader", and takes thirty seconds to read the name Spinoza on Lucien's book before "taking his revenge" by throwing the book with all his might against the wall (p. 18). The fragile binding of the book collapses and the pages scatter across their shared room, all-too-obvious symbols of the frailty and weakness of traditional intellectualism in contemporary Haiti. The displacement of intellectualism by the discourse of violence is further suggested when Little Joe takes out a pistol from his pocket, places it on the table "to replace the book" and states: "that is called a Glock, it's my college degree" (p. 18). Little Joe has few words to articulate his philosophy, but Lucien reads in his eyes his scorn for a life of "hesitating between your dream of a normal life in a normal country . . . and the strength to tear down from the tree the branch that they won't let you have" (p. 19). Life to Little Joe is "like a weapon, and a weapon fires shots". His own "plan for society", he holds in his hands, "and it opens all doors" (p. 19). Little Joe is in many respects like Chauvet's thugs in *Amour*, a disenfranchised, black working-class Haitian seeking retribution and gaining it freely. As in Chauvet's novel, the fact that the working classes' revenge is historically justified – no one can deny that the elite have systematically repressed Haiti's poor – creates a moral confusion, where binary concepts of right and wrong disintegrate.

In *Bicentenaire,* Lucien is painfully aware of the fragility of his own position, his own solution, and he recognizes that there is a kind of "wisdom in the violence" of Little Joe, for "even in [Joe's] delirium, he is able to see the truth". Lucien is sensitive to the lack of resolution in his fellow students, their growing lassitude and imminent retreat into the university libraries. Moreover, he tacitly agrees with the other students' view that in this "true-false city . . . only the rich can afford to be twenty years old" (pp. 44–45). The notion of the truth is therefore destabilized, as ideas of justice and liberty crumble before the wordless truth of Joe, who "saw truly" and who "speaks the truth" (pp. 44–45). The novel's twisting, confusing and contradictory morality is exemplified when Little Joe and his gang steal the car of the cynical doctor, the object of Julien's silent hatred. Learning that he is a doctor, Little Joe asks if he is "one of those do-gooders who look after protesters and write up reports for human rights organizations" (p. 102). The doctor, who "has never been able to like the poor" (p. 101), answers no, but without looking at his assailants, which leads Little Joe to ask if his mother did not teach him that it was impolite to have a conversation with people without looking at them (p. 103). There is a strong sense in this scene of the doctor getting his comeuppance and of Little Joe almost as a Robin Hood figure, righting social wrongs that the books and words of Lucien have never been able to correct. As Little Joe casts the shoeless doctor onto the city streets, the novel's morality takes one further twist, when Joe orders the doctor to "In the future, do a little bit of voluntary work", thereby contradicting his own initial disdain for "do-gooders" (p. 104). In this way, morality floats and is contingent upon social context. Consequently, once more, rigid categories of good or bad collapse. Little Joe's bad-guy act is just that; an act, a role constructed from movies, video games and black gangster figures in the music he listens to. He may be bad, but he is bad in a different way to the doctor, whose bourgeois complacency is a sign of a longstanding social malaise in Haiti. Likewise, as in an early scene where an impoverished mother beats her children for beating each other, in the novel's Haiti "one cannot say who was the torturer, and who were the victims" (p. 12).

Even if Lucien retains something of the aura of the *La Ruche*–style, 1946-era student militant, Trouillot's subtle destabilization of conventional notions of truth begs one fundamental, unsettling question: just who is the true revolutionary in his novel – Lucien or Little Joe? Up until the final chapter of the novel, time almost literally ticks by; the characters' actions are reported with the precise times they took place. The careful demarcation of time ends however, as the march turns into a chaotic free-for-all, and protesters flee the shots of the police and Little Joe's hired band of thugs. In the final chapter, "no one can say what the exact time was. Watches were out of synch. Watches did not tick in the same direction" (p. 111). In this chapter, then, time is uncertain and unspecified; it could be any time from 1804 to the bicentenary. The stakes are the same, the players are the same, and the violence is the same. Given this temporal uncertainty, and the sense that present time is indistinguishable from any period from the last two hundred years, the figures of Lucien and Little Joe are themselves less solidly anchored in the present than they first appear. They are both products of the late twentieth century, but at the same time seem to recall the two great revolutionary leaders, Toussaint and Dessalines.

In his commitment to reason, reading and moderation, Lucien reincarnates many of the qualities attributed in popular and official histories to Toussaint, "the black Consul", the "gilded African", "the black Napoleon" and, for many Europeans, the acceptable face of the Haitian Revolution. Little Joe, on the other hand, the unrelentingly violent, unreconstructed thug, recalls Dessalines, the illiterate tyrant, "the most unregenerate of Haitian leaders" and the unsettling antithesis to the rational Toussaint. In the European imagination, Dessalines has been registered as "nothing but an African savage", with none of the redeeming qualities of Toussaint.[7] In a hyperbolic phrase that could equally be applied to Trouillot's Little Joe – who is "happy to destroy anyone who gets in his way" (p. 84) – the Haitian historian Thomas Madiou describes Dessalines as a "thunderbolt of arbitrariness".[8] If Toussaint was at least publicly an ardent Catholic, Dessalines was, as the historian Gustave d'Alaux says, "mixed up with the papas" and at times would bear magic talismans into battle to protect himself.[9] Similarly, in *Bicentenaire*, Little Joe "had retained the memory of the mysteries", and he ritually spreads his red neckerchief on his bed, places on it a pin, three leaves of artemisia, and an image of Saint Jacques le Majeur, folds it up, puts it in his jeans pocket, picks up his Glock and crosses himself before setting out on his own particular battle (p. 87). In suggesting a connection between "the mysteries" and violent despotism, Trouillot recalls Frankétienne's statement in *Ultravocal* (1968) that "wherever idolatry triumphs, liberty dies". Little Joe's red kerchief, moreover, connects him to Frankétienne's tyrant, Mac Abre, who also wears a red neckerchief (p. 184).[10] Both figures are in turn linked iconically to Dessalines, "the liberator, with his red silk scarf".[11]

If Dessalines has remained in the European imagination as the epitome of the black savage, his place in Haitian culture is more ambiguous. The only one of the trinity of revolutionary leaders to achieve apotheosis, Dessalines has, as Dayan says "gradually acquired unequalled power in the Haitian imagination".[12] It is perhaps significant that what Dayan calls the "state cult of Dessalines" was inaugurated on the centenary of Haitian independence, when the new national anthem, the "Dessalinienne", was first sung, and one hundred years before the publication of Trouillot's novel. If the literate elite have recuperated Dessalines as "the Great One", "the Savior", "the Lover of Justice", and "the Liberator", he is, to Vodou initiates, a "far less comforting or instrumental" figure. As Dayan points out, "The image of Dessalines in the cult of the people remains equivocal and corruptible: a trace of what is absorbed by the mind and animated in the gut. How inevitable are the oscillations from hero to detritus, from power to vulnerability, from awe to ridicule: a convertibility that vodou would keep working, viable, and necessary."[13]

In his presentation of Little Joe, Trouillot seems sensitive to the ambiguities and oscillations that surround the violent tyrant-saviour figure in the Haitian imagination. The final disintegration of ordered, chronological time in his novel takes his characters and their situations out of the specific situation of the bicentenary and encourages a reading of them as timeless manifestations of an unending, recurring history. The truth and purity that Lucien recognizes in Little Joe's violence reflects the popular retention of a belief in what Dayan calls "the potency and virtue of atrocity".[14] Even if Lucien dies an innocent, struck down by a shot from Little Joe's group, Trouillot is careful to suggest that neither brother is any less a product of the revolution that the novel commemorates. The bicentenary serves only to heighten the ambiguities of a revolution that is fêted the world over as an unthinkable act of anticolonial heroism, but which is still lived in Haiti as an imperfect liberation that solved few of the problems of the dispossessed, and that gave birth to the deep animosities that resurface in the novels of Trouillot, Lahens and Chauvet. The closing image of *Bicentenaire* emphasizes the ambiguities of commemorating Haitian independence, and further implies that history in Haiti is lived as an unending, deadening confusion. Lucien's corpse lies on the street, his eyes still open, fixed on the official banners that have accumulated, palimpsest-like over time: "the old ones, the new, some bigger than others, mixing in their disorder past, present, future. The largest one. The one that could not be missed. The colours are striking, half blue, half red: 2004, year of the bicentenary" (pp. 121–22).

Notes

1. Anténor Firmin, *The Equality of the Human Races*, trans. Asselin Charles (1885; repr., Champaign: University of Illinois Press, 2002), lvi. Parts of my my analysis in this chapter have been published in Martin Munro, *Exile and Post-1946 Haitian Literature: Alexis, Depestre, Ollivier, Laferrière, Danticat* (Liverpool: Liverpool University Press, 2007).

2. Georges J. Petit and Jacques Roumain, "À la jeunesse", *Le Petit Impartial*, 7 March 1928, reprinted in Jacques Roumain, *Œuvres complètes*, ed. Léon-François Hoffmann (Madrid: ALLCA XX, Collection Archivos, 2003), 463.

3. Georges J. Petit and Jacques Roumain, "Manifeste à la jeunesse", *Le Petit Impartial*, 4 April 1928, reprinted in Jacques Roumain, *Œuvres complètes*, 468.

4. J. Michael Dash, *Literature and Ideology in Haiti, 1915–1961* (London and Basingstoke: MacMillan, 1981), 101.

5. Marie Chauvet, *Amour, Colère, Folie* (Paris: Gallimard, 1968); Yanick Lahens, *Dans la Maison du père* (Paris: Le Serpent à Plumes, 2000); Lyonel Trouillot, *Bicentenaire* (Arles: Actes Sud, 2004). Subsequent references to these works appear parenthetically in the text. All translations are my own.

6. Joan Dayan, *Haiti, History, and the Gods* (Berkeley and Los Angeles: University of California Press, 1995), 120.

7. Ibid., 17, 20.
8. Ibid., 121 (quotation).
9. Ibid., 24 (quotation).
10. Frankétienne, *Ultravocal* (1972; repr., Paris: Éditions Hoëbeke, 2004), 39, 184.
11. Dayan, *Haiti, History, and the Gods*, 17.
12. Ibid.
13. Ibid., 28.
14. Ibid., 29.

Index

abolitionism
    British anti-slavery campaign, 71, 75
    literature of, 50
    role of women in, 48
Adams, Henry, on US debt to Haiti, 17–18
Africa, European view of, 2–3, 53
African-American art
    Harlem Renaissance, 63–69
    Jacob Lawrence, 61–85
    politicization of, 63–67
African diaspora
    depiction of in *L'Ouverture* series (Lawrence), 72, 79
    Schomburg Library collection, 69–70, 84n50
Africanism, 165
d'Alaux, Gustav, 173
alienation, of Haitian diaspora, 122–23, 142
Alston, Charles, 64, 72, 82n14, 83n30
    Harlem Arts Workshop, 65–66
    Magic and Medicine (murals), 66
Altman, Janet Gurkin, 128
Aravamudan, Srinivas, *Tropicopolitans*, 52, 53
Arcade, Eugene, 30
architectural traditions (Louisiana), Haitian influence on, 30, 34, 38n20
Aristide, Jean-Bertrand, 19
    parallels with Toussaint, 43–44, 56n6

Bâ, Mariama, *So Long a Letter*, 123–24
Banks, Russell, 100
Bannarn, Henry, 65, 66, 83n30
Beard, Charles, *Toussaint L'Ouverture*, 70
Beard, John R., *Toussaint L'Ouverture: A Biography and Autobiography*, 70–72
Bearden, Romare, 62, 65
Bell, Madison Smartt
    All Souls' Rising, 97–98, 99, 101
    cruelty, of women, 102–4
    depictions of violence, 100–101
    as outsider in Haitian literature, 100
    The Stone the Builder Refused, 45, 56–57n10
Benjamin, Walter, 122, 128
Bernasconi, Robert, 88
Bhabha, Homi, 41, 52, 136
Blackburn, Robert, 66
black Marxism, 49–50, 51, 164–65
black nationalism
    in *Amour* (Chauvet), 165–67
    arts, politicization of, 63–67
    Marcus Garvey, 63, 66
Blumenbach, Johann Friedrich, 88
Bonaparte, Napoleon. *See* Napoleon
Bourke-White, Margaret, 72
Braziel, Jana Evans, 137
Buscaglia-Salgado, José, *Undoing Empire*, 51

Index

Caco rebellion, 19, 164
Carby, Hazel
　Race Men, 48
　Toussaint as black male hero, 49–50
Caribbean
　as diaspora, 143, 149–50
　"Toussaint complex", 44
Caribbean literature, non-Caribbean authors, 100
Carpentier, Alejo, *The Kingdom of this World*, 97, 98, 103, 109n13
Catlett, Elizabeth, 74
Cerami, Charles, *Jefferson's Great Gamble*, 14–15
Césaire, Aimé, *Cahier d'un retour au pays natal*, 50, 150–51
Charlier, Etienne, *Aperçu sur la formation historique de la nation haïtienne*, 46
Chauvet, Marie, 96, 163
　Amour, 165–67, 172, 174–75
Christophe, Henri, 2, 6
colonialism
　citizenship of African people in colonial society, 3, 21n4, 53
　as male-defined world, 96–99
　"postcolonial" defined, 44, 56n8
　postcolonial interpretations of Toussaint, 41–60
　and Rights of Man, 53
　and self-hatred, 163–65, 168
　silence as anti-colonial resistance, 168
colour hierarchy, 86–94
　in Griot movement, 165
　in Kant's definition of race, 87–88
　role of skin colour in moral hierarchy, 88–89, 94n7
Condé, Maryse, 48
Conlin, Joseph, *The American Past: A Survey of American History*, 12–13
Cook, Elizabeth Heckendorn, *Epistolary Bodies*, 128
Cooper, Anna Julia, 48
Creole language
　colour distinctions in, 96
　influence of Haitian refugees on, 29–30, 34, 37n6
　role in migrant reordering of identity, 145
　in slave communications, 118–20
creolization
　in Haiti, interruption of, 96
　and hybridity, 50–51
　influence of refugees on Louisiana culture, 29–30, 36
Crisis, 63
Cuba, migration of Haitian refugees, 28
Cullen, Countee, 65
cultural credentialing, 125
cultural identity
　as aspect of gender and heritage, 146
　continuity of Haitianness, 143
　and nationalism, 134–39
　as process of translation, 149–50
　psychological colonialism, and self-hatred, 163–75
　transformation of national identity, 136
cultural traditions
　continuity of by refugees, 33–34, 36, 38n20
　in Louisiana, influence of Haitian refugees on, 30

Dadié, Bernard, 55
Danticat, Edwidge, 98, 122–33
　After the Dance: A Walk Through Carnival in Jacmel, Haiti, 122, 150, 153–54
　Breath, Eyes, Memory, 130, 138, 140, 141–42, 145–46
　Brother I'm Dying, 122
　"Caroline's Wedding", 130–31
　"Children of the Sea", 129–30
　The Dew Breaker, 124, 126–27, 128–29
　female-centred *rasin* of, 126–27
　Haitian oral culture, use of, 124
　Krik? Krak!, 123, 126, 129–30
　letter motif, 123–24, 128–29, 140
　mask motif in, 157–58, 159
　on practice of "testing", 130, 133n19

short story cycles, 129–30
use of writer's "I", 157–58, 159
writer's return, and identification of landscape and self, 150, 152–55
on writing, 127–28
Danticat, Rev. Joseph N., 139
Dash, J. Michael, 129
on American attitudes to Haiti, 16
Davies, Carole Boyce, 146
Davis, David Brion, *The Problem of Slavery*, 47
Davis, Gregson, *Aimé Césaire*, 151
Dayan, Joan, 132n8, 174
Debergue, Constant, 30
Debien, Gabriel, 32
DeConde, Alexander, French reoccupation of Louisiana, 10, 23n21
Dédé, Edmond, 30, 33
Dédé, Sanité, 34
de Duras, Mme, 95
de Gaulle, Charles, 56n4
Déjour, Julien, 32
Depestre, René, 98, 154
Desdunes, Rodolphe, 30, 32
Nos hommes et notre histoire, 35, 37n11
Dessalines, Jean-Jacques, 6, 7, 52, 54, 57–58n15, 88
as antithesis of Toussaint, 173
as black Napoleon, 78
cult of, 174
diasporic writers
discourse of return, 149–62
and identification of landscape and self, 150–55
and (self)-identification, 155–60
Divers, Michelet, 159
Dominican Republic, 1937 massacre, 126, 132n12
Douglas, Aaron, 63, 72
Dr John, 34
Dubois, Laurent, 135
Du Bois, W.E.B., 63, 67
Haiti, 69
Duval-Carrié, Édouard, 45
Le Général Toussaint enfumé, 49

Duvalier, François "Papa Doc", 165
appropriation of Vodou, 125, 132n8
as Baron Samedi, 154
Duvalierism, 19
resistance to, 126–27
and spiralist movement, 101–2, 109n9

Edmondson, William, 67
education
and cultural transmission, 33–34
Howard University, 63
influence of Haitian refugees on, 28, 31, 38n15, 39n27
Endore, Samuel Guy
Babouk, 111–21
biographical novels, 111
critique of US imperialist interests, 111–13
The Curse of the Werewolf (film), 111
The Werewolf of Paris, 111
ethnicity
essentialist romance of, 125
and postcolonial identity, 42, 49, 59n32

Fanon, Frantz, 145
Faragher, John Mack, *Out of Many*, 12, 13
femininity
cruelty, of women, 102–4, 105–7
portrayals of in Caribbean literature, 51, 97, 106, 107
feminist writing, of Danticat, 123–24, 126–27
Ferguson, Moira, *Colonialism and Gender Relations from Mary Wollstonecraft to Jamaica Kincaid*, 95
fetishization of historical figures, 41
Fick, Carolyn, 46
Fignolé, Jean-Claude, 95, 97, 109n11
Aube tranquille, 98, 104–7, 110n19
on Caribbean pathology of expectations, 102
cruelty, of women, 102–4, 105–7
depictions of violence, 100–101
spiralist movement, 101–2, 109n9

Index

Fillidori, Matthieu (*Génération FLNC*), 43
Firmin, Anténor, *The Equality of the Human Races*, 164
folk culture, Haitian
    practice of "testing", 130, 133n19, 141–42
    in pro-democracy movement, 126–27
    rasin (roots) movement, 125–26
France
    de Gaulle as latter-day Toussaint, 56n4
    Haitian reparations, demands for, 19, 134
    Napoleonic Wars, 76–77
    Peace of Amiens, 7
    recognition of Haitian independence, 4
    relations with US, 18–19, 27n51
    Treaty of San Ildefonso, 5
Frankétienne, 101, 136
    Ultravocal, 174
Freemasonry, 29, 31, 33
French Revolution
    Haitian Revolution, recognition of, 4, 21n6
    status of women during, 95

Garvey, Marcus, 63, 66
Gates, Henry Louis Jr., 47, 48
Geggus, David, 59n32
Geggus, David, *Haitian Revolutionary Studies*, 41
gender relations
    as aspect of cultural identity, 146
    and postcolonial identity, 42, 48
Génération FLNC (documentary), 43
Genovese, Eugene, 51
Glissant, Édouard, 55
    on cultural affiliation, 140
    culture as dynamic process, 159–60, 162n50
    historical silence, 46
    Le Discours antillais, 42
    Monsieur Toussaint, 49, 50, 56–57n10, 57–58n15
    "Toussaint complex", 44
Glover, Danny, 45

Gottshalk, Louis, *Notes from a Pianist*, 33–34
Gouges, Olympe de, 95–96
Griot movement, 165
Gropper, William, 68
Grosz, George, 68

Haiti
    1937 Dominican Republic massacre, 126, 132n12
    "addiction to death", 103
    Africanism, 165
    Caco rebellion, 19, 164
    colour discrimination, and class conflicts, 134–35, 163–75
    contemporary US policy towards, 19–21
    cycles of oppression as post-revolution redux, 135
    depiction of in *L'Ouverture* series (Lawrence), 73–74
    French demands for reparations, 19, 134
    Griot movement, 165
    Henri Christophe, 2, 6
    indigenism, 164–65, 166–67
    "mulatto legend" of, 49, 51
    as postcolonial case study, 47
    Sténio Vincent, presidency of, 165
    US occupation of, 19, 133n13, 134, 164–65
Haitian-Americans
    Haitianness of, 136–38
    perceptions of otherness, 142
    social segregation of, 140–42
    tenth department (in North America), 135–36
Haitian diaspora
    alienation of, 122–23, 142
    artistic expression of, 137–39
    cultural identity in migrant Haitian communities, 134–48
    migrant experience of, 143–45
    migration patterns, 28, 36n1, 36n4, 96, 135–36
    pride of origin, 32–33

Rara music as transnational cultural form, 126
Haitian literature
  in diasporic communities, 137
  as historiographic metafiction, 98–99
  nationalism and cultural identity, 146–47
  non-Haitian authors, 100, 122–33
  portrayal of white women, 96–97
  spiralist movement, 101–2, 109n9
Haitianness
  articulation of in migrant postcolonial context, 139–40
  and cultural continuity, 143
  cultural expression in diaspora identity, 136–38
  Haitian literary identity, 137–39, 146–47
Haitian Revolution
  as crisis of linguistic intelligibility, 111
  depiction of in *L'Ouverture* series (Lawrence), 75–78
  emigration of planter society post-Revolution, 96
  English view of, 71
  European view of, 173
  invisibility of in white historiography, 2–4, 8–21, 21n6
  Napoleon's reconquest of Haiti, cost of, 4–5, 6–7, 23n15
  role of in Louisiana Purchase, 6–8
  St Domingue refugees in New Orleans, 14, 28–40
  as transcultural movement, 135
  treatment of in US "survey course" textbooks, 11–13, 26n34
  tri-racial element of, 76
  as the "unthinkable", 116–17, 120, 120n1, 121n7
  in US historiography, 8–21
  as US policy, 8, 9–10, 24n22
Hall, Stuart, 136, 139–40, 147, 159
  Caribbean as diaspora, 143, 149–50
Hallward, Peter, 135

Halpine, Susana, 72–73, 77
Hamilton, Alexander
  on Jefferson's negotiations with Napoleon, 5–6
  on role of Haitian Revolution in Louisiana Purchase, 7–8
Harlem
  Caribbean immigration to, 63
  Great Migration of African Americans, 62–63
Harlem Renaissance, 62–69
  Federal Theatre Project, 69
  Harlem Artists Guild, 66
  Harlem Arts Workshop, 65–66, 67
  Harlem Community Art Center, 64
  Harmon Foundation support, 63–64
  Schomburg Library, 65, 69–70, 84n50
  Utopia House, 64, 69
Harmon, William E., 63
Harmon Foundation, 63–64
Hegel, G.W.F., 2
  master-slave dialectic, 47
Herder, Johann Gottfried, 88
hero creation, 45–46, 57n14
  male heroes in Caribbean history, dominance of, 48–49
Hills, Patricia, 74
Hirsch, Marianne, 146
historiographic metafiction, 97, 98–99
historiography
  interpretation of US history in "survey course" textbooks, 10–11, 24n26, 25n27, 25n29
  interpretations of historical memory, 41–42
  invisibility of Haitian influence in Louisiana, 35–36
  invisibility of Haitian Revolution, 2–4, 8–21, 26n37, 26n43, 27n49
  mythologization of Toussaint, 45–46
  of Negro history, 72
  treatment of black independence, 16
  treatment of Napoleon in US "survey course" textbooks, 12–13, 25n31

Index

Hoffman, Léon-François, 101, 110n14
    and Haitian literary identity, 138–39
Hugo, Victor, *Bug-Jargal*, 51, 56–57n10, 97, 98, 109n12
Hunter, Donna, 53
Hurley, Anthony, 42, 55, 56n8
Hutcheon, Linda, 97
hybridity, 42
    and creolization, 50–51
    and postcolonial identity, 48
hybridization, and racial mixing, 88, 89, 92–93

identitarian positionality of migrant experience, 136–38
indigenism, 164–65, 166–67
Institute of the Black World, *Small Axe* lectures, 48
invisibility
    of Haitian cultural influence in Louisiana, 35–36
    of Haitian refugees in New Orleans, 29
    of Haitian Revolution, 2–4, 8–21
    historical silence, 46
    of oppressed people, 2
    role of race in, 16–17
    of white women in colonial plantation society, 96–99

Jamaica, migration of Haitian refugees, 28
James, C.L.R.
    The Black Jacobins, 41, 42, 47–48, 50, 53, 55
    invisibility of Haitian Revolution, 4
Jefferson, Thomas
    and Haiti, 8, 9
    and Louisiana Purchase, 4–5, 7–8, 14–15, 22n13
Jenson, Deborah, 43, 56n6
Johnson, James Weldon, 63, 66
Jones, Art, 45
Jones, W.M.A., 44
Joseph, Ronald, 66
journalism, influence of Haitian refugees on, 28, 30–31, 33, 38n14, 39n28
Julien, Eileen, 125

Kadish, Doris, 48
Kant, Immanuel, definition of race, 87–88, 94n7
Karlstrom, Paul, 79
Kastor, Peter, *The Louisiana Purchase: Emergence of an American Nation*, 14
Kennedy, Roger, *Mr Jefferson's Lost Cause*, 15
King, Nicole, *C.L.R. James and Creolization*, 50
Kleist, Heinrich von, 93n1
    "appearance and being", use of, 89, 90, 91
    colour symbolism of, 89–90, 91
    The Engagement in Santo Domingo, 86–94
Knight, Gwendolyn, 65, 66
Kollwitz, Käthe, 68
Korngold, Ralph, *Citizen Toussaint*, 41
Kukla, Jon, *A Wilderness So Immense*, 15

Lachance, Paul, 32, 35
Laferrière, Dany
    autobiographical fiction, 156–57, 161n29, 161n34
    on fusion between literature and life, 152
    Haitian literary identity, 137, 138, 139
    on Haitian mythology, 156
    J'écris comme je vis, 156–57
    Pays sans chapeau, 150, 155, 156, 157
    use of short studies, 151–52
    use of writer's "I", 156–57, 158–59, 160n4, 161–62n34
    writer's return, and identification of landscape and self, 150–55
Lahens, Yanick, 136
    on coherence of Haitian culture, 137, 147
    Dans la maison du père, 165, 167–69, 174–75
Lamming, George, 55
Lamming, George, *Pleasures of Exile*, 47
Lange, Dorothea, 72
language
    biopolitical significance, 119–20

as biopower, 117–19
connection between words and meanings, 115–16, 119–20
cultural politics of translation, 111–21
hybrid cultural practices, 140–41
and loss of voice, 133n14
in oral culture, 127–28
power of in slave communications, 113–15
role in migrant reordering of identity, 145
silence(s) in, 113, 117, 120, 127, 163, 167–69, 171–72
Lanusse, Armand, 30
Les Cénelles, 35
Laveau, Marie, 35
Lawrence, Jacob, 61–85
as American griot, 72
in Civilian Conservation Corps, 64
critical recognition of, 74, 77, 79
influences on, 62–69
The Life of Toussaint L'Ouverture, 61, 69–80, 80n1
The Migrants, 62
Museum of Modern Art exhibitions, 67, 83n39
technique and composition, use of, 72–78
Utopia House, 64
Works Progress Administration (WPA) Federal Art Project, 65–66
Leclerc (brother-in-law of Napoleon), 6
Le Gardeur, René, 32
Lejeune, Phillippe, 156
literature
death and zombification, 152, 153–54
discourse of return, 149–62
epistolary letter, 123–24, 128, 129
historiographic metafiction, 97
literary ghettoization, 100
mask motif in, 104–7, 110n19
spiralist movement, 101–2, 109n9
status of women in, 96–99
Livingston, Robert, Louisiana Purchase negotiations, 5–6, 7

Locke, Alain
African art, 67
The New Negro, 63–64
Lorimer, Denis, 165
Louisiana
architectural traditions, influence of Haitian refugees on, 30, 34, 38n20
culinary traditions, influence of Haitian refugees on, 34, 39n33
education, refugee influence on, 28, 31, 39n27
folk culture, resistance to Americanization post-Purchase, 35
as frontier society, 30
Haitian cultural influences post-Revolution, 28–40
journalism, refugee influence on, 28, 30–31, 33
music, influence of Haitian refugees on, 30, 33–34, 36, 39n30
occupational patterns of Haitian refugees, 30, 37n9
survival of Gallic culture in, 31, 32–33
Voodoo, 29, 30, 34–35, 36, 38n19. *See also* New Orleans
Louisiana Purchase
invisibility of role of Haitian Revolution in, 8–21, 25n31, 26n37, 27n49
New Orleans purchase negotiations, 5–6
treatment of in US "survey course" textbooks, 12–13, 14–15, 25n31, 26n43
Treaty of San Ildefonso, 5, 7
and US rise to dominance, 1–2, 4–5, 22n10, 22n13

Madiou, Thomas, 173
Magnier, Bernard, 156
Martineau, Harriet, 47
The Hour and the Man, 50
Matisse, Henri, 63
Matthewson, Tim, on Haitian Revolution as US policy, 8, 9–10, 24n22, 26n43
McAlister, Elizabeth, 126

INDEX

McKay, Claude, 63, 65, 66, 80n1
Meiners, Christoph, 88
Messenger, 63
mimicry
    as element of agency, 53
    postcolonial identity and, 42
    in post-emancipation Haitian society, 51–53
    as strategy of resistance, 52
miscegenation, 86–94
    as racial mixing, 88, 89, 92–93, 109n13
Monroe, James, New Orleans purchase negotiations, 5–6, 7
moral hierarchy, role of skin colour in, 88–89, 94n7
Moreau de Saint-Méry, M.L.E., 38n13
Moreau de Saint-Méry, M.L.E., *Topographic Description of the Island of Saint-Domingue*, 96, 107
Morrison, Toni, 97
Mudimbe-Boyi, Elisabeth, 52, 53, 55
Murrin, John, *Liberty, Equality, Power*, 12
music
    in diasporic communities, 137
    influence of Haitian refugees on, 30, 33–34, 36, 39n30
    Rara music, 126, 132n9

Napoleon
    alternative expansionsism of Republican Empire, 44
    attempt to reconquer Haiti, 4–5, 6–7, 134
    cinematic representations of, 57n11
    depiction of in *L'Ouverture* series (Lawrence), 77–78
    Louisiana Purchase, French reoccupation of, 4–5, 7, 9–10
    Peace of Amiens, 7
    treatment of in US "survey course" textbooks, 12–13, 15
National Association for the Advancement of Coloured People (NAACP), 63
national identity, in literary definitions of Haitianness, 137–39

nationalism, and cultural identity, 134–39
Neruda, Pablo, *Canto General*, 44
Nesbitt, Nick, 47, 53, 137
New Orleans
    Books of Wills, 35
    Congo Square dances, 33, 36
    Haitian cultural influences post-Revolution, 28–40
    invisibility of Haitian refugees in, 29
    journalism, refugee influence on, 30–31
    purchase negotiations, 5–6
    refugees, ethnic community of, 31–33
    St Domingue refugees in, 14
    survival of Gallic culture in, 31, 32–33, 35. *See also* Louisiana
New York Age, 63
Nixon, Rob, 47

Ollivier, Émile, 98
Onuf, Peter, 15
oral culture
    and literacy, 125, 127–28
    relationship to written narrative, 123–24, 131
    in writing of Danticat, 124. *See also* storytelling
orality
    cultural politics of, 125–26, 130–31
    and writing, 124–25, 129
Orozco, Jose Clemente, 68

paternalism, and female inferiority, 95, 97
Péralte, Charlemagne, 164
Petit, Georges J, 164
Philocrète, René, 101
Picasso, Pablo, 63
plantation society
    Creole marriage, 104
    as male-defined world, 96–99
    moral dilemma of the Enlightenment, 99, 104–7
    racial mixing, 109n13
    violence in, 102–4
    white women in, 95–110
Pluchon, Pierre, 41

Index

Plummer, Brenda Gayle, 8
postcolonial identity
    in Haitian historiography, 42
    role of gender in, 48–49
    treatment of in literature, 46–50
postcolonialism
    collapse of anti-colonial ideal, 54
    genealogy of, 41–42, 55
postcolonial literature
    representation of Toussaint in, 45–46, 47
    status of women in, 96–99
    writing as form of agency, 47–48

race relations
    class divisions, role of, 170–74
    colour discrimination, and class conflicts in Haiti, 163–75
    in Dominican Republic, 132n12
    racial ideology of Griot Movement, 165
    role of white women in colonial race relations, 104–6, 107–8
    role of white women in colonial society, 98–99
    white superiority, maintenance of in slavery, 117, 121n8
racial ambiguity, 89, 91, 92
racial hierarchy, 86–94
    race, definition of, 88–89, 93n1, 94n7
Ramsay, David, on Louisiana Purchase, 4, 7
Randolph, A. Philip, 63
Raynal, l'Abbé, *Histoire des Deux Indes*, 53, 75
Rhys, Jean, 100
Rivera, Diego, 68
Roark, James, *The American Promise*, 13
Robinson, Cedric J., 49–50
Roumain, Jacques, Haitian indigenism, 164–65
Roup, Pierre, 33
Rüsch, Erwin, 41

Said, Edward, 41
Saint-Eloi, Rodney, 154
Sala-Molins, Louis, 104
Savage, Augusta, 63, 64–65
    black nationalism, 66–67

Schomburg, Arturo A., 69
Schomburg Library, 65, 69–70, 84n50
Schwarz-Bart, André, 100
Scott, David, 44
    Conscripts of Modernity, 41, 53–55
    Refashioning Futures, 54
Seifert, Charles Christopher, 67
Séjour, Louis Victor, 30
Séligny, Michel, 30
Shelton, Marie-Denise, 141
Siqueiros, David, 68
slavery
    and abolitionism, 48, 50
    as antithesis of liberty, 3
    in *Babouk* (Endore), 113
    British anti-slavery campaign, 71, 75
    as component of US expansion, 25n28
    depiction of in *L'Ouverture* series (Lawrence), 74–75
    influence of Haitian refugees on Louisiana slave culture, 29–30
    language, power of in slave communications, 113–15, 118–20, 120n4
    in postcolonial literature, 47
    punishments for escape, 117
    reimposition of by Napoleon, 6, 13
    slaves as Haitian refugees, 31–32
    white superiority, maintenance of in slavery, 121n8
    women, status of compared to slavery, 95
Snaër, Samuel, 30
Sofka, James, 14
Spain, role of in Louisiana Purchase, 4, 5, 7, 22n10
Spivak, Gayatri, 41
Steele, Elizabeth, 72–73, 77
storytelling
    in *Babouk* (Endore), 114
    influence of Haitian refugees on, 30
    and intersubjective communication, 128
    as visual art, 72. *See also* oral culture
Stovall, Lou, 80
Suk, Jeannie, 47
    "postcolonial" defined, 44, 56n8

Index

theatre arts, influence of Haitian refugees on, 28, 38n19
Thierry, Camille, 30
Toussaint Louverture, François Dominique, 18, 58n20, 88, 173
- as black male hero, 48–49
- Christianity, impact on, 71
- cinematic representations of, 45, 57n11
- as conscript of modernity, 54
- death of, 6, 44–45
- ethnicity, 49, 59n32, 71–72
- fictional biography of, 97–98
- as George Washington of Haiti, 78, 80
- *The Life of Toussaint L'Ouverture* (paintings), 61, 69–80
- "mulatto legend", 49, 51
- mythologization of, 41–42, 44, 45–46, 56n4
- parallels with Aristide, 43–44, 56n6
- postcolonial ethnicity, 49
- postcolonial interpretations of, 41–60
- in postcolonial literature, 45–46, 47
- as symbol of anti-colonial struggle, 43–46

Toussaint pitchers, 47
translation
- connection between words and meanings, 115–16, 119–20
- cultural politics of, 111–21
- role of in cultural identity, 149–50

transnationalism
- in the Caribbean, 136
- and cultural hybridity, 139–40
- and migration, 134–48
- in migratory life, 123–24
- Rara music as transnational cultural form, 126

Trouillot, Lyonel, *Bicentenaire*, 165, 169–75
Trouillot, Michel-Rolph, 13
- on invisibility, 2, 4
- on silence(s), 113, 163
- on slave networks of communication, 120n4
- *Ti difé boulé sou istoua Ayiti*, 46

on the "unthinkable", 116–17, 120, 120n1, 121n7
United States
- American national myth, 17, 25n27
- *Babouk* (Endore) as critique of imperialist interests, 111–13
- black nationalism, 63, 66–67
- civil rights organizations, rise of, 63
- contemporary policy towards Haiti, 19–21
- debt to Haiti, 17–19, 20–21, 27n50
- foreign relations of, 18–19, 27n51
- Great Depression era, 62–69
- Great Migration of African Americans, 62–63
- Haitian Revolution in US historiography, 8–21, 24n26, 25n29
- interpretation of US history in "survey course" textbooks, 10–11
- Jazz Age, 63
- Louisiana Purchase, role in US rise to dominance, 1–2, 4–5, 7–8
- Negro experience in, 61–62, 68–69
- occupation of Haiti, 19, 133n13, 134, 164–65
- slavery as component of US expansion, 25n28
- St Domingue refugees in New Orleans, 28–40
- treatment of Napoleon in "survey course" textbooks, 12–13
- Works Progress Administration (WPA) Federal Art Project, 65–66

universal historiography, and translation, 111

Vergès, Françoise, 102
Vodou
- appropriation of by "Papa Doc" Duvalier, 125, 132n8
- Baron Samedi, 154
- cult of Dessalines, 174
- Rara music, 126, 132n9
- Virgin Mary association, 133n13

Voodoo, in Louisiana, 29, 30, 34–35, 36, 38n19

Walker, Keith, 123–24
Walvin, James, 48
Wheat, Ellen Harkins, 69
White, Hayden, 97
Wollstonecraft, Mary, 95
women
    in Haitian society, 144
    marivaudage, 99
    paternalism, and female inferiority, 95, 97
    role of in abolitionism, 48
    role of white women in colonial race relations, 98–99, 104–6, 107–8, 108n5, 109n13
    white women as Other in colonial society, 107–8
    white women in colonial society, 95–110
Wood, Marcus, 43, 47, 50

Woodruff, Hale, 63, 72
writing, as form of agency
    autobiographical fiction, 156–57, 161n29, 161n34
    biopower of, 117–19
    black journals, 63
    discourse of return, 149–62
    and orality, 124–25, 129, 131
    in postcolonial literature, 47–48, 58n20
    technology of distance, 123
    writer's "I", and (self)-identification, 151, 155–60, 160n4, 161–62n34

Yee, Jennifer, 51
yellow fever, 6, 13–14, 26n36, 78

zombies, and zombification, 152, 153–54

Contributors

Martin Munro is Associate Professor of French and Francophone Literature at Florida State University. He is the author of *Shaping and Reshaping the Caribbean: The Work of Aimé Césaire and René Depestre* (2000) and *Exile and Post-1946 Haitian Literature: Alexis, Depestre, Ollivier, Laferrière, Danticat* (2007), and co-editor, with Elizabeth Walcott-Hackshaw, of *Reinterpreting the Haitian Revolution and Its Cultural Aftershocks* (2006). He is a member of the *Small Axe* editorial collective, and is currently working on rhythm in New World cultures.

Elizabeth Walcott-Hackshaw is Lecturer of Francophone Caribbean Literature and Nineteenth-century French Poetry at the University of the West Indies, St Augustine, Trinidad. She is the author of articles on the Caribbean cultural landscape as presented in the works of Gisèle Pineau, Yanick Lahens, Edwidge Danticat and Marie Chauvet, and co-editor, with Martin Munro, of *Reinterpreting the Haitian Revolution and Its Cultural Aftershocks* (2006). Her first collection of short stories, *Four Taxis Facing North*, was published in 2007.

Edward E. Baptist teaches in the Department of History at Cornell University. He is the author of *Creating an Old South: Middle Florida's Plantation Frontier Before the Civil War* (2002) and the co-editor of *New Studies in the History of American Slavery* (2006). His forthcoming publications include *The Half That Has Never Been Told: How the Expansion of Slavery in the US Shaped African Americans, The US, and the World* and *The Historical Encyclopedia of Slavery in the Americas*.

CONTRIBUTORS

Nathalie Dessens is Professor of American History at the University of Toulouse. After working on slavery from a comparative perspective, she has refocused her research on nineteenth-century Louisiana. Her publications include *Myths of the Plantation Society: Slavery in the American South and the West Indies* (2003) and *From Saint-Domingue to New Orleans: Migration and Influences* (2007). She is currently working on the correspondence of Jean Boze, a St Domingue refugee who lived in New Orleans from 1809 to 1842.

Charles Forsdick is James Barrow Professor of French at the University of Liverpool. His recent publications include *Victor Segalen and the Aesthetics of Diversity* (2000); *Travel in Twentieth-Century French and Francophone Cultures: The Persistence of Diversity* (2005); and *Francophone Postcolonial Studies: A Critical Introduction* (2003; co-edited with David Murphy). He is currently completing books on representations of Toussaint Louverture and on the travel writing of Ella Maillart, and is co-editing (with David Murphy) *Postcolonial Thought in the Francophone World*. He is editor of the Liverpool University Press series "Contemporary French and Francophone Cultures".

Kathleen Gyssels is Professor of Francophone Postcolonial Literatures at the University of Antwerp. She is the author of *Filles de solitude: Essai sur les autobiographies fictives de Simone et André Schwarz-Bart* (1996) and *Sages sorcières? Révision de la mauvaise mère dans* Beloved *(Toni Morrison),* Praisesong for the Widow *(Paule Marshall), et* Moi, Tituba, sorcière noire de Salem *(Maryse Condé)* (2001). Her forthcoming book compares anglophone and francophone voices from the African diaspora.

Brenna Munro is Assistant Professor of English at the University of Miami. She is working on a book provisionally titled *Queer Constitutions: Sexuality, Literature, and Imagining Democracy in South Africa*, and is interested in queer postcoloniality, Africa and its diasporas.

H. Adlai Murdoch is Associate Professor of French and Francophone Literature and African-American Studies at the University of Illinois, Urbana–Champaign. He is the author of numerous articles and of *Creole Identity in the French Caribbean Novel* (2001) and *Decolonizing Representation: Migratory Metropolitan Caribbean Identities in Literature and Film* (forthcoming), and the co-editor (with Anne Donadey) of *Postcolonial Theory and Francophone Literary Studies* (2004).

Contributors

William Scott is Assistant Professor in the Department of English at the University of Pittsburgh, where he teaches twentieth-century American and African-American literature, critical theory, and cultural studies. He is the author of several articles and is currently completing a manuscript on novels about industrial workers' strikes, entitled *Troublemakers: Power, Representation, and the Fiction of the Mass Worker in the United States*.

Wendy Sutherland is Assistant Professor of German at New College of Florida. Her research focuses on the eighteenth-century German bourgeois drama and deals specifically with the portrayal of the black and the construction of race in such works. She is currently working on her manuscript *Staging Blackness and the Construction of Whiteness in Eighteenth- and Early-nineteenth-century German Bourgeois Drama*.

Carolyn Williams is Associate Professor of History at the University of North Florida. Her main teaching and research interests are US gender studies, multicultural studies and public history. She has published several articles in anthologies and encyclopedia entries and is the author of *Historic Photos of Jacksonville* (2006).

www.ingramcontent.com/pod-product-compliance
Lightning Source LLC
Chambersburg PA
CBHW021828300426
44114CB00009BA/373